Managing
the
CIVIL SERVICE

Managing
the
CIVIL SERVICE

JOHN GARRETT

Foreword by
The Rt. Hon. Denis Healey, MP

HEINEMANN: LONDON

William Heinemann Ltd
10 Upper Grosvenor Street
London W1X 9PA

LONDON MELBOURNE TORONTO
JOHANNESBURG AUCKLAND

First published 1980
© John Garrett 1980

SBN 434 90655 7

Printed in Great Britain by
Willmer Brothers Limited
Rock Ferry, Merseyside

Contents

Foreword

By The Rt. Hon. Denis Healey, MP

In 1964 I found myself in my first Ministerial job as Secretary of State for Defence, responsible not only for helping to revise Britain's defence policy at a time when our military commitments exceeded our economic capacity, but also for the efficient management of nearly a million men and women, divided roughly equally between the armed services and civilians, many of whom were working in great industrial establishments like the dockyards and ordnance factories. I held the job for five years.

Though at that time the general tradition in Whitehall was that the first responsibility of higher civil servants was to advise their Minister on policy, in the Ministry of Defence management was of at least equal importance. Even the largest multi-national corporation have rarely faced management problems quite so extensive as those involved in the British and American Polaris programmes.

The strains imposed on defence management by a growing shortage of resources led the ministry in Britain, like its counterpart in the US, to pioneer the introduction of new management techniques in the Civil Service like programme budgeting, systems analysis and critical path programming and to apply cost/benefit techniques at all levels.

I found also that the existing systems were inadequate for the complex policy decisions I was called upon to make by applying political judgment to operational and scientific data. So I set up a small personal 'cabinet' called the Programme Evaluation Group to ensure that I asked the right questions and got relevant answers in time – with alternatives when suitable.

Neither in the Ministry of Defence nor in the Treasury, where I later served for almost as long, did I find significant party political bias among my Civil Service advisers, although the vested interests of institutions are as apparent in Government as in the private sector. And of course an honest judgment is always influenced by strong personal convictions. The best of my civil servants and of my military advisers had an intellectual ability and breadth of experience I have never found surpassed, and the average were above the average in other comparable walks of life.

Yet I have no doubt that the exceptionally long and uninterrupted history of our Civil Service, and the way in which it operates the committee system – the nuclear village of Whitehall, as anthropological observers have well described it – rendered it inadequate for the sort of rapid change which all countries have had to face, particularly over the last ten years. Moreover, at the interface between government and private industry, which is of growing importance in many departments, government officials are too often at a serious disadvantage, both in knowledge and experience, compared with their counterparts in, say, France or Japan.

Mr John Garrett is himself a management consultant by profession. He has spent much of an exceptionally active political career in studying the problems of the British Civil Service, particularly its problems of management. This latest book, following on *The Management of Government* which he published in 1972, provides a comprehensive description of the attempts of successive governments to come to grips with the management of the Civil Service in a period of exceptionally rapid change, and gives a penetrating insight into the problems. It puts into a more balanced perspective some of the criticisms which have been fashionable in recent years among those who wrongly attribute to bureaucratic sabotage or political prejudice behaviour which arises too often from the sheer intractability of the process of Government in Britain as it is now conducted.

Preface

Managing the Civil Service describes developments in the administration of central government departments over the last decade, in respect of both the advance of management techniques and the response to demands for greater public accountability. It examines the results of the attempts to reform and modernize the Civil Service started by the Fulton Committee in the late 1960s and carried forward with diminishing enthusiasm by subsequent governments. It concludes that reform is needed more than ever as government has grown more complex and secretive, and proposes a programme of development to improve the management of the Civil Service and its accountability to Parliament and the public.

J.G.

I

Introduction

This book examines developments in the management of government in Britain in the 1970s. It considers the results of the report of the Committee on the Civil Service (The Fulton Report, 1968) and of the new style of government announced by the Conservative administration of 1970–4; the implications of the proposals for administrative reform made by the House of Commons' Expenditure and Procedure Committees in 1977 and the policies proposed by the new government in 1979.

Each of these developments has had a different emphasis, reflecting changing political ideas of administrative reform. The Fulton Report was concerned with making the Civil Service a more effective instrument for the modernization of Britain; it emphasized improved management processes and the need for a new kind of manager to run them. The Heath administration of 1970 emphasized structural changes in central government, the National Health Service, and local government and sought to apply what were then thought to be the latest ideas in business organization to public administration. From 1974 onwards, a new assertiveness appeared in the House of Commons and the emphasis changed to the need for an increase in the effectiveness and scope of Parliamentary scrutiny, a reduction in official secrecy and a concern with the public accountability of government. The 1979 Conservative administration then came in intending to roll back government, reduce its interventionist role and abolish major functions.

The result of all this has been a most turbulent decade for the Civil Service and a severe blow to the self confidence of an institution which had always, in its upper levels at least, considered itself an inviolable shrine of intellectual excellence, administrative competence and stability. The Fulton Committee attacked the basic assumptions on which the members of the higher Civil Service selected and nurtured themselves, it demolished the principles on which they had governed the country for a hundred years and it described what they saw as their unique professionalism as amateurish. Both Fulton and the Heath

1

government told them that management, which they had always seen as a rather inferior activity for businessmen, was what mattered and that their concept of 'administration' was out of date. They were given a mass of confusing and sometimes contradictory directions: one year it was policy to establish non-departmental agencies, the next it was policy to abolish quangos*; one year long-range planning was in, the next across-the-board cuts in expenditure; one year managerial accountability was all the rage, the next public accountability; one year a new sensitivity and care in personnel management, the next a unilateral abrogation of Civil Service payment agreements. An occupation which had for generations enjoyed the highest public and Parliamentary esteem was suddenly vilified for being too well paid, too well pensioned and too luxuriously staffed. The generals of departments, accustomed to instantaneous response from a disciplined and unquestioning army of officials, found that their troops went on strike. From some quarters even their integrity was questioned and they were accused of sabotaging government policy.

Though it is clear that the Civil Service was ripe for a shake-up and that some of the criticisms and prescriptions (particularly those from the Fulton Committee) were fully justified, there is no doubt that the Civil Service at all levels has been deplorably treated in this decade to the point where its morale and in some ways its effectiveness has been wantonly damaged. Few politicians and commentators have taken the trouble to understand the organization, management, style and tasks of our Civil Service before launching proposals for radical change. It suits many of them to shuffle on to the Civil Service the blame for weaknesses in our society, our economy and our constitutional arrangements rather than to examine these fundamental problems.

In this book, the prime concern is with the way in which the management of the Civil Service has developed in the decade since new directions for management were set out by the Fulton Committee. The central topics which are discussed are organization, planning, control, accountable management and personnel practices. This structure matches that of the author's *The Management of Government*, published by Pelican in 1972, which discussed the origins and background of the Fulton Report and its management concepts, the report itself and the results of the first year or so of its implementation. This is to some extent a sequel to *The Management of Government* carrying forward the development of each topic to the present time. It incorporates some material from the earlier book (by kind permission of Penguin Books Ltd) where this is necessary to set the scene for the developments which are described here. Reflecting the concerns of

---

* Quasi-autonomous non-governmental organizations.

2

the time and the author's translation from management to politics, in the final chapters it discusses the relationship of the Civil Service to Parliament.

The earlier book ended on a note of cautious optimism. In 1971 it looked as if the Fulton lessons had been learned and it seemed that the Civil Service had embarked upon modernizing itself. Changes were under way in planning and control systems, organization structures and man-management. We shall see that a few of these changes were seen through to completion. However, the optimists had over-estimated the capacity of a huge and long-established organization to change its ways, particularly when top management was not committed to change and the political will for change was not maintained. All large organizations, unless kept under constant pressure, develop arrangements to stifle change and ensure a quiet life with steady growth. It is not surprising, therefore, that in general the Civil Service of 1980 is not much different from the Civil Service of 1968. A central failure has been the reluctance of the Service to reform its recruitment, training, promotion and, particularly, its grading structure so as to open up its top general management levels to the technically qualified: the 'new breed' of managers which Fulton rightly saw as the key to the improvement and modernization of the management of British government. The top management of our large and technically complex departments of state is still dominated by generalist arts graduates from public schools and Oxbridge. Almost as important, the Civil Service College, intended as the source of the new professionalism in management, producing not only a stream of new managers but also a stream of new ideas, has never functioned as it was intended because of neglect by the higher Civil Service. The Civil Service Department, created as a powerful instrument of organizational change – even headed by Prime Ministers – has made little impact on departmental autonomy in the field of personnel management and efficiency services. In the field of management information and performance measurement, of crucial importance in policy planning, control, accountability and Parliamentary surveillance, a few departments (DHSS, Inland Revenue, Manpower Services Commission) have developed new systems while others have done virtually nothing. Here and there, progress has been made on Fulton lines: in management by objectives (though now virtually abandoned); in merging career classes (though slowly); in improving office environments and in training but there has not been any sense of pushing through the great strategy for development which Fulton envisaged. After 1969 no politician with sufficient weight cared sufficiently to understand the strategy or to see the importance of reform.

Nevertheless, since 1968 the Service has been obliged to examine every aspect of its management and to try out new management ideas in a more open way than ever before. There has been fairly constant comment and criticism and the Service has been kept in the public eye. Until the 1960s it was accepted simply as part of the national furniture: a pillar of our way of life, reassuringly solid and unchanged, widely believed to be a model for the rest of the world. The Fulton Report, the first public enquiry into the Civil Service since 1854, took the covers off and revealed an institution dangerously unfitted for its present day tasks. Since Fulton, the efficiency and the effectiveness of the Service has continued to be questioned and increasing Parliamentary interest has given rise to the first House of Commons select committee enquiry into the Civil Service for over a hundred years and its proposal that in future the Service be kept under regular review by such committees. Other committees of the House have engaged in open struggles with the Executive: over the Crown Agents, Chrysler, the British Steel Corporation and Treasury policy. The new House of Commons select committee system introduced in 1979 could lead to continuous probing and enquiry.

Another welcome result of Fulton and its sequels has been that the study of the management of government is coming to be accepted as part of the study of management. For many years public administration has been treated in Britain, unlike the United States, as a branch of 'political science' rather than as a branch of management. Top civil servants and academics alike saw 'management' as something to do with trade and industry and no relevance to government except in such insignificant matters as office layout, forms design and the assessment of the qualities of office machines. Managers in government belonged to the lower executive and technical classes. Fulton showed that modern government departments are huge managerial entities with problems of organization, planning and control which are found in all large enterprises though with the particular problem of having to operate in a political environment. Though we still do not yet have 'government schools' as we now have business schools and management education for officials in central government is wholly inadequate at least more work is being done in the field and the mandarins cannot brush the relevance of management studies aside as easily as they used to.

It is clearly essential that the management of an institution which affects every aspect of our national life, and directly controls many of them, which employs 750,000 people and spends £44 billion in a year should receive the closest scrutiny and attention. It is also important that its task, its style, its structure and its systems are understood. In this chapter we briefly examine its tasks and the peculiar management style which developed to deal with them before turning to structures and systems in later chapters.

The Management Task

The Management Consultancy Group which reported to the Fulton Committee defined the total management task of the Civil Service as:

(a) formulation of policy under political direction
(b) creating the 'machinery' for implementation of policy
(c) operation of the administrative machine
(d) Accountability to Parliament and the public.[1]

Political direction makes itself felt in frequent and sometimes radical changes in the content or emphasis of policy. Civil servants are expected to be able to adapt to rapid change, at the time of a change of government, for example, and to implement entirely new policies without any break in continuity. Prime Ministers frequently reshuffle not only their Cabinet colleagues but also whole departments and agencies, so that the Civil Service has to cope almost overnight with the creation and dissolution of substantial organizations (e.g., The Land Commission, The Prices Commission, the Manpower Services Agency) on the basis of political decisions which may have hardly taken managerial considerations into account. Public accountability requires meticulous attention to the maintenance of equity in implementing decisions and in dealing with specific cases. It requires elaborate arrangements to insure consistency in the application of policy within, and between, departments. The greatest care has to be taken in accounting for public assets and for the regularity and proper authorization of expenditure. Elaborate recruitment and promotion procedures have to be operated to ensure the equitable treatment of applicants and staff.

The tasks of civil servants are defined, to varying degrees of clarity, by the legislation which they have to operate. Once the legislation is in existence, they have to deal with whatever case or problem arises within its field of operation. In addition, over large tracts of legislation, the responsibility for implementation lies not in the originating department but with such external bodies as police forces, regional health authorities or local authorities. In this situation, the department tends to be expected, in the eyes of its 'publics', to carry the responsibility for action over which it has little executive authority: to make and adjust policy in the light of results on which it has inadequate information; to supervise the implementation of policy at a level far removed from where implementation takes place.

The constraints of 'managing in a political dimension' inevitably have an effect on management style. Sir Derek Rayner, a businessman brought into government in the early and late 1970s as an adviser on management, has said: 'efficiency in the Civil Service is dependent, as in business, on motivation and whereas in business one is judged by overall success, in my experience the civil servant tends to be judged by failure. This inevitably conditions his approach to his work. . . .'[2] The civil service manager is obliged to concentrate on the avoidance of mistakes, to emphasize precedents and established procedure and to adopt a custodial and equitable style rather than the entrepreneurial style which is expected in most organizations. Similarly, the objectives of a civil service manager may be less tangible, and are usually less quantifiable, than those of a manager in a commercial organization. He is expected to carry out the requirements of his Minister, to secure value for money both within the department and in external agencies, tightly to control growth in staff in the face of an increasing workload and to provide a wide range of services and benefits to the community efficiently, equitably and effectively.

Nevertheless, in spite of these added difficulties, managers in the Civil Service are still faced with the fundamental management task of deploying resources to meet departmental objectives and in many, perhaps most, areas they have to do so in a largely unchanging environment. They have to manage processes for handling transactions and information, for budgeting, planning and personnel management which are similar to those found in any large organization. It was the failure of the higher Civil Service to recognize the similarities and its emphasis on the peculiarities of managing in a political dimension which led it to adopt some of the practices for which it was so heavily criticized in the Fulton Report. The most obvious of these practices was the career class system discussed in the next section.

The Mandarins and Other Classes

In 1853, Sir Stafford Northcote and Sir Charles Trevelyan reported on the organization of the permanent Civil Service.[3] They found that admission to the Civil Service had been sought after by the unambitious, the indolent and the incapable, with the result that the public service suffered both in internal efficiency and in public estimation. The Northcote-Trevelyan report produced four main reforms as required to create an efficient body of permanent officers: entry into the Civil Service by competitive examination; promotion on merit, as assessed by the reports of superiors; the placing of first appointments on a common footing throughout the Service; and the establishment of a proper distinction between 'intellectual' and 'mechanical' labour. For the superior situations involving intellectual work 'endeavours should be made to secure the services of the most promising young men of the day, by a competing examination on a level with the highest description of education in this country'. The distinction between this work and the mechanical work of the lower class of clerks (copying, posting accounts, keeping diaries) was left to the discretion of the chiefs of offices.

In 1874, the Playfair Committee allocated routine work to a 'Lower Division' of clerks with a tested knowledge of reading, writing and arithmetic, and intellectual work to a 'Higher Division' (called the First Division after 1890) mostly of graduates. In 1920 a joint staff and management committee on the Organization of the Civil Service[4] considered career arrangements in the Service and proposed a division of administration and clerical work into three categories. The lowest category of work, 'the application of well defined regulations, decisions and practices to particular cases', was given to the Clerical Class, to which entry was regulated by a competitive examination approximating to the standard at the intermediate stage of a secondary-school course (today's O-level). This class was later sub-divided into a General Clerical Class (requiring five O-levels on entry) and a Clerical Assistant Class (two O-levels). The middle category of work was defined as 'the critical examination of particular cases of lesser importance not clearly covered by approved regulations or general decisions, initial investigations into matters of higher importance and the direction of small blocks of business'. In its upper ranges, it was concerned with matters of internal organization and control, 'with the settlement of broad questions arising out of business in hand or in contemplation and with the responsible conduct of important questions'. This category was given to the Executive Class, recruited from secondary-school leavers by an examination at the standard of today's A-level. The highest category of work was described as concerned with the formation of policy, the co-ordination and improvement of government machinery, and with the general administrative and control of the departments of the public service. This work was laid to the Administrative Class, whose members were usually recruited from university graduates with first-class or second-class degrees. From the late nineteenth century onwards increasing numbers of professionally qualified staff (solicitors, engineers, doctors) were required by departments. In 1921 Service-wide classes of scientists and scientific assistants were set up and in 1946 similar classes of engineers, technicians and draughtsmen.

By the middle 1960s there were forty general 'Treasury classes' whose members were employed in a wide variety of departments and over 1,400 'departmental classes' whose members worked in a single department. Policy making and financial control rested with the 2,500 members of the Administrative Class; middle non-technical management with the Executive Class (numbering 48,000) and clerical work with two Clerical Classes (170,000). Virtually every job in the Service belonged to a class and most classes had a hierarchy of grades within them representing different levels of responsibility, age or length of service. There were Treasury classes which spanned specialist work from middle to upper management, e.g. the Works Group of Engineers, Architects and surveyors (11,500) and the Scientific Officer Class (4,000) and there were supporting Treasury classes of technicians, typists and cleaners. Some departmental classes were also large, e.g. that of the 24,000 Tax Inspectors while some had half a dozen or fewer members. An officer's career was normally within his class but it was possible for some to be promoted from a lower to an upper class. Many officers were promoted from the Clerical to the Executive Class and some from the Executive to the Administrative Class and promotion from technician to the Works Group and the Scientific Officer Class was not uncommon. 'Horizontal' transfers between classes were rare because of the rules relating to qualifying ages, academic attainments and experience. The class system was reinforced by organizational conventions which generally assumed that separate classes should be organized in separate organizational units (see Chapter 4).

The Fulton Committee found that the career class system greatly handicapped the effective management of the Civil Service and recommended its abolition (see Chapter 2). It also attacked the fundamental and unique principle on which the system was based: that the control of departments should be exclusively in the hands of the 'generalist' senior managers of the Administrative Class and that technically- and professionally-qualified officers of the specialist classes should generally be subordinate to them. It observed that many departments operated in highly complex technological and social environments calling for both administrative and specialist expertise and that the practice of placing the policy-formulation, management, financial, legislative and ministerial-support functions with administrators and advisory functions with specialists was outdated. This practice sprang from a belief in 'the expert on tap, but not on top' or, as the staff association representing the Administrative Class said in evidence to Fulton, it reflected 'the generally accepted principle in this country that non-specialists should take the major policy decisions on behalf of the community as a whole'.[5]

The case for a top management composed of generalists which, as we shall see, is still being argued today, is that the overwhelmingly important task in running a department is coping with political turbulence and that the main requirements for doing so are: very wide experience of the processes of policy-making; fluency in writing and speech and the ability to summarize complicated arguments; social acceptability among one's peers and the competence to cope with crises in a detached and objective way. Administrators, it has been said, are a group 'who, whatever the subject matter of their particular work, may be said to specialize in the awareness of Ministerial responsibility'.[6] The Fulton Committee said that one result of this specialization was that 'few members of the class actually see themselves as managers, that is as responsible for organization, directing staff, planning the progress of work, setting standards of attainment and measuring results, reviewing procedures and quantifying different courses of action . . . much of their work is not managerial in this sense; so they tend to see themselves as advisers on policy to people above them, rather than as managers of the administrative machine below them'.[7]

Over the decades, an elaborate mythology grew up around the natural superiority of the generalist administrator. He could be relied upon to construct a defensible position for his Minister, he was alert to threats to his department, he could sift through all the conflicting advice coming the Minister's way, he knew how to propagate his department's view through the government machine: he was a 'politician's politician',[8] a 'statesman in disguise'.[9] The possessors of these skills came from a very narrow social and educational background. A very high proportion of those who reached the top levels of the class came from public schools and had arts degrees from Oxford or Cambridge. They joined the Service straight from university on a training and promotion scheme (as 'Assistant Principals') which gave them exceptional prospects and switched from job to job with great rapidity, almost always in headquarters policy divisions. The frequency of job rotation, at around two- or three-year intervals, was to enable them to gain wide experience of their departments and absorb the department ethos and to prevent the staleness and a loss of detachment which might result from 'too great a familiarity with the problems in hand'.[10]

It was observed by many critics and confirmed by the Fulton Committee that this administrative style had a number of weaknesses. It was not suited to a managerial role in which complex technical evaluations were required to precede political decision-making. It placed a low valuation on management, quantified analysis, planning and peformance measurement. It could not easily mobilize technical, scientific and management skills to address a national problem. It tended to be remote from the preoccupations and perceptions of ordinary people and to be incompetent, however benevolent, in personnel management. It was detached from the worlds of, for example, industrial relations, comprehensive schools and industrial management. It was quite unfitted for the conduct of the interventionist and technocratic industrial policy which was seen as the direction for Britain in the late 1960s.

The critics hammered its amateurism and elitism, sometimes in an exaggerated and unfair way. The criticism of generalism became mixed up with criticism of the public school and Oxbridge ascendancy so that that administrators were to some extent able to characterize a well-founded concern about administration practice as class-motivated spite. The absence of any coherent plan for reform arising from the diagnosis of the Fulton Committee encouraged resistance and delay and, as we shall see from the following chapters, the opportunity to reconstruct our Civil Service on lines more appropriate to the needs of late twentieth-century Britain was largely missed.

References

1. *Committee on the Civil Service, Report*, (June 1968), Cmnd. 3638 Vol. II, para. 303.
2. *Expenditure Committee, Eleventh Report*, (July 1977), HC 535, Vol. II, p. 659.
3. NORTHCOTE and TREVELYAN, *Report on the Organization of the Permanent Civil Service*, reprinted in the *Committee on the Civil Service, Report*, (1968) Vol. I, Appendix B.
4. Civil Service National Whitley Council, *Report of the Joint Committee on the Organization of the Civil Service*, (1920).
5. *Committee on the Civil Service, Report*, (June 1968), Vol. V(I), Memorandum 15, para. 3.
6. SISSON, C. H., *The Spirit of British Administration*, (Faber & Faber, 1959), p. 13.
7. *Committee on the Civil Service, Report*, (June 1968), Vol. I, para. 18.
8. BRAY, J. *Decision in Government*, (Gollancz, 1970), p. 66.
9. FRY, G. R., *Statesmen in Disguise*, (Macmillan, 1969).
10. *Committee on the Civil Service, Report*, (June 1968), Vol. II, para. 73.

II
The Fulton Report
and
'A New Style of Government'

The Fulton Committee was very much a product of its time. Its time was the brief period of Harold Wilson's technological revolution, 1964–7. After thirteen years of opposition, the Labour Party came to power on a new deal programme of modernizing Britain through the application of science, technology and the best management practices. The command generation of British society, the Establishment, was to be replaced by technologically-trained thrusters. Moribund industries, led by incompetent and complacent directors who had presided over decades of decline, were to be reorganized into powerful groups capable of competing with the alarmingly successful Germans and the rising Japanese. Industrial reconstruction was to be masterminded by new institutions: the Industrial Reorganization Corporation, the Ministry of Technology and the Department of Economic Affairs and was to be systematically supervised through a national plan. A Civil Service which was strongly suspected of being dominated by a core of top officials ('the establishment of mandarins') with no knowledge of, or feeling for, technology or management, few of the skills required for industrial reconstruction and an aversion to radical change was no instrument for such a revolution and had to be modernized as well.

In February, 1966 the Committee on the Civil Service was set up under the chairmanship of Lord Fulton 'to examine the structure, recruitment and management, including training, of the Civil Service and to make recommendations'. The Prime Minister, Mr Wilson, in his introductory statement to the House of Commons, said that the decision to set up a committee was reached in view of the changes which had taken place in the demands placed upon the Civil Service and of the changes in the country's educational system and that the time had come to ensure that the Service was properly equipped for its role in the modern state.

The Evidence

In evidence to the Fulton Committee, the Treasury's[1] main suggestion

11

was that the Executive and Administrative Classes should be combined so as to give one line of promotion through a general management class from the level of clerical supervisor to the top posts in a department. It considered that there should be an enlarged graduate entry, a proportion of which ('roughly equivalent in size to the present Assistant Principal entry') might be 'starred' (i.e. picked out for rapid promotion) on the basis of academic record and performance at the selection stage. The necessity for identifying an élite group arose from the need to give the most able an especially attractive career and because departments could give special training to only a few. The Treasury also suggested the merger of the Administrative with the Specialist Classes above the level of the top of the Assistant Secretary scale (the fourth level down the hierarchy) and the provision of training for senior specialists so as to fit them for general management, though it pointed out that policy posts would usually continue to go to those who had spent their careers in general administrative work because these posts primarily required expertise in administrative processes.

The First Division Association,[2] representing the Administrative Class, found even the Treasury's proposals too radical to stomach. 'Starring' the right kind of graduate they found insufficiently exclusive for their members – 'many of our assistant principal members . . . assure us they would not have been interested in joining under these conditions. They saw a real incentive in seeking to join what they regarded as an élite. . . . They will only see a lowering of the graduate entry standards and, in place of membership of an élite, a vague promise of preferential treatment.' On the question of the primacy of the lay administrator, the FDA said that he had to bring to bear on any issue all the wider considerations that were relevant, while the role of the specialist was to speak on the scientific or technical merits of a particular course of action: 'We do not believe these roles can be combined.'

The Institution of Professional Civil Servants,[3] representing most of the specialist classes in the Civil Service, attacked the Treasury's evidence as inadequate and unreal in seeking to keep the specialist in a subservient role and to perpetuate the mystique of the lay administrator. It proposed the abolition of all the class divisions above the level of administrative Principal (the fifth level down the hierarchy) and proposed three broad career groups: the Technology Group, the Science Group and the Administrative Group including technical and junior classes. Responsibility should be placed on the man doing the job – for instance the specialist engineer should be responsible for seeing his work through, rather than having it vetted and approved by an unqualified administrator. Jobs should be open to the best man available rather than one from a particular academic or career background:

in future no man should be effectively barred from any level or from participating in policy or from giving advice directly to the Minister because of his profession. The work of formulating policy and of management should be open to all talents.

The evidence sent to the Committee by the Labour Party[4] was widely interpreted at the time as a list of complaints against the Civil Service which Ministers had accumulated in two years of office. It drew attention to the fact that the Civil Service now managed a highly complex techno-industrial society – a job calling for more specialized technical skill than the generalist could provide. In a highly publicized section, it criticized the amount of information withheld from Ministers which made some of them 'tools of their departments a good deal of the time' and said that 'inter-departmental committees of officials are a particularly effective way of undermining the authority of Ministers'. It proposed that an incoming Minister should have the right to appoint a personal *cabinet* of assistants who would have access to him and to all the information of his department. 'Its function would be to act as a political brains trust to the Minister, to act as an extra pair of eyes and ears, to stimulate him.' It also proposed that the temporary appointment of expert advisers in 'posts of confidence' who would have direct access to the Minister. It opposed the Treasury's proposal for 'starring' an élite group of graduates and supported the merger of the Administrative and Executive Classes and the upper levels of these with the Professional Classes. It recommended that 'administrative' training should be given to professionally qualified entrants to fit them for administrative jobs; that improved training should also be given to non-graduates so that they could also compete for the highest posts; that the personnel management function of the Treasury should be transferred to the Civil Service Commission; that careers should be better planned so that an official acquired a steadily widening range of experience and was not expected to move between totally unrelated jobs. It proposed a more vigorous and determined attempt to recruit people from universities other than Oxbridge and with other than arts degrees, an enlarged Centre for Administrative Studies and the provision of middle and senior management courses for both administrative and professional staff.

The Fulton Committee commissioned two pieces of evidence which heavily influenced its report: a study by a Management Consultancy Group and a Social Survey. The Management Consultancy Group[5] studied the jobs of civil servants in twenty-three 'blocks' of work in twelve departments. The group found that over half of the direct-entry administrators they had interviewed had degrees in history or classics. They found that most lacked training or experience of management techniques and they commented on their rapid movement from job to job. They concluded that the work of the Administrative Class suffered because of lack of continuity in the job, lack of management skills and experience and a largely irrelevant educational background. The group paid particular attention to the relationships between administrators and specialists. They discussed all the standard arguments for excluding specialists from the line of management and from financial control. These were that administrators were more cost-conscious than specialists; that they relieved scarce specialists of non-specialist work; that they could best co-ordinate the work of the different specialists; that they could set specialist matters in the context of Ministerial policy and their knowledge of the administrative machine; that they had the fluency to synthesize various specialist and administrative views in a form on which decisions could be based; that the work of specialists benefited from critical scrutiny by the intelligent layman who, by virtue of his detached viewpoint, could spot unnecessary expenditure. They then put the opposing arguments. They had found that, particularly in matters of financial control, administrators did not have the competence to challenge the specialists except on obvious or relatively trivial points; that the division of decision-making between specialists and administrators resulted in delay and inefficiency (misunderstandings arose, papers were sent to and fro, time was occupied by explanation); that since administrators frequently changed jobs, specialists often found themselves having to explain the technical background to laymen. They observed that in industry specialists were frequently empowered to spend funds without having their decisions under continuous scrutiny by laymen – cost-control was a feature of the training of architects, engineers and surveyors, for example; that there was no evidence that specialists were unsuited to the role of policy-makers – accountants and engineers were prominent in the policy areas of large companies; that there was no evidence that specialists could not quickly assimilate knowledge of the working of the government machine; that specialists resented their subordinate status and this hindered the recruitment of top-class professionals and that where the common task was divided between specialists and administrators, no one individual had clear management responsibility. They concluded that in administrative/technical areas the manager should usually be a specialist who had acquired training and experience in the administrative procedures of government and that it was essential that top posts should be open to specialists with the appropriate qualifications.

In its final chapter, 'Management and Organization', the Consultancy Group concluded that the career class structure was a major obstacle to efficient management in the Service and proposed the replacement of all classes by a system of pay bands, a 'unified grading structure' based on job evaluation. The group then went on to suggest lines of research into a new managerial style for the Service based on the definition of objectives and priorities for organizational units; forms of organization derived not from the hierarchies of career classes but from the definition of managerial objectives; rewards related more to merit than to seniority; more sophisticated forms of management accounting and control; greater delegation of authority to individual managers supported by procedures for assessing accountability and for measuring managerial effectiveness. To establish the long-term policy framework for these systems of objective-setting and control, they said that new high-level departmental planning units were required.

The Social Survey commissioned by the Fulton Committee was carried out by Dr A. H. Halsey, head of the Department of Social and Administrative Studies at Oxford and Mr I. M. Crewe of the University of Lancaster and was published in September 1969.[6] It found that until very recently the Administrative Class had tended to be more, rather than less, socially exclusive, with an increasing proportion of its direct entrants coming from the middle classes and having been to public schools. No fewer than 85 per cent of those directly recruited between 1961 and 1965 were middle-class in background (as compared with 64 per cent in 1951–5) in a period when the universities were drawing an increasing proportion of their students from working-class backgrounds. The Survey also found that 'the type of subject studied at university by graduate recruits to the Administrative Class is remarkable when compared with foreign experience and with British business and professions'.[7] No less than 71 per cent had arts degrees, mainly in history and classics, in marked contrast to their equivalents in the US government service, who mostly had degrees in science or social studies, and in France, where administrators were trained in economics, law, public administration, finance and statistics. Some 73 per cent of direct entrant Administrators in 1961–6 had been to Oxford or Cambridge – nearly the same as the immediate post-war period and considerably higher than during the war. In contrast, the proportion of all students graduating from Oxbridge had declined from 22 per cent before the war to 14 per cent in the early 1960s. The survey also found a marked decline in the quality of recruits to the Administrative Class (as measured by class of degree). The authors of the survey concluded that 'there is reasonable ground for questioning the effectiveness of Civil Service recruitment'.

On the day this 'damning survey'[8] was published, the Civil Service Department published a report on the interview system by which most direct entrant administrators are selected, made by a Committee under the chairmanship of Mr J. G. W. Davies, an assistant to the Governor of the Bank of England.[9] The Davies Report said that the selection

15

system was one to which the public service could point with pride; that there had been a distinct and progressive change in the type of candidate entering the competition since 1964; that there was no evidence of bias in the system and that there was no fundamental weakness in it. It said that the selection board provided equality of opportunity and maintained an appropriate balance between the personal and intellectual qualities which were needed in the Administrative Class. The *Financial Times* reported that 'senior civil servants are clearly delighted and relieved that the Davies Report has come down so overwhelmingly in favour of the present selection system'.[10]

The Report

The Fulton Committee reported in June 1968. The first chapter of its report began: 'The Home Civil Service today is still fundamentally the product of the nineteenth-century philosophy of the Northcote-Trevelyan Report. The tasks it faces are those of the second half of the twentieth century. This is what we have found; it is what we seek to remedy.' It concluded that the structure and practices of the Service had not kept up with its vastly increased responsibilities. The Service was inadequate in six main respects:

First, it was still essentially based on the philosophy of the amateur (or 'generalist' or 'all-rounder'). This was most evident in the Administrative Class, which held the dominant positions in the Service. 'The ideal administrator is still too often seen as the gifted layman who, moving frequently from job to job within the Service, can take a practical view of any problem, irrespective of its subject matter, in the light of his knowledge and experience of the government machine.'[11]

Secondly, the system of classes in the Service seriously hindered its work.

Thirdly, many scientists, engineers and other specialists were not given the responsibilities, authority or opportunities they ought to have.

Fourthly, too few civil servants were skilled managers. Members of the Administrative Class, in particular, who were allotted the major managerial role in the Service did not see themselves as managers of departments but as advisers on policy to those above them.

Fifthly, there was not enough contact between the Service and the rest of the community. There was not enough awareness in the Service of how the world outside Whitehall worked, how government policies would affect it and of the new ideas and methods which were developing in the universities, in business and in other walks of life.

Finally, the Committee had serious criticisms of personnel management. Career planning was rare, senior civil servants were moved too frequently between unrelated jobs and there was insufficient encouragement and reward for individual initiative and performance.

After discussing the tasks of the modern Civil Service, recruitment and the class structure, the promotion of efficiency, the central management of the Service and relationships with the community, Fulton made 158 recommendations. The most important of these were:

1 A classless service should be created. The Committee recommended the abolition of all occupational classes and their replacement by a unified grading structure based on job evaluation (i.e. the relative value of every job in the Civil Service should be analysed and fitted into about ten pay grades).

2 Administrators should specialize, particularly in their early years of service, in specific subjects; for example, in economic and financial affairs or in social affairs. The basic principle of career management should be progressive development within a specialism. In the recruitment of graduates for administrative work the relevance of their university studies to their future work should be an important criterion. Those graduates appointed without relevant qualifications should be required to take a special training course.

3 Specialists should be allowed to carry more responsibility and the obstacles preventing them from reaching the top should be removed.

4 A Civil Service College should be created to provide training in administration for specialists, post-entry training for graduates recruited for administrative work, courses for the best school leavers, post-experience courses in management and in particular management techniques.

5 Movement in and out of the Service should be facilitated by arrangements for transfer, temporary appointments and transferable pensions.

6 The principles of accountable management should be applied to the Service; that is, individual managers should be held responsible for their performance, measured as objectively as possible.

7 Each department should have a management services unit capable of carrying out efficiency audits involving all aspects of the department's work at all levels.

8 Departments should have planning and research units with responsibility for long-term policy planning. These units should be headed by Senior Policy Advisers who would have direct and unrestricted access to the Minister.

9 The central management of the Service should be made the responsibility of a new department, the Civil Service Department, which should absorb the functions of the Pay and Management side of the Treasury and those of the Civil Service Commission.

Its official head should be designated Head of the Home Civil Service.

10 The government should set up an inquiry to make recommendations for getting rid of unnecessary secrecy.

The Response

The publication of the Fulton Report provoked loud cries of outrage from top people. A reference in it to 'the tradition of the "all-rounder" as he has been called by his champions or "amateur" as he has been called by his critics' (which Sir James Dunnett, one of the Permanent Secretaries on the Committee later called 'a fair statement of fact'[12]) particularly caused offence. The report was called rude, abrasive, indiscriminating, notorious, commonplace, and shameful. Former administrators in the House of Lords were particularly upset.[13] The House of Commons[14] generally welcomed the report and the Prime Minister announced that the government accepted its recommendations for the abolition of the classes, the setting up of a Civil Service Department and a Civil Service College. He could not accept that in future preference should be given by the Service to graduates with relevant degrees.

Implementation of the Fulton Report got off to a rapid start. The Civil Service Department came into existence on 1st November 1968, taking over the responsibilities of the Pay and Management Divisions of the Treasury and the Civil Service Commission. Sir William (now Lord) Armstrong was appointed Head of the Civil Service and was welcomed as a good choice for the task of seeing through the Fulton reforms. 'It was an important coincidence that at the time when criticism of the Civil Service was at last inducing reform there should be a man at the top of it who saw his lifework as a reformer. The personality of Sir William Armstrong may emerge historically as a more important factor than the Fulton Commission, for no bureaucratic reform is possible without strong support from inside. In 1968 Sir William Armstrong took over the job of head of the Home Civil Service, including the new Civil Service Department and committed himself – with publicity unprecedented for a civil servant – to implementing the Fulton reforms. . . . When the Report of 1968 was accepted, Armstrong was the obvious man to carry it through.'[15]

The Civil Service College was opened in April 1969 with a capacity of 800 places in Sunningdale, London and Edinburgh. Work on the unified grading structure began with 'vertical' mergers of classes. The Clerical, Executive and Administrative Classes were merged into an Administration Group and the Scientific Officer Class and its supporting classes into a Science Category in 1971. The Works Group and some of its supporting technical classes were reconstituted as a Professional and Technology Group in 1972. Since then, Treasury and departmental classes have been absorbed into existing or new occupational groups and these have been associated in three main categories. Thus, the Economist, Information Officer, Librarian and Statistician Groups were associated with the Administration Group in a General Category. Various technical groups were associated with the Professional and Technology Group in a Professional and Technology Category. Smaller categories were set up for those classes which apparently could not readily be absorbed into the General Category: e.g. training staff, data processing operators, lawyers. By late 1977 the three categories accounted for about 70 per cent of the non-industrial Civil Service and a further 20 per cent was being considered for absorption. This would leave about fifteen general classes (including accountants and doctors) and about twenty significant departmental classes (mostly in the Inland Revenue and the Department of Social Security) outside the category system.

In January 1972 the first sign of progress appeared in merging the classes 'horizontally', the essential step in achieving Fulton's unified structure. The top 650 (now 860) officials at Permanent, Deputy and Under Secretary levels in the Administration Group and their equivalents in other classes (top scientists and economists, for example) were placed in a new Open Structure and it was proposed to extend this structure downwards, next to the Assistant Secretary level, then to Principal level and so on until the whole Civil Service was 'open'. A report by the joint official/staff side saw no technical difficulty in opening the structure at least down to Principal level.

Unfortunately, at that point the progress of unification stopped and it became known that the Civil Service Department was not inclined to continue with it. It was said that the exercise was complicated and that some Civil Service unions were opposed to it though it is interesting that it stopped at exactly the point (Under Secretary) recommended to the Fulton Committee by the Treasury in 1966. We shall see from the next chapter that the Civil Service Department maintained some years later that there were less expensive ways of giving specialists access to general management jobs though the House of Commons Expenditure Committee was not convinced by the argument. We shall also see that the new graduate trainee scheme introduced by the CSD in response to the criticisms of the narrowness of the educational and social backgrounds of Assistant Principals did not fulfill Fulton's objectives either. In general, the reforms Fulton proposed for changing the top management of the Service have not yet been implemented.

A Review

Comment and debate on the Fulton Report focused almost exclusively on the criticisms it made of the characteristics of the two thousand or so top administrators and its call for their jobs to be made open to specialists. The Committee saw this reform as the essential first step to improving the management of the Service while its critics saw it as an expensive irrelevance. Introducing the unified grading structure would be a lengthy and complicated task in that hundreds of jobs would have to be analysed and evaluated and the lower down the hierarchy the process is taken, the more the jobs that have to be studied. There were only 570 jobs at the Under Secretary level when it was brought into the Open Structure but there would be nearly four times that number at the Assistant Secretary level and twenty times that number at the Principal level (though many jobs at these levels are already linked for purposes of pay).

Job evaluation on this scale can also be costly in that the work of fitting many separate pay grades into a few consolidated ones would involve some 'rounding up', i.e. increasing the pay of some grades or individuals. The Civil Service Department has said that the opportunity to round up was severely limited by the incomes policies of the 1970s. In addition, it is clear that there has been opposition to unification from the Society of Civil and Public Servants representing the Executive Class who see the prospect of jobs which had been reserved for their members being taken by specialists – 'We do not believe that the Administration Group should be viewed as the happy hunting ground for the frustrated careers prospects of others.'[16] Given these difficulties, it is understandable that the Civil Service Department tried to open up career opportunities for specialists by means other than the unification of the classes. Within the new categories, restrictions to promotion were removed. Executives now more freely move into senior jobs and, more noticeably, some scientists and technicians who could not achieve the academic qualifications required by the former Scientific Officer Class but who were capable managers of scientific work can now move into managerial positions.

The problem remains, however, that the best specialists still have many obstacles to overcome before they can get into general management. While classes, groups and categories exist it is unlikely that the specialist can obtain sufficient experience of administration – handling ministerial work, policy making, legislation and financial control – early enough to fit him for jobs in the Open Structure while he is still young enough to compete for them. Under the present arrangements, we shall continue to have a top management cadre in the Civil Service who are not well equipped to apply scientific method, quantitative analysis and technical experience to the problems of government, though the need grows more pressing every year. As Lord Fulton said to the Expenditure Committee: 'It is depressing that after a long rumination the Civil Service, by and large, came out against the Open Structure – accepting it at the top but not far enough down the Service to capture these talented scientists and having captured them to put them to the service of the nation.'[17]

Even without unified grading, the expertise and management competence of the administrative cadre could have been much improved if the government had accepted the Fulton Committee's recommendation that graduates recruited for administration should be required to have 'relevant' qualifications. It put the argument for relevance in this way:

'To give preference for relevance is to adapt to the needs of today the old principle that the Service should seek to recruit those it believes best equipped for work in government. . . . Today when the tasks of government have changed, the Service should seek to recruit those equipped for the new tasks. First-degree courses based on the study of modern subjects especially attract many young people with a positive and practical interest in contemporary problems, political, social, economic, scientific and technological. These problems will yield their solutions only to the most concentrated assaults of minds equipped through rigorous and sustained intellectual discipline with the necessary apparatus of relevant ideas, knowledge, methods and techniques. We therefore wish the Civil Service to attract its full share of young people motivated in this way, with minds disciplined by undergraduate (and post-graduate) work in the social studies, the mathematical and physical sciences, the biological sciences or in the applied and engineering sciences.

There is also evidence that most undergraduates want jobs in which they can make direct use of their university studies. In recent years the Service has not properly recognized this, giving the general impression that it is more concerned with the quality of a man's degree than its relevance to the work of government. This, in our view, has discouraged applications from graduates whose interest and studies are focused on modern problems. Thus post-war recruitment to the Administrative Class has run counter to the increased trend in the universities towards the study of the problems of the modern world. Therefore, to be attractive to this growing number of graduates, the Service should declare its special interest in the relevance of their studies. In this way, too, the Service would be attracting its recruits from a wider range of degree subjects than those from which administrators have traditionally been drawn.'[18]

The government, under pressure from the universities who saw the proposal as a suggestion that the State should try to influence what they taught, rejected the relevance argument and the pattern of arts graduate recruitment continues. As Lord Crowther-Hunt, a member of the Fulton Committee, said to the Expenditure Committee: 'if I were giving a son advice – you asked for this – on how to get into the modern Civil Service today I would say "be born in Social Classes I or II, go to a public school, read Classics at Oxford for preference and you have on that basis the best chance for getting to the top of the Civil Service".'[19]

Fulton made many other very important recommendations for the improvement of the management of departments and these are discussed in later chapters. Unfortunately, many of them were not very clear and some were confused. For example, changes which its Consultancy Group suggested should be the subject of research programmes (new forms of organization, new management controls, performance auditing) were promulgated by the Committee as full-blown principles of management without any further evidence or deeper discussion. The Consultancy Group's proposed management planning units became Fulton's policy planning groups in which a planning function and a Ministerial *cabinet* were confused and the Group's job evaluation scheme was mixed up with 'end results analysis'. Moreover, the Committee left the implementation of these new systems to the Civil Service Department, i.e. a detached part of the Treasury without the Treasury's authority, and proposed no means of monitoring its results. The whole programme relied on a massive change of attitude on the part of top administrators who objected to the propect of upheaval and who were smarting from the most penetrating criticisms of their competence and social characteristics.

In addition, the Committee missed several areas of enquiry which were central to modernizing the Civil Service. First, it made no reference to the audit of departmental efficiency other than that carried out by departments themselves or by the proposed Civil Service Department. The need for an external audit body which can override departmental autonomy has since become clear. Secondly, it hardly touched on departmental systems of budgeting and expenditure control. A number of important reforms proposed by the Committee under the heading of 'Accountable and Efficient Management' could not have been carried out without very great prior changes in the information systems operated by departments and the design of new procedures for planning, objective-setting and the measurement of performance. Fulton indicated the need for the measurement and analysis of the performance of departments but did not consider the extent to which government accounting and statistical information needed to be reconstructed to meet the requirements of its new management methods. We shall see that the pressure for changes in this field has increased in recent years as a result of demands by Parliamentary committees for improved Parliamentary scrutiny. The Committee also devoted the bulk of its enquiry to the characteristics and behaviour of the higher Civil Service and spent very little time on the problems of the lower grades, their attitudes and their morale; problems which came home to roost before long.

A New Style of Government

The Fulton programme had hardly been started when the government changed and Civil Service reform took off in a new direction. Whereas Fulton had called upon the Service to develop management techniques which were derived from practices in large scale industry and commerce but adapted to public administration and which required the most careful preparation and implementation over many years, the new emphasis was on rapid cost-cutting through 'businesslike' methods. Conservative politicians tended to dismiss Fulton's views about the importance of changing the nature of the top management of the Service as socialist egalitarianism. They wanted to cut what they saw as wasteful bureaucratic procedures by the adoption of the methods used by efficient businesses, like Marks and Spencer Ltd which had recently had a very good press for its campaign to reduce paperwork. The Civil Service was therefore faced with both implementing the long-term Fulton reforms, though with no great pressure from the government, and the new efficiency drive. In addition, the Conservative government also required them to implement 'a new style of government' involving substantial organizational changes, new budgetary control systems and new routines for policy analysis (these are described in later chapters). It is no wonder that the Fulton programme was pushed into the background.

The blame for the confusion between long term reform and short term cost cutting cannot be laid entirely at the door of the Conservatives. A few months after Fulton reported, in November 1968, the Labour government had decided to try business methods in the Service as a means of reducing manpower. The Panel of Businessmen for Civil Service Manpower Review was set up under Sir Robert Bellinger and included eight businessmen. Accompanied by CSD staff and by officials of the departments under review it carried out assignments in thirteen government departments by March 1970. Apparently, they found that economies could be made in reducing excessive checking and monitoring of work, in the greater delegation of authority, in charging higher fees for services, and in the simplification of schemes which departments had to administer. The panel recommended improved internal audit schemes in departments and that there should be a 'conscious and directed' effort to counter the inevitable pressure to increase the numbers of staff. The savings suggested by the panel were not large: they concluded that substantial savings could be made only if Ministers, Parliament and the public were willing to accept changes in practices which might change levels of service. The CSD politely said that it had been helpful to have a basis of comparison between the methods used in Government service and modern industry and commerce. The Bellinger panel was ended by the Conservative government in 1970 and was replaced by a new team of businessmen.

The new Conservative approach apparently began in 1967 when Mr Ernest (later Lord) Marples, a successful businessman and former Minister 'went off round the world on a managerial fact-finding mission and bored his colleagues into taking the subject seriously on his return'.[20] Mr Marples was reported as persuading Mr Edward Heath to support a 'public sector research unit' to find out 'why elected politicians so rarely got their undertakings carried out'.[21] Mr Marples was assisted by Mr David Howell, MP, and they were advised by sympathetic businessmen. In September 1969 a seminar was held at a management training centre, Sundridge Park, to discuss the application of business methods to government. After the Sundridge Park meeting groups of businessmen and politicians were set up to produce proposals but they had completed only a general survey when the election of June 1970 was called.

On taking office, Mr Heath appointed Mr Richard Meyjes of Shell International to head a team of five businessmen who were to apply new methods to government. 'As the business team sees it, the Civil Service tries to carry out three tasks of government: advising Ministers on policy; running regular administration (for instance tax collecting, where rules and precedents are already laid down); and managing vast enterprises such as the National Health Service or the education services. The businessmen think the Civil Service performs the first two tasks well, and the third – which requires business and managerial training – badly.'[22]

In May 1970 the Conservative Political Centre published *A New Style of Government* by David Howell, MP:[23] 'A Conservative View of the Tasks of Administrative, Financial and Parliamentary Reform Facing an Incoming Government'. Mr Howell wrote that administration, often thought to be a matter for civil servants and not for politicians, was central to government policy. 'The work of the Civil Service Department is of the highest political importance. There is all the difference in the world between the reform of government machinery and procedures under a party which believes in more government and one which believes in less. . . . Under the latter, it becomes, or should become . . . a key instrument in the drive for public economy and in the process of transforming functions and activities back to the private sector or running them down altogether.'[24] Mr Howell's new style included a new planning and control system based on stating the objectives of government functions in terms of outputs (basically Programme Budgeting – see Chapter 5); a new body in the Treasury for evaluating government programmes; a reorganization of central government departments on the basis of small policy-making head-quarters staffs and executive boards, agencies and task forces (see Chapter 4) and the increased recruitment of managers from industry.

Some of these ideas were repeated in the White Paper of 1970 *The Reorganization of Government* which said that the administration had pledged itself to introduce a new style of government and proposed the amalgamation of departments and new arrangements for policy and expenditure analysis with the aim of 'less government, and better government carried out by fewer people'.

We shall see that the new style had a substantial impact on the machinery of government, a more modest effect on policy and expendi-ture planning and almost none on the size of government. Many of its objectives could have been achieved more effectively by a commitment to the Fulton ideas for accountable and efficient management, i.e. the patient development of systems properly tuned to the requirements of public administration rather than ideas lifted from business practice. Moreover, the ideas which were lifted from business were just about to become out of date. They were heavily influenced by the enthusiasm of the 1950s and 60s in British industry for economies of scale and large conglomerate forms of organization structure. These ideas also found their way into the reorganization of the National Health Service and of local government where they have proved to be of doubtful worth. By the 1970s there was a growing awareness of the diseconomies of scale and the very great problems of managing large organizations and much thought is now being given to ways of unpicking the organiza-tions that were created by the enthusiasts of a decade ago.

During the period of the Labour Government, 1974–9, there was little progress on Civil Service reform. There were some improvements in the presentation of expenditure plans and work on accountable management proceeded but the development of personnel management was virtually halted by public expenditure cuts and labour relations problems. We shall see that an attempt by the Expenditure Committee to get the Civil Service to re-start the Fulton programme was un-enthusiastically received by the government, which had clearly lost interest in the matter.

The Conservative government of 1979 immediately initiated a pro-gramme of Civil Service manpower cuts as part of a policy to reduce public expenditure. Departments were required to produce proposals for reductions of up to 20 per cent, involving the abandonment of large spending programmes and probably, the abolition of major divisions of departments. Once again, the proposal was made to introduce business methods in departments as a means of making them smaller and more efficient. A member of the 1970 Meyjes team of businessmen, Sir Derek Rayner of Marks and Spencer was brought in to lead 'the war on waste'. Within a few months he and his small team were reported as having identified savings of £70 million a year[25] as a result of looking briefly at, for example, the costs of paying Social Security benefits, the cost of food supplies to the Ministry of Defence and the Treasury's growing use of paper. As Fulton had done, he criticized the provision of services (e.g. stationery and accommodation) to departments on allied service or no-charge basis. However, neither the across-the-board cuts in staff nor the piecemeal attack on individual elements of cost appears to be better than the systematic improvement of efficiency and effectiveness which would have resulted from the application of the Fulton Committee's principles of managerial accountability or the development of its ideas on regular efficiency audits.

References

1. *Committee on the Civil Service, Report*, (June 1968), Vol. 5, Memorandum 1.
2. ibid., Memorandum 15.
3. ibid., Memorandum 36–39.
4. ibid., Memorandum 47.
5. ibid., Vol. II, *Report of a Management Consultancy Group*.
6. ibid., Vol. III(i), *Social Survey of the Civil Service*.
7. *Social Survey*, p. 400.
8. DEAN, M., 'Whitehall Elite Holds Its Own', *Guardian*, (25 September 1969).
9. *Report of a Committee of Enquiry*, 'The Method II System of Selection', (September 1969), Cmnd. 4156.
10. EVANS, R., 'No Oxbridge Bias in Top Grade Appointments', *Financial Times*, (25 September 1969).
11. *Committee on the Civil Service, Report*, (June 1968) Vol. I, para. 15.
12. DUNNETT, Sir J., 'The Fulton Report', *Institute of Public Administration*, (1969), p. 31.
13. *House of Lords Debates*, (24 July 1968), Vol. 295, No. 122, Cols. 1049–1194.
14. *House of Commons Debates*, (21 November 1968), Vol. 773, No. 17, Cols. 1542–1681.
15. SAMPSON, A., 'The New Mandarins', *Observer*, (28 February 1971), p. 19.
16. *Expenditure Committee, Eleventh Report*, (July 1977), HC 535, Vol. II, p. 518.

17. Expenditure Committee, op. cit., Vol. II, p. 468.
18. *Committee on the Civil Service, Report*, (June 1968), Vol. I, para. 77.
19. Expenditure Committee, op. cit., Vol. II, p. 474.
20. WATT, D., 'Why the Tories Want More Whizz Kids in Whitehall', *Financial Times*, (21 November 1969).
21. BELOFF, N., 'Heath Adds the Marks and Sparks Touch to Whitehall', *Observer*, (21 July 1970).
22. BELOFF, N., op. cit.
23. HOWELL, D., 'A New Style of Government', Conservative Political Centre, (1970).
24. HOWELL, D., op. cit., p. 8.
25. NORTON-TAYLOR, R., 'Whitehall Wasting £70m a Year', *Guardian*, (12th October 1979).

III
The Expenditure Committee :
Recruitment,
Training and Grading

Until the reform of the select committee system in 1979, the General Sub-Committee was one of the most effective of the 'subject' sub-committees of the House of Commons' Expenditure Committee. The General Sub-Committee had as its field of reference policy and management in the Treasury, the Inland Revenue, the Civil Service Department and such bodies as HMSO and the Central Office of Information. It usually concentrated on Treasury policy and gradually tried to develop its role into a Parliamentary committee on economic affairs. Its annual enquiry into the Public Expenditure White Paper became an examination of Treasury ministers and officials on the management of the economy, fiscal and monetary policy, economic forecasting, public expenditure planning and control and the scope and form of national accounting and financial information and its reports provided valuable material for the national debate on the British economy. Its advisers, notably Mr Wynne Godley and Mr Terry Ward, of the Department of Applied Economics of Cambridge University, provided it with critical analyses which enabled its members effectively to challenge Treasury policies. In its last few years, the sub-committee invited outside specialist bodies to contribute papers and thus provided a forum in which the Treasury had to justify and explain its actions and proposals.

From May 1976 to July 1977 the General sub-committee examined the Civil Service. Its enquiry, the first into the Civil Service by a House of Commons Select Committee for over one hundred years, began as a review of developments in the Civil Service since the Fulton Report but rapidly widened into the consideration of pay and pensions in the Service; the relationships between ministers and civil servants and Parliamentary power of control and surveillance over the central administration. It strongly emphasized the need for the increased public accountability of the Service through better information and new Parliamentary machinery, indicating the strong concern felt by back bench MPs that the Executive had gained too much power at the expense of Parliament. This important report[1] was received very coolly by the Government and its Observations,[2] published in March 1978, promised action on only the most minor of the Expenditure Committee's recommendations. The Committee felt so strongly about this treatment of its report that it issued a brisk response to the Government's observations in a further report in July 1978. After months of urging, the Government allowed a debate on the report in January 1979.

In later chapters of this book detailed consideration is given to the Committee's comments on the machinery and organization of government, personnel management, efficient and accountable management and Parliamentary surveillance. In this chapter, the Expenditure Committee's report and the Government's reactions to it will be examined in relation to the central Fulton theme of the characteristics of the top management cadre of the Civil Service: the mandarins.

Recruitment

The Expenditure Committee concentrated, as the Fulton Committee did, on the recruitment arrangements for the hundred or so administration trainees who entered the Service every year rather than those for the thousands of clerical and executive staff and specialists, because these trainees are the people who are groomed, with exceptional care, to occupy the top jobs in departments.

The administration trainee (AT) scheme had been introduced as a result of Fulton's criticisms of the Assistant Principal procedure, an arrangement for selecting a small group of young graduates for accelerated promotion in the administrative field. Under the new scheme, external graduate recruits and internal applicants, with honours degrees or two years' service, are selected for the AT grade. It was expected that there would be 250–300 AT appointments per year, with 175 recruited externally and the remainder from within the Service. Selection is by a written test, a two-day selection procedure with written tests, interviews and group exercises and a final interview. It has never been clear what weight is given to the objective written tests as compared with the subjective interviews. Once in the grade, ATs spend two to four years in a variety of postings lasting nine months to a year and two eight-week periods of training at the Civil Service College. For their first two years ATs are on probation. If at the end of that period they are judged satisfactory, their status as ATs is confirmed and they are eligible to be 'fast streamed', i.e. promoted to the HEO(A) grade with the expectation of reaching the lowest rung of top management, the Principal grade, in a further two to three years during which it was originally planned that they go on another ten-week course at the College. It was expected that about one-third of ATs would be fast streamed, but in practice around 80 per cent have been, though a far higher proportion of external than internal recruits have found their way into the fast stream. Those who fail are 'main streamed' back into the executive grades. Members of the HEO(A) grade continue to receive a variety of short postings before being promoted to Principal and most are expected to reach at least the Assistant Secretary grade. There are also arrangements for sideways transfer for late developers from the executive and specialist grades into the HEO(A) grade: there is an average of seven such transfers a year.

It was hoped that the new scheme would bring into the Service a wider range of new entrants than the traditional public school and Oxbridge educated arts graduate and would give a chance to able young people already in the Service to get into the fast stream for promotion. After six years of the scheme's operation, analyses prepared by the Civil Service Department showed that 21·6 per cent of the applicants for the AT entry were Oxford or Cambridge graduates but that those two universities provided 50 per cent of AT appointments. In 1975 and 1976 Oxbridge (which account for 12 per cent of total university output) accounted for no less than 60 per cent of the appointees. They further showed that 28 per cent to 36 per cent of applicants had attended independent schools and 50 per cent to 62 per cent of appointees had done so. The bias towards public schools was partly due to the Oxbridge bias, because two-fifths of Oxbridge undergraduates come from independent schools. However, the Expenditure Committee noted that in the case of recruits from other universities, 8·6 per cent of applicants were from independent schools as compared with 21·3 per cent of recruits. 'This makes it look as if the Civil Service Commission not only reinforces an Oxford and Cambridge bias, but also creates a bias which either does not exist in other universities or is much smaller there,'[3] the Committee commented. It also observed that a survey carried out by Lord Franks had shown that at Oxford ex-independent schoolboys obtained on average a poorer class of degree than other Oxford graduates, i.e. the dominance of public school entrants lowered the quality of its graduates to some extent. Analyses of the AT intake also showed that 42·5 per cent of applicants and 56·7 per cent of recruits were arts and humanities graduates and 65 per cent of applicants and 80 per cent of appointees were from socio-economic classes I and II.

Lord Crowther Hunt submitted to the Committee a detailed examination of the statistics on recruiting. He pointed out that the graduate entry into the AT grade was considerably larger than that into the pre-Fulton Assistant Principal grade and that this should lead to the expectation that there would be a broadening both in the type of recruit and of appointee. In fact the Oxbridge bias was somewhat greater than

30

at the time of Fulton's social survey, the public school bias somewhat less and the arts bias considerably greater. Lord Crowther Hunt went on to examine the pattern of increasing graduate recruitment at the Executive Officer level, the entry point for middle management. Three hundred graduates had come into the Service at this grade in 1968 (5 per cent of the total recruitment to the grade) and 1,800 in 1977 (50 per cent of the total). In this case, the pattern of academic subject, type of school and university was very similar for both applicants and recruits. Lord Crowther Hunt's analysis pointed to the conclusion that the system of selection for high flyers was more biased than at the time of the Fulton report, though the system of selection for middle management showed no apparent bias. He concluded that the selection arrangements for ATs were too subjective.

The AT scheme had been disappointing in another respect. Instead of recruiting up to 175 candidates externally and 75 to 125 from inside the Service, between 1971 and 1975 125 to 129 came from outside and only 17 to 55 from serving officers. From 1976–80, an average of 103 per year were external and 43 per year internal recruits. It was not surprising that internal applicants had fallen from 1,172 in 1971 to 593 in 1975. In their joint evidence to the Expenditure Committee, the Society of Civil and Public Servants (representing the Executive grades) and the Civil and Public Services Association (representing the clerical, typing and allied grades) stated their belief that the scheme favoured external graduates as against experienced internal candidates. 'The scheme has failed to provide real opportunities for serving staff and so it has not achieved the declared aim of opening the higher levels of the Service to the most able, regardless of method of entry.'[4] Moreover, the bias against internal candidates was reinforced in the decisions on which ATs were fast streamed. The unions said that nearly all external ATs had been fast streamed, whereas an internal AT had only a 50 per cent chance of being fast streamed. A survey by the CSD's Behavioural Science Research Division had shown that whereas the performance of ATs from within the Service was at least as good as the performance of externally recruited ATs when streaming decisions and ratings of future potential were made internal candidates did less well. The unions concluded that the scheme had positively discriminated against in-service staff, contrary to an agreement made in 1971 with Staff associations. Not surprisingly, it had become increasingly discredited.

The two unions had other complaints against the scheme. Nearly all the work given to ATs was policy work in London and little attempt had been made to give them experience of the day-to-day work and problems of most civil servants. Since the selection procedures were too concerned with academic ability to identify those most capable of performing well in management, the scheme was producing too many 'academically orientated' policy makers. In placing a low valuation on performance and managerial ability, the scheme excluded the experience and ability of executive and clerical officers from being used in developing a 'higher management which understood what it was managing'. The large number of external ATs were denying executive grades the opportunity to do policy work. Far from providing the opportunities envisaged by Fulton, the unions said, the scheme was worsening the career prospects of middle grade officers. The Civil Service had devoted an enormous amount of effort to the AT scheme: it had accounted for 24 per cent* of the training undertaken by the Civil Service College (as against 6 per cent devoted to the training of graduate specialist staff) and officials appearing before the Committee appeared to be hard pressed to explain the disappointing way it had worked out.

Sir Douglas Allen, Head of the Home Civil Service, was tackled on the question of bias in selection during oral sessions of the Committee. He acknowledged bias 'in the statistical sense': 'and I would not quarrel with that sense'. One possible explanation, 'which most of us would find difficult to accept' is that there was 'a correlation between the talents which the Service is looking for and the ability to get high incomes, that these talents are inherited and therefore rather more public school people come in because they have inherited some talents and their parents have been wealthy enough to send them to a public school'.[5] In passing, he drew attention to the heavy representation of Oxbridge in the House of Commons. The Civil Service Commission thought that the results of its selection procedures for ATs were partly due to a long-standing tradition in certain kinds of school and Oxbridge colleges of encouraging people to include the higher ranges of public service among their career choices. It seemed that a high proportion of able school leavers entered Oxbridge, a high proportion of Oxbridge graduates were encouraged to apply for the AT scheme and a high proportion of them did well in the qualifying tests. The Commission said it would welcome more candidates from other universities and polytechnics. If a candidate had had a 'disadvantageous upbringing' then 'in a sense he could be regarded as getting a little extra mark against his name'[6] and they had modified the tests to ensure that scientists and engineers were not placed at any disadvantage. The Commission were guided by a document which described the personal qualities and intellectual characteristics which were to be looked for in Administration Trainees. This document, it transpired, had been

---

* By 1978–9 this was reduced to 15 per cent.

prepared in 1946 by Professor Burt* in conjunction with Dr Anstey and had been in use until 1974 when it had been revised by Dr Anstey. The revised document was supplied to the Committee.[7] It set out such essential qualities as 'good all-round intellect', being able to carry due 'weight' in discussion; being clear in expression on paper ('in an increasing number of jobs numeracy will be almost as important'); being able to work with people; having a feeling for 'ordinary people'; having a general interest in current affairs; having drive and determination. It made some interesting observations on those who might merit promotion in the fast stream. Its authors thought that it might be tempting to look for stereotypes that correlated with selection or non-selection for early advancement, 'e.g. the administrator as against the manager; the conceptual thinker as against the practical man; the man of ideas as against the non-original thinker'. However, they argued that this would not do: there were very important managerial posts in the upper reaches of the Service. 'There is a place among those selected for early promotion for the manager, the practical thinker and the non-originator.' That certainly put management in its place: a second-rate occupation for practical men, in esteem well below the all-round good chap, the natural top administrator and policy maker. In effect, while the Civil Service had been paying lip-service to the Fulton recommendation for a radical change in the way in which it recruited its young high flyers, its criteria for selecting them had never changed. It had simply allowed a few internal candidates to join them. The elaborate and very costly AT scheme produced a top management stream that was at least as socially and educationally exclusive as the scheme it replaced, it had done very little for able people already in the Service and had probably worsened their prospects. The Service had also ignored the Fulton proposal that it should look for and encourage a considerably larger number of late entrants, people with experience of the world of industry and commerce and other parts of the public service. The practice of allowing entry to the Service at Assistant Secretary had been abandoned and the number of mature Principal entrants had fallen from forty-six in 1968 to seven in 1977. After an increase to twenty-four in 1978 the direct entry scheme for Principals was stopped in 1979 as a result of the government's ban on recruitment.

The Committee concluded that the Civil Service Commission might be rather inbred and proposed adding to its membership a majority of outsiders. It also suggested that more people who were not civil

---

* 'In Burt's analysis – expressed in a famous paper, Intelligence and Social Mobility – the class system appears as the economic reflection of a genetically determined order of human merit.' *Sir Cyril Burt and the Great I.Q. Fraud*, by Oliver Gillie, *New Statesman* 24.11.78. This article concluded that Professor Burt 'was one of the most formidable confidence tricksters British society has produced'.

servants should be added to final selection boards and that the selection method should be changed: 'it is almost bound to inspire criticism since it depends more on interviewing applicants than on written examinations ... it ought to be modified so that its objectivity can be demonstrated to the public'.[8] After examining training in the Civil Service, when it concentrated almost entirely on the training given to ATs, the Expenditure Committee came to the conclusion that the AT scheme should be abolished and replaced by uniform entry arrangements for all graduates.

The Government's observations on the Report accepted the recommendation that outsiders be added to the Civil Service Commission and to selection boards, though they would not accept that these should be in a majority. It defended the selection procedure for ATs by saying that it was based on thirty years experience, had been widely copied by outside organizations and had been approved as recently as 1969 by the Davies Committee. However, it agreed to review the selection procedure and said that the AT scheme was being reviewed by a committee of officials who would take the Expenditure Committee's views into account.

In November 1978 the Government published the report of the committee set up to review the Administration Trainee scheme.[9] This committee, consisting of eleven administrators and two outsiders, admitted that faults had been discovered in the scheme, though it rejected charges of bias in selection. It reiterated the faith of the Civil Service in the generalist principle: staff who were to progress to the highest levels of the Service needed 'a wide range of abilities and experience', a high level of 'all round ability' and the capacity 'to adapt quickly' to particular jobs among the wide range of activities in departments. It was crucial that the Civil Service continued to recruit some of the very best graduates. Seniority rules governing the progress of staff up the administrative hierarchy was a significant constraint on promoting 'the very best staff' while they were still young enough to get to the top with the right mix of experience. Good quality graduates were attracted to the AT scheme by the prospect of early promotion and some of the best of them would not have been attracted to the Service if they had had to enter it with all the others of their age group. A separate high quality entry was required and to attract it first rate prospects including early promotion had to be offered. It is worth reminding ourselves at this stage that the review committee were not writing about all graduates, but only about graduates, mostly in arts subjects, destined for the administrative line of command. As far as they were concerned, it was unthinkable that the Service should try to give accelerated promotion to engineers, accountants, scientists, economists or sociologists – people with training related in some ways to dealing with the problems of modern Britain – into top general management and policy making. The review committee briefly rejected the Expenditure Committee's proposal to put all entrants on an equal footing, saying that it did not believe it was safe to rely on performance in a few early jobs to identify staff of high potential.

What most bothered the review committee was the radical change in the direct Executive Officer entry. Originally intended for 'A' level school leavers, the proportion of graduate entrants at this level had risen from 4 per cent in 1964 to 48 per cent in 1977, 1,500 to 2,000 of them a year, 70 per cent with first or second class degrees. These executives and their union strongly objected to the selection of a separate 150 graduates, with no better qualifications but a 'superior' background, for special training, special postings to Ministers' private offices and exceptional promotion. The review committee, very much more sensitive to the strictures of the union than those of the House of Commons, had to find a way of giving a better chance to some of the Executive Officer entrants while safeguarding the fast promotion route for young graduates of the traditional type. It admitted that much talent in the Service was not being drawn into the AT scheme; that the scheme took up resources which could have been better devoted to the development of talent in the executive grades and that there were faults in the fast streaming arrangements, that the training was unsatisfactory and that ATs had not received a wide enough range of work experience. This was the Civil Service establishment showing a new deference towards the Executive grades, formerly always thought of as good, sound NCO types who did as they were told but who were now turning into tough, educated and articulate young people wanting a fair crack at the good jobs.

The scheme proposed by the review committee was that some 200 to 300 Executive Officers should, after one to five years' service, go into a two- or three-year development programme. The best of these, some 30 to 60, should be selected for a HEO(D) grade where they would be joined by 50 to 60 Administrative Trainees who had served a two-year probation. HEO(D)s would be in a fast stream who would reach the Principal level after a further two years' service which would include short periods of training.

In a section on 'the place of specialists', the review committee repeated the CSD's view that a number of opportunities existed for specialists to transfer into administrative work (though they knew that the association representing specialists had described these opportunities as 'illusory' to the Expenditure Committee). It proposed a few new opportunities: specialists could apply for the AT entry, for the Executive development programme and for direct entry to the HEO(D) grade. The review committee did not expect that these proposals would result in 'a major flow' of young specialists into administration. It clung to the view that most specialists wanted to spend their careers in specialist work and would find administration unappealing.

The proposed scheme was an improvement over its predecessor in that the programme of experience was somewhat wider than that given to present ATs and there would be more opportunity for a few of the best Executive Officers. However, it still gave an advantage of several years and possibly other advantages to the AT type who would doubtless continue to be selected in a way which favoured candidates of a particular social and educational background. The main objections to it were that it was still based on the idea that an officer caste of generalist arts graduates were the best people to take charge of departments. The review committee seriously proposed that a few scattered weeks of training and a change of jobs every one or two years would turn an Oxford classicist (as many of them still are) into a manager and decision-maker in industrial, or transport or penal policy. It simply failed to recognize any value at all in relevant training or qualifications for what are some of the most important management jobs in Britain. In January 1980 the CSD responded to this report by announcing an administration trainee scheme involving 50–100 trainees drawn in equal numbers from serving Executive Officers and new graduate recruits who, after training, would go into an HEO(D) grade. The executive development scheme was dropped.

In December 1979 the Civil Service Commission published the report of the Committee on the Selection Procedure for the Recruitment of Administration Trainees dealing with the charge of bias in the recruitment of ATs. The Committee consisted of five Civil Service Commissioners and two outsiders. Not surprisingly, it praised 'the inherent fairness' of the selection procedure and said that the main problem was that insufficient graduates of universities other than Oxbridge applied for the AT grade. The discrimination in the selection procedure, it said, was essentially related to the needs of the job and the qualities required in an administrator in the Civil Service. It discussed these qualities in the customary terms: a good all-rounder with commonsense and 'a general interest in current affairs', though it thought that in future numeracy (the ability to understand quantitative terms, to interpret diagrams and to grasp simple statistical concepts) needed more emphasis. It failed, as usual, to see that the continuing definition of the job in terms of all-round generalism was the central fault in the system.

The Civil Service College

The section of the Expenditure Committee's report on training concentrated exclusively on the Civil Service College which had been set up as a result if the Fulton Report, though it provided less than 10 per cent of total Civil Service training. The College, which was intended by Fulton to be the power house of the reformed Civil Service, teaching the new style of management, carrying out practical and relevant research and spreading new ideas throughout the Service, had come under criticism early in its life.

In September 1974 Mr R. N. Heaton, formerly a Deputy Secretary at the Department of the Environment, and Sir Leslie Williams, formerly Secretary of the National Staff side of the Civil Service, produced a report on Civil Service training[10] much of which was devoted to the problems of the Civil Service College. The Heaton-Williams report said that few people would claim that the College had lived up to the expectations of its founders and it had not won the confidence of the Civil Service. It had not been a forum for the discussion of important Civil Service problems or for the promotion of a greater understanding between civil servants and the outside world. It had been expected to provide a wide range of courses: 'it is as though the same institution were expected to combine the roles of All Souls and an adult education centre with some elements of technical education and teacher training thrown in for good measure'.[11] Criticisms of the College were widely and consistently voiced: the lack of clarity in the College's objectives, the poor quality of much of the teaching, the over-academic nature of some of the courses and their lack of coherence, the confused lines of responsibility in the organization of the College and its lack of involvement in the life and work of the Civil Service. Heaton and Williams considered that there should be greater emphasis on training to develop practical management capabilities and that this could be achieved by the appointment of a Director to take charge of management training programmes. There should be a shift away from the teaching of management through individual subjects and personnel management and industrial relations training should be emphasized. They also commented on the College's unique diarchical form of organization, with Directors of Studies responsible for academic work, and, in parallel, Directors of Programmes (Assistant Secretaries) responsible for the organization of courses. This arrangement led to confusion over responsibilities, to tension that was not always creative, to tasks falling between the two sides and to the 'carve-up' approach which had led to each faculty contending for what it considered to be its right share of the 'cake'. The report, echoing what Fulton had said about the need for integrated rather than parallel hierarchies (see Chapter 4), recommended that groups of programmes should be made the responsibility of a single individual who would head a mixed team of academics and civil servants and who would be the best man for the job, regardless of whether he were an academic or a civil servant. The

37

College had great difficulty in attracting sufficiently high quality academic staff because it could offer them only five-year contracts and no opportunity for promotion, and departments did not give a high value to a period at the college for their best assistant secretaries. Heaton and Williams recommended promotion and transfer opportunities for academics at the College and recognition that service at it should count for promotion for the Civil Service staff employed there.

Fulton envisaged the College as uniquely well placed to conduct research into administration and the machinery of government but Heaton and Williams observed that research commissions from departments had been very few and far between and the College had carried out very little research. Links with departments were weak: very few departmental training officers of their staffs had ever visited the College. Administration trainees, whose needs received a disproportionate amount of attention 'to the detriment of the no less pressing needs of others less highly favoured',[12] were highly critical of the College. They found courses too long, with too much straight lecturing, not always of a very high quality, with not enough work on problems and case studies and, being based on watertight academic disciplines, lacking in coherence.

Soon after the Heaton-Williams report was published the National Whitley Council set up a joint official and staff side committee to consider its recommendations. It issued a final report in 1976.[13] By this time, the College had been reorganized under four directors of programmes, to whom the academic staff reported, though directors of studies continued to be responsible for academic staff in their own subject areas, and a director of management studies had been appointed (there is now an integrated structure of six directors). A liaison committee had been set up to improve contact between the College and departments and the College had held an open day for departmental training officers. The Civil Service Department's overall responsibilities for training were to be the subject of another review.

In November 1976, Professor Grebenik, the Principal of the College since its inception, produced his sixth annual report on the eve of his retirement. It was a vigorous response to the attacks that had been made on the College and implicit in it was a strong criticism of the Civil Service Department. 'Anyone charged with the direction of the college as it is at present would have found difficulty in achieving divergent, and sometimes inconsistent, objectives supported by different pressure groups.... I would express the strong hope that an explicit decision on the nature and objectives of the college will be taken in the near future.... I now regard it as a matter of regret that the decision to expand training facilities in 1970 diverted our energies from giving greater attention to more fundamental problems of college objectives. ... Unless the role that the college is expected to play in the life of the Civil Service is properly defined, the task of its Principal will continue to be one of difficulty and frustration and the results of his labour unlikely to please anyone.'[14]

Professor Grebenik complained that recent cuts in public expenditure had fallen disproportionately on the College – it had been required to save £$\frac{1}{2}$ million of its £2$\frac{1}{2}$ million annual expenditure and had therefore been forced to close its Edinburgh centre. Soon after the Heaton-Williams study it had been the subject of a management review (an internal consultancy study – see Chapter 7). A college was not susceptible to an examination by the methods of efficiency studies and, he said, members of the review team had no previous experience of an educational institution and may not fully have appreciated its problems. The review had, for example, proposed increasing the teaching loads of academic staff apparently on the basis of assessing only the resources that were necessary for repetitive presentation of existing courses. The team's terms of reference had precluded it from making a fundamental re-examination of the objectives of the College.

Professor Grebenik went on to point to the difficulties of recruiting suitable academic staff when they could not be offered permanent appointments and had to look for posts elsewhere after two or three years. Whereas in similar institutions administrative staff existed to support the academic staff, in the College administrators regarded academics as unpractical theorists, attempting to teach their grandmothers to suck eggs. Administrators played a large part in discussions on course content and regarded academics as temporary outsiders who could not be trusted to understand the training needs of the Civil Service. Both administrators and academics served so short a time at the College that there was a waste of acquired expertise. In constructing the training programme it was necessary to obtain the approval of the Civil Service Department, Establishment Officers in departments and the staff side. Their views did not always coincide with those of the College or with each other leading to unsatisfactory compromise. Surely, he said, the College had the right to expect the support of the Civil Service? Trainees were quick to sense the lack of support. One establishment officer, writing to the College about the AT course regretted that he could not convince his ATs of the value of the training because he himself was not convinced! Trainees were often disappointed with the College. Teaching them critically to examine accepted procedures and then returning them to an environment in which they were unable to promote change was a recipe for frustration and cynicism and an invitation to regard college training as academic, of no practical value, or even downright useless.

Professor Grebenik said he did not apologize for the academic nature of some of the College's work: there was a need for the problems of the public sector to be examined in a scholarly way. He was disappointed by the attitudes in some quarters of the Civil Service, even among those responsible for training, towards scholarship and research. Accusations of academicism was one aspect of this attitude, and the disappointing reception by departments of proposals for research was another and these had had discouraging effects on the morale of the academic staff. If the College carried out more high-level training, the best academic staff could be attracted to it but it could offer, for example, only a $2\frac{1}{2}$-day course for newly appointed Under Secretaries.

The College had two alternatives, he said: either to be developed as a training centre, in which case it would be staffed by instructors, it would not carry out research and would not achieve a reputation for academic distinction, or to concentrate on more advanced aspects of training needed in the Civil Service, possibly operating on a smaller scale, and becoming a university for the Civil Service in which discussion and research were encouraged and attacks on it for academicism were ended. What was needed was a decision on what it was supposed to be.

In evidence to the Expenditure Committee, the staff side of the National Whitley Council, representing all the Civil Service unions, said that the College had done a first class job in teaching operational skills such as data processing and management services but repeated earlier criticisms of its work in management. Staff side representatives told the Committee that the College was overacademic rather than practical and failed to hold the interest of students. Mr Stanley Henig,[15] a former member of the College staff, referred to the lack of autonomy of the College as a small part of the Civil Service Department empire. He criticized the reorganization of the College in 1975, aimed at producing a single line of management. He considered that this had meant effective demotion for the academic wing of the College: the academics found themselves increasingly in the position of specialist advisers to be called on at the discretion of generalist administrators. The CSD was exercising tighter control over a College which looked ever more like part of a government department and less like an academic institution. Academics had no career prospects: the new directors of programmes posts were strictly reserved for career civil servants. Student performance was not graded (though the students graded the teachers) and trainees found lengthy courses irksome, particularly when they found it difficult to relate work at the College to their own prospects. Mr Henig's impression was that the College was wished on to the Civil Service by the Government in response to the Fulton Report and there was little belief in its long term value. In oral evidence, Mr Henig observed that the Civil Service absorbed the College as soon as it was set up, so that it became part of the Civil Service it was supposed to reform. On that basis its fundamental task was impossible and it never had any chance of succeeding.

Lord Crowther Hunt,[16] in evidence to the Expenditure Committee, said that the main reasons for the disappointing performance of the College were that it had seen its main function as training generalist administrators, some of whom had no knowledge whatsoever of the problems of modern Britain, and that it had not geared its research effort to the needs of departments. He considered that it should be a requirement that a graduate recruited for administration should have acquired the basic corpus of relevant knowledge before he came into the Civil Service College. He drew a parallel with the French Ecole Nationale D'Administration (ENA) and pointed out that the examination to get into that institution was in the relevant subjects of modern government. The Fulton Committee, he said, did not want to keep out those who had not studied relevant subjects but said 'you should go back to the university for a year to catch up with the problems of modern government before you actually get admitted to the Civil Service College'. If the Civil Service had adopted relevance of study as a criterion for recruitment, there would be a major response from universities and polytechnics and this would cut down on the amount of training necessary at the College on subjects which candidates should have dealt with before they went to it. Fulton, he said, had also thought that the College would train people from Shell, ICI and local government alongside civil servants. He referred to the contact between the French Civil Service and French nationalized and private industry through ENA: Fulton had envisaged the Civil Service College as something like ENA adapted to English conditions.

ENA

The General sub-committee went to Paris to examine the work of ENA, which has a very high reputation for producing remarkably able top civil servants. The school has an annual intake of about 150 students, with 100 coming from outside the Service and 50 from within. Of the external students, 80 will have gone from school at 18 to a university for three to five years studying for a law degree in a Law faculty and a diploma in economics from an Institute of Political Studies, at which they also prepare for the ENA entrance examination. The other 20 will have passed through one of the *grandes écoles*, institutions which run parallel to the university system. These entrants must be under 25 and will have spent five or six years in higher education preparing for admission to ENA. The 50 internal entrants, usually graduates, are selected by competitive examination each year and must be under 30 with four or five years' service. They prepare for entrance to ENA at Institutes of Political Sciences and the Civil Service allows them one year of paid study leave if they have a degree, two or three years if they do not. Entrance to the preparatory institute is also by competitive examination, with three times as many places being offered as there are at ENA. The entrance examination to ENA involves six days of written tests and four or five days of oral tests and covers law, economics and social affairs. On admission to ENA, students become civil servants. The course lasts two and a half years with only one month's holiday each year: it is thus the equivalent of five years in a university. In the first year, students are placed in an embassy or a prefect's office where they work as assistants. In the second year, students spend nine months at ENA studying economics, administrative law, international and social affairs and there are also courses in accountancy, mathematics, computer techniques and foreign languages (one compulsory, a second optional). Teaching is by visiting lecturers, usually from the Civil Service, and stress is laid on a practical problem-oriented approach to these subjects. For the last two months of the second year, two-thirds of the students are placed in private industry and one-third in the public sector. The final half year is spent in seminar work in groups on two general topics under very senior people from outside: Ministers, members of the opposition, civil servants and top union officials. ENA has only four permanent directing staff: senior civil servants see lecturing at the school as a worthwhile part of their career. On the basis of continuous assessments and regular written tests, ENA graduates are placed in an order of merit. The top graduates can pick places for themselves in the élite corps of the Civil Service (the Council of State, Court of Accounts, Finance Inspectorate, diplomatic corps) and receive a distinction for life which will ensure that they will get to the top of the Civil Service or to a leading position in some other part of French national life. Many of them reach top policy-making posts in government in their 40s and move on into the public or private sector. Their training instils a strong feeling of the special quality of state service and a sense of the national interest.

Professor F. F. Ridley, specialist adviser to the Expenditure Committee, wrote a memorandum for it on ENA and the characteristics of its graduates.[17] He commented that the French Civil Service was élitist, in that it recruited an academic 'cream of the cream' and deliberately segregated officials throughout their careers on the basis of their academic achievements early in life. Since the élite was selected at under 30, there was no way in which somebody outside it could get to the top through management competence. This élite technocracy were accused of intellectual arrogance and confidence in their own answers. Professor Ridley observed that in the past this had reflected the weakness of the French political system and the inability of politicians to control the administrators. 'The British political system is probably strong enough to balance a more professionalized civil service, so that one could have the benefits of a greater expertise without the risks of technocarcy.'[18] Professor Ridley also referred to the movement from specialist or professional tasks to managerial and policy-making posts within the service or outside, particularly by engineers. 'As a result, there are probably fewer "psychological" barriers between the worlds of administration, technology and business than in Britain.'[19] In France, the state trains its administrators in such a way that the private sector finds them as well qualified for management as graduates of élite business schools. When these officials move into the private sector they retain 'a sense of the public interest', a phrase often repeated to the members of the committee in their interviews in France.

The Expenditure Committee was much impressed by ENA, as the Fulton Committee had been. The ENA system produces young civil servants of formidable expertise, fully equipped to handle the problems of modern government and driven by the idea of service to the state. Their occupation of key positions in government, the public and private sectors has been an important contributory factor to the successes of the French economy in the 1960s and 1970s. The Committee felt that Britain could certainly do with a Civil Service of that calibre, though preferably without all the élitist emphases. One essential lesson they drew from their examination of ENA was the importance of insisting on relevant qualifications for the future top management of the Service. The Committee proposed the creation of a new higher management training system in the Civil Service for existing civil servants entry to which would be based on an examination in 'specific subjects of relevance', e.g., constitutional law, economics, international affairs, the domestic political process and management and planning in government. All potential applicants should be given the opportunity by their departments to study the subjects of their entrance examination to the required level. The course itself should consist of relevant academic work, seminars and problem-solving case studies lasting rather longer than the twenty weeks of the AT college course and 'on the job training' of two to six months. Students from such national institutions as the National Health Service, local government and the foreign service should also be trained on the new course. The Committee had neither the time nor the expertise to fully work out its new higher management training arrangements or to detail the link between it and career arrangements for young graduates. What was clear, however, was that it wanted a total break with the traditional views of the British Civil Service on what training was appropriate for potential top managers in the Service and who should undergo it. It found, as Fulton did, that the expertise and competence of the higher civil service in Britain had to be raised and to do so the service had to insist on relevant qualifications and tough, practical training for people with managerial skills.

Unified Grading

We have seen from Chapter 2 that the Fulton Committee considered that a unified grading structure, involving the abolition of the separate career classes in the Service and their replacement by a single structure, was crucial to the improvement of efficiency, the development of accountable management, improved organization structures and the professionalization of top management. We have seen that the government to which it reported fully supported the concept of unified grading. We have also seen that after some progress had been made in reforming the grading structure, though not in a way which would fully open up a path for specialist staff to get into the top management positions, the development of a unified structure was brought to a halt.

The Expenditure Committee enquired into the reasons for the failure to proceed and consulted Sir Harold Wilson, MP, who had been particularly keen on the reform, Mr Edward Heath, MP, and Lord Armstrong, who had been expected to implement it.

Sir Harold said, 'I think there was an immediate burst of activity after Fulton came out and it was very much under Prime Ministerial direction. I got the impression – I hope that I am not being unfair – that by 1969 it was tailing off a bit.'[20] Sir Harold went on to say that his Principal Private Secretary, Mr Michael Halls, 'kept trying to warn me round about 1969 onwards that the thing was losing steam. In fact, he started producing memoranda for me.' Mr Halls died just before the change of government. Sir Harold said that there were so many urgent problems at the time that he was not able to give his mind sufficiently to the question. He agreed that the unified structure was still a major issue. Mr Heath simply said that as Prime Minister he had been concerned to see that officials with technical backgrounds were given the opportunities for promotion that Fulton proposed.

Lord Armstrong could not recollect that he had ever publicly given his full support to the Fulton recommendations, saying that he was 'very, very careful, very careful indeed' to say only that the appearance of the Fulton report was a great opportunity for new ideas to come through – 'an icebreaker'.[21] Once he had come to the question of unifying the class structure below Under Secretary he began by being 'quite prepared to examine this, though I was not particularly impressed' (*this* was government policy at the time!) and the more he went into it the more he found it impractical, mainly because of the difficulties of aligning the different salary rates of different jobs (a problem that any other large technical organization deals with as a matter of course). In one part of his evidence Lord Armstrong said that the classes appeared to have been abolished to Mr Wilson's satisfaction and in another that given the difficulties of abolishing them he had decided to approach the Fulton objective by another means: giving increased opportunities to younger specialists to try out work in generalist areas.

The Civil Service Department's justification for not persevering with unified grading bore a strong resemblance to the views of Lord Armstrong. The Department had found the removal of barriers between the classes a complex and costly task below the Under Secretary level and some trade unions (those which represented posts into which specialists might move) opposed it. The Department reported to the Expenditure Committee that 'through the re-structuring of the Service has not taken the precise form envisaged in the Fulton Report, the objectives which Fulton have set have been and will continue to be met in ways which are deemed to be the most effective given the inevitable constraints on suitable resources'.[22] These ways were said by the Department to be a variety of improved personnel practices: training, job appraisal, career interviewing and other techniques had been designed to develop the individual's potential; arrangements had been introduced to enable scientific and other specialist staff to acquire and use administrative and managerial skills; barriers to movement between the classes, groups and categories had been, or were being, removed and appointment to top posts was open to all, irrespective of their background. The Civil Service Department pointed to the fact that of the 860 posts at Under Secretary and above in the open structure nearly 40 per cent were filled by people whose earlier service had been wholly or mainly in specialist grades. The Department never made it clear whether those specialists were in general management and policy posts or still in advisory positions.

It was true that many restrictions on promotion had been removed after the Fulton Report. There was free upward movement for the most able within the Administration Group (leaving aside the exceptional scope for ATs) and the barriers to promotion within the Science Category and the Professional and Technology Category had been much reduced. The question was what new opportunities had been opened up for movement from these categories and other specialist classes into the Administration Group where the top general management and policy jobs were? Could there be any real opportunities for such movement without a unified grading structure?

The Civil Service Department maintained that the movement of specialists into administration had been assisted by the creation of 'opportunity posts', usually between the levels of Executive Officer and Assistant Secretary, for which members of more than one group were

45

automatically considered. Some were 'open' posts for which any suitable officer could be considered (in late 1975 the Department said there were 1,300 of these) and others were 'limited' and restricted to certain groups agreed with the staff side (there were 2,080 of these). Over 300 of the incumbents of these posts were, in late 1975, of a different discipline from their predecessor. There was also the lateral transfer scheme to allow movement between groups and classes at roughly equivalent levels, either for a two-year term or permanently. In the twelve months to September 1975 there had been at least 75 temporary and 100 permanent lateral movements. There was the Senior Professional Administrative Training Scheme (SPATS) which was open to those civil servants at Principal level in all specialist groups and classes who had been identified as having the potential to reach more senior levels. Those selected for the scheme were trained for three months at the Civil Service College and then normally spent two years in an administrative post at headquarters, often as Principals. The majority then returned by choice to their specialism. Between 1972 and 1976, 128 specialists had received the formal training element of the scheme and 78 had been given experience postings (of whom 5 had opted to stay in administrative work) and between 1976 and 1980, 89 officials were accepted for the scheme. Arrangements had also been made to give early promotion to specialists so that they might reach the open structure young enough to compete with administrators. Some specialists had also been promoted into the open structure outside their own fields, though the Department admitted that most specialists in the structure were occupying specialist and not policy jobs.

The Institution of Professional Civil Servants (IPCS), representing the specialists, was far from satisfied with these arrangements, as they made clear to the Expenditure Committee in evidence.[23] They pointed out that the restructuring of the classes into groups and categories had still left, in the field covered by their membership, 17 general classes and over 1,000 grades which had not been touched by structural reform and nothing had been done to rationalize them. Since there were only minor differences between pay grades in the Administration Category and the professional and scientific groups they could see no major obstacle in the way of extending unified grading down to Principal level. They said that fewer than 300 open posts existed in the 21,000 posts at Principal level and above. They considered that improved personnel management practices were complementary rather than alternatives to introducing unified grading. In answer to the Civil Service Department's assertion that the open structure, opportunity posts and lateral movement had given opportunities to specialists to participate in activities outside their specialisms, the IPCS said 'in practice, nothing has materially changed. The open structure now differs little in composition from that in 1968–70.'[24] In January 1970, 62·5 per cent of the posts at and above Under Secretary were occupied by administrators and in July 1976 the figure was 58·9 per cent. In January 1970 10·3 per cent of the posts in the open structure were held by scientists and in July 1976 10·2 per cent; the figures for professional and technical staff were 6·8 per cent and 6·5 per cent. Virtually all of these specialists were working in specialist fields: there had been no perceptible movement into policy-making positions. The IPCS said the intake to the scheme for training specialists in administration was only twenty-five per year. The early promotion scheme involved small numbers of specialists and none of them were being promoted as young as ATs were. Ten times as many administrators as specialists were being promoted to Principal level before the age of 29, and six times as many were promoted to Assistant Secretary level before the age of 45. The IPCS said that only 430 'open' posts had been created in the Administration Group and there had been only 44 lateral moves by specialists into administration. Within the specialist classes career prospects varied very widely, as Fulton had found, with particularly poor opportunities for accountants. The IPCS concluded that though both the Government and the official side of the Whitley Council accepted the objectives of the reform of the grading structure they had not been achieved and that the new avenues for advancement which the Civil Service Department claimed were open to specialists were illusory.

It was clear that the Civil Service Department had tried to give opportunities for specialists to get into administration without introducing unified grading. It had spent time and money creating a variety of new schemes but had failed materially to affect the underlying problem. Its approach was palliative and piece meal and it had signally failed to deal with the discrimination against expertise observed by the Fulton Committee, primarily because of its total dedication to the principle that generalists should occupy the top posts in the Service, regardless of the effect that this might have on efficiency and on the effectiveness of management and policy making.

Report and Response

It was clear from the evidence received by the Expenditure Committee that in management recruitment, training and grading the intentions of the Fulton Committee had not been met by the Civil Service in the decade after its report, despite Government backing. The AT scheme still produced a socially and educationally exclusive fast stream of high flyers, most of them with no qualifications for the important posts for which they were destined and professionally qualified specialists, needed more than ever before in departments, were still denied equal opportunity to compete for top management jobs. We have seen that the Committee proposed a wholesale reform of recruitment and training: a uniform entry system and the development of a staff course for middle management based on the French ENA. It also proposed that the Civil Service Department should resume the process of unified grading, observing that the lack of progress in this reform was simply due to the lack of priority given to it, and recommended that unification proceed down to Assistant Secretary as soon as possible and that work should begin on unifying the structure down to the Principal level.

The Committee criticized – as the Fulton Committee had done – the frequency with which members of the Administration Group were moved from job to job, merely with some vague idea of giving them experience. This further example of the generalist principle in action had been shown by the Fulton Committee to lead to substantial inefficiencies. Fulton found that administrators changed jobs less than three-year intervals, on average, but by the time the Expenditure Committee investigated the question, this frequency appeared to have increased (the average length of service of Under Secretaries and Assistant Secretaries was $2\frac{1}{2}$ years or less in the DOE; between 2 and $2\frac{1}{2}$ years in the Department of Industry and between $1\frac{1}{4}$ and $1\frac{3}{4}$ years at the Treasury).[25]

The Government's reply to the Expenditure Committee, in March 1978, was cautious, defensive and vague in tone. Whereas the 1968 government had broadly accepted the criticisms of the Service made by the Fulton Committee and had immediately undertaken to implement the most important of them, the 1978 government clearly had no stomach for administrative and Parliamentary reform. It did little more than reply to each recommendation briefly, usually saying that the Committee's observations would be taken into account. It gave a particularly frosty reply to the Committee's ideas on improved Parliamentary surveillance of the Civil Service (see Chapter 9).

The Government dismissed the Committee's proposals for a new selection and training procedure for higher management by simply endorsing the principle of 'mid-career developmental training' but said that promotion prospects should not depend on having been through a training course. On unified grading, the Government said that it was not willing to impose such a structure on unwilling unions or to pay a high price in terms of additional wage costs to secure their agreement. Nevertheless, in view of the Expenditure Committee's endorsement of the Fulton Committee's argument for unified grading, the Civil Service Department would examine further, with the National Staff Side, the extension of unification down to Assistant Secretary and, in the light of that examination, consider a further extension to

Principal. The Government stressed the cost of these exercises without ever referring to any benefits for the management of the Service.

The Expenditure Committee was very dissatisfied with the Government's observations and took the unusual course of action of replying to them. In July 1978 it published its response, saying that it felt that some of its most important proposals on the management of departments had not been taken sufficiently seriously. It repeated its call for the abolition of the AT scheme 'because we are not satisfied that any such procedure, based on "fast-streaming" a selection of recruits, could give equal opportunities for all potential top managers'.[26] It preferred an arrangement, customary in other large organizations, whereby all entrants, whether school leavers or 'generalist' or 'specialist' graduates, were required to prove themselves for some years in the service of the organization before being selected for promotion to the highest posts. The Committee re-emphasized the importance of its proposed higher management training scheme and repeated that entrants to the course should have prepared themselves by study in such relevant subjects as law, economics, international affairs and management and the course itself should emphasize the management of government. The Government had ignored several important observations made by the Committee: on the need to train civil servants alongside outsiders and on the unnecessary and inefficient frequency with which senior civil servants changed jobs.

The Committee ended by saying that its aim was to examine the Civil Service in its huge and complex task of managing the Government machine; to discuss its responsiveness to political initiative and to emphasize its belief in increasing the accountability of the Service to the House of Commons. It considered that important questions remained to be answered. 'Our duty as the custodians of Parliamentary democracy is to continue to ask them.'[27]

References

1. 'The Civil Service', *Expenditure Committee, Eleventh Report*, Session 1976–77, (July 1977), HC 535.
2. *Government Observations on the Eleventh Report from the Expenditure Committee*, (March 1978), Cmnd. 7117.
3. *Expenditure Committee, Eleventh Report*, (July 1977), para. 9.
4. *Joint memorandum submitted by the Society of Civil Servants and the Civil and Public Services Association to the Expenditure Committee, Eleventh Report*, Vol. II, p. 487, para. 114.
5. *Expenditure Committee, Eleventh Report*, (July 1977), Vol. II, p. 809, Q. 1982.
6. ibid., Vol. II, p. 252, Q. 651.

7. ibid., Vol. II, p. 269.
8. ibid., Vol. I, p. xxi, para. 15.
9. *Administration Training Review Committee, Report*, Civil Service Department, (November 1978).
10. *Civil Service Training*, Civil Service Department, (September 1974).
11. ibid., p. 14, para. 53.
12. ibid., p. 24, para. 5.61.
13. National Whitley Council Joint Committee on Training, *Final Report of the Joint Review Sub-Committee*, (1976).
14. Civil Service Advisory Council, *Principal's Annual Report to the Advisory Council*, 1975–6, (November 1976), p. 18, para. 31.
15. *Expenditure Committee, Eleventh Report*, (July 1977), Vol. II, p. 191.
16. ibid., Appendix 48, p. 1090.
17. ibid., Appendix 31, p. 982.
18. ibid., p. 984.
19. ibid., p. 989.
20. ibid., p. 788.
21. ibid., p. 656.
22. 'The Response to the Fulton Report', *Expenditure Committee, Eleventh Report*, (July 1977), Vol. II, p. 21, para. 111.
23. 'Reforming the Civil Service', *Expenditure Committee, Eleventh Report*, (July 1977), Vol. II, p. 529.
24. ibid., p. 546, para. 88.
25. GARRETT, J., MP, *Memorandum to the Expenditure Committee, Eleventh Report*, (July 1977), Appendix 1.
26. 'Response to the Government's Observations on the Committee's Report on the Civil Service', *Expenditure Committee, Twelfth Report*, Session 1977–8, (July 1978), HC 576, para. 4.
27. ibid., para. 19.

IV
The Structure
and
Machinery of Government

Government departments are headed by Permanent Secretaries and reporting to them are, in some departments, second Permanent Secretaries, but more usually Deputy Secretaries. Some departments have top specialist posts (e.g., economic, legal, scientific advisers) at or around Deputy Secretary level. All departments have three headquarters 'staff' groups; the Minister's private office, headed by his Private Secretary, which provides a Ministerial secretariat; a Finance Division and an Establishments Division. The Finance Division is concerned with the preparation of annual estimates and five-year public expenditure forecasts, sanctioning and controlling expenditure, dealing with the Treasury on financial procedures and cases and maintaining accounts. The Establishments Division is concerned with controlling the numbers employed in the department, employment and welfare matters, training and personnel development, relations with staff associations, the provision of office equipment and services, and efficiency ('management services') studies and deals with the Civil Service Department on policy on these questions.

Deputy Secretaries co-ordinate and generally oversee the work of Under Secretaries, or their equivalents, who head the major units of organization. These units (which may be called divisions or departments) deal with a major aspect of the department's business (for example in the Home Office: Fire, Police, Criminal, Prisons, Probation, etc; in Agriculture: Horticulture, Animal Health, Economic Policy, External Relations, Land use, etc). In a very large department, such as the Department of Health and Social Security, there may be twenty or more of these divisions. In some departments there are divisions of specialist staff sufficiently large to be headed by a scientific or professional civil servant at the Under Secretary level (for example Directorates of Economics and Statistics, Information, Building or Design, Research) and most sizeable research establishments are headed by scientists at this level (Chief Scientific Officer).

The sub-unit of the division, which may be called the branch, is headed by an Assistant Secretary or his equivalent in the specialist grades. It is at this level that the organizational separation of career classes often becomes apparent. The general convention, at the time the Fulton Committee reported, was to separate 'policy' work from executive and specialist work in different hierarchies. Thus, reporting to a divisional Under Secretary there might be policy or administrative branches headed by Assistant Secretaries and staffed by Principals and members of the executive and clerical grades, executive branches managed and staffed by members of the executive and clerical grades, and specialist branches, directorates and inspectorates staffed by members of the specialist classes (for example engineers, research officers, scientists, planners, architects, technical officers). This separation of administrative work from specialist and executive work gave rise to parallel and joint hierarchies described by Fulton's Consultancy Group, i.e., units of administrators and specialists engaged on a common task but organized in separate units. The practice was (and in many cases still is) in departmental headquarters to divide the total range of activities necessary to operate a particular piece of legislation or policy according to the characteristics of education and experience represented by the career classes. Administrators handled the policy, Ministerial, legislative and Parliamentary aspects of a case and supervised the executive machinery by which routine cases were processed and specialists contributed advice and technical inputs. Outside headquarters, in regional and local offices and research establishments, there are usually units of specialist or executive and clerical staff with relatively few senior administrators.

Fulton on Organization

The Fulton Committee proposed the creation of a new Civil Service Department (CSD) consisting of the Civil Service Commission, with its responsibilities for selection and recruitment, and the pay and management divisions of the Treasury, which covered personnel management, staffing, the control of numbers employed and efficiency services. The reasons for this new arrangement for the central management of the Service were the need to separate an expanded personnel management function from financial control and to create a 'separate institution with a single-minded devotion to its own professional purpose . . . in a position to fight, and to be seen fighting, the Treasury on behalf of the Service'.[1] Fulton thought that the staffing of the department was of critical importance. Its responsibilities called for staff with experience of personnel management and organization, both inside and outside the Service, on long-term and short-term appointments. Departments should be prepared to release some of their best men for a period of service in the CSD which would include some of the most challenging and creative jobs that the Service had to offer. Fulton also considered it important that a number of appointments at senior levels should be made from outside the Service of people with experience of managing large organizations and that the CSD should include such specialists as scientists and engineers. The Department should include a planning unit for examining new developments in personnel management, training and management techniques and making the Service 'a model of progress in its field for others to follow'.[2] The CSD should report to the Prime Minister, who should delegate day-to-day responsibility to a non-departmental Minister of appropriate seniority who should also be a member of the Cabinet. Fulton said that the expanded role of the CSD should not be allowed to develop into a take-over by central management of responsibilities that properly belonged to the other departments: its main role should be to encourage the use of the most modern techniques rather than itself to implement the changes that were needed in departments. However, it had a special part to play in assisting reorganization at the higher levels of departments and should be in a position to call all departments to account for failure to use the recommended techniques and to put in its own men to investigate any departmental organization and to recommend improvements.

Within departments, Fulton recommended that there should be planning units headed by senior policy advisers who, on matters of long-term policy developments, should report direct to Ministers. This recommendation is discussed in Chapter 5. The Committee also recommended that departmental O & M (management services) sections should be upgraded in scope and quality so that they could take on 'efficiency audits involving all aspects of the department's work at all levels . . . in particular, special attention should be paid to studies designed to improve organizational efficiency'.[3] This recommendation is discussed in Chapter 7.

The Fulton recommendation with potentially the most far-reaching organizational effects was that 'accountable units' should be established within departments. Accountable units were described as units of organization 'where output can be measured against costs or other criteria, and where individuals can be held personally responsible for their performance'.[4] The Committee proposed that 'executive' areas of work should be designated as separate managerial commands or 'centres' and that the managers of these centres should be made accountable for the results they achieved as compared with pre-determined budgets or standards. In 'administrative' areas, concerned with policy and administrative matters, a similar concept of centres based on 'management by objective' should be introduced. The Committee thought that to enable organization by centre to be introduced certain other reforms would have to be undertaken. First, responsibilities which were diffused when several departments or branches had substantial interest in the same matter should be concentrated in one man or a team, who would have the responsibility for assembling the relevant material and putting forward observations. Secondly, there was scope for reducing the number of levels in the hierarchy of most departments. With 'flatter' structures, there could be a more precise allocation of responsibility and authority. Thirdly, the separation of administrators and specialists in parallel and joint hierarchies not only prevented the specialists from exercising the full range of responsibilities normally associated with their professions but also obscured individual responsibility and accountability: no single person at any level had clear-cut managerial responsibility for the whole task. The best organization for work involving administrative and technical expertise was a single integrated organization (or centre) under a single head, who should be the man with the most appropriate qualifications for the job. At lower levels administrators and specialists should be integrated in teams or unified hierarchies.

The Committee took these ideas from the report of its Consultancy Group, which had come to the conclusion that some of the organizational conventions of the Civil Service hindered its work. The Consultancy Group advocated experiments in new organizational forms related not to the traditional structure of class and grade, but to operational needs as demonstrated by an analysis of the objectives and key functions of departments. It then outlined an approach to organization based on teams, groups and 'centres' of staff of mixed backgrounds and qualifications. There appeared to be need for high-level functional and service staffs serving the top management of departments – certainly for planning and possibly in some departments for management services: data processing, operational research, efficiency studies, training and development. At operating levels, the Group proposed the creation of managerial units or 'centres' based upon accountability for costs and results: 'budget centres' in areas where output could be measured; 'responsibility centres' in areas where the measurement of output was difficult or impossible. Within these centres, analysis might show scope for some modification of the rigid hierarchy in favour of 'looser' team groupings and less closely described individual jobs. These ideas for functional groups and centres would work, the Group suggested, only within a framework of greater delegation to managers of authority over resources and if supported by entirely new systems of information, planning and control.

Finally, Fulton considered whether there were areas of Civil Service work which could be 'hived off' from the central government machine and entrusted to autonomous public boards or corporations. It had been put to the Committee that accountable management would be most effectively introduced when an activity was separately established outside any government department and that this solution should be adopted for many executive activities, especially the provision of services to the community. Such bodies would be outside the day-to-day control of Ministers and the scrutiny of Parliament, though Ministers would retain powers to give them directions when necessary. The Committee had been impressed by the application of this principle in Sweden where small central departments dealt with policy and operational management was hived off to autonomous agencies. There were a wide range of executive activities in British government – the Royal Mint, air traffic control, parts of the social services – to which the principle of hiving off might be applied and it had already been applied to the Post Office and the Atomic Energy Authority.

Drawing the line between autonomous bodies and central government would raise parliamentary and constitutional issues beyond the Committee's terms of reference and it could go no further than to suggest an early and thorough examination of the possibility of a considerable extension of hiving off.

The Reorganization of Government

As we saw in the last chapter, before the arrival of the new government in 1970, David Howell, MP, had poposed major changes in the organization of government departments in his booklet *A New Style of Government*.[5] One of them was a new 'central capability' in the Treasury for the analysis of government programmes and the efficiency of their implementation. This unit could be developed, after the development of new accounting systems and greater delegation to departments, into a Department of the Budget, combining resource allocation, programme analysis and the Civil Service Department functions of management services and manpower control. Mr Howell proposed the reorganization of departmental functions on the basis of small central bureaucracies delegating executive authority to boards, agencies and task forces concerned with specific functions. Each central department would also contain a unit capable of reviewing spending programmes and assessing aims and objectives. He also suggested a Ministry of Industry, covering industry, trade and employment policy, supervising agencies concerned with aid to exporters (possibly largely in the private sector) and with employment exchanges, training and labour disputes conciliation. There would be a small Commission for Protection and Conservation, under the Lord Chancellor, with responsibility for 'safeguarding the position of the individual in modern society' and surmounting a cluster of agencies and boards with delegated powers. These agencies would deal with employee protection, consumer protection, policy for shareholders and investors and environmental pollution. There would be a Minister for Infrastructure heading a department concerned with policies for housing, transport, power, ports and telecommunications and responsible for executive agencies and project groups engaged in implementing policies in these fields. The result of all these proposed structural alterations would be a cabinet reduced to 16 or 17: this 'would symbolize as nothing else the determination of the new administration to provide a new style of government for Britain in the 1970s'.[6] New recruits from industry and commerce would have to be brought into the Civil Service, men who could adjust to the public sector and yet who understood how to wind things up; here Mr Howell quoted the use being made by Governor Reagan of California of business talent in weeding out and terminating unnecessary public activities.

In October 1970 the Conservative government's White Paper: *The Reorganization of Central Government*[7] said that weakness had shown itself in the apparatus of policy formulation and the quality of government decisions. In order to remedy this situation, the government had reviewed its functions and organization with the aims of improving policy formulation and decision taking; critically examining the activities of government; matching the responsibilities of departments to coherent fields of policy and administration and ensuring the adaptability of the government machine. The fulfillment of these aims would improve the efficiency, openness and responsiveness of government. The principles of the reorganization were rigorous analysis of policies, action and expenditure; the organization of departments on the basis of grouping related functions and the creation of a capability at the centre of government for assessing the relative priorities of departmental programmes and policies in relation to strategic objectives.

The White Paper suggested a number of advantages in grouping functions together in departments with a wide span of policy: the capacity to implement a single strategy and to resolve conflicts within the line of management rather than by interdepartmental compromise; the ability to manage large programmes and to apply analytic techniques; more direct identification of Ministers and more open communication between government and the public and a capacity to contribute more effectively to the formulation and development of the Government's overall strategy. Unified departments would be less open to the risk of being parochial and would therefore be more answerable to Parliament and the community at large. Within them, executive blocks of work would be delegated to accountable units of management, thus lessening the load on departmental top management.

On these principles, the Ministry of Technology and the Board of Trade and parts of the Department of Employment were combined as a new Department of Trade and Industry. The advantages of this merger were said to be the combination of internal and international aspects of commerce and industry; the simplification of industry's contacts with Government; the existence of a single minister for the allocation of resources to industry, both public and private, and ease of dealing with EEC questions. The Secretary of State for Trade and Industry would be supported by two Ministers, to each of whom would be delegated a particular range of functions.

The second new development was the designation of the Aviation Group of the Ministry of Technology as a Ministry of Aviation Supply to which it was proposed to add, after further study by a project team, defence research and development and procurement. In fact, in 1971 Aviation Supply was disbanded and its functions split between the Ministry of Defence and the Department of Trade and Industry.

The White Paper went on to observe that because of the interaction of housing, transport and planning, which were among the main functions of local authorities, and because these activities gave rise to acute and conflicting requirements and were having an ever-increasing impact on ordinary people a new form of organization was needed to deal with them. It was therefore proposed to unify the Ministeries of Housing and Local Government, Public Building and Works and Transport into a single Department of the Environment. Here again, in addition to the Secretary of State, Ministers would be appointed in full charge of the 'functional wings' of the Department – Local Government and Development, Housing and Construction and Transport Industries. The new Department would have the leading responsibility for regional policy.

Overseas aid was brought into the Foreign and Commonwealth Office under a Minister of Overseas Development with powers delegated from the Foreign Secretary. Responsibilities for children were transferred from the Home Office to the Department of Health and Social Security to match the integration of personal social services in local authorities brought about by the Local Authority Social Services Act of 1970.

In the next section of the White Paper, the Government made proposals for improving the methods by which collective policy decisions were taken in relation to their strategy as a whole and to public expenditure. The structure of interdepartmental committees, each concerned with a separate area of policy, needed to be reinforced by a clear definition of government strategy. For lack of such a clear definition of strategic purpose and under the pressure of day-to-day problems governments were always at risk of losing sight of the need to consider all their current policies in relation to their longer-term objectives and to alternative policy options and priorities. The task of producing a strategic definition of objectives, analysing priorities and alternative causes of action was formidable and could only be approached gradually. A beginning would be made by setting up a small multi-disciplinary Central Policy Review Staff (CPRS) in the Cabinet Office, under the supervision of the Prime Minister but working for Ministers collectively. The public expenditure planning process was also to be developed. The annual Public Expenditure Surveys (see Chapter 5) did not provide all the information needed by Government to balance the claims of competing blocks of public expenditure. They did not show the explicit objectives of expenditure in a way which would enable a Minister's plans to be tested against general government strategy, nor did they contain detailed analyses of existing programmes and of major policy options on them. The team of businessmen in the Civil Service Department were developing a system of regular reviews which would provide this information. This system (later announced as the Programme Analysis Review system, or PAR – see Chapter 5) would emphasize the definition of objectives and the expression of programmes as far as possible in output terms. The review of the tasks of departments was continuing, so as to define accountability and to explore the possibilities of stopping some government activities altogether or transferring them to the private sector. There would be a fresh look at the scope for dispersing Civil Service work from London to other parts of the country.

In the following four years, the concept of 'agencies' within departments was further developed. A Defence Procurement Executive was established in the Ministry of Defence, headed by one of the business team, Mr (later Sir) Derek Rayner. The Employment Services Agency and the Training Services Agency were set up in the Department of Employment (in 1973 these two were placed under a Manpower Services Commission); the Property Services Agency was established in the Department of the Environment; the Industrial Development Agency, headed by a Minister, was created in the Department of Trade and Industry and the Central Computer Agency, bringing together elements from the Civil Service Department, the Treasury, the Department of Trade and Industry and HMSO, was set up in the Civil Service Department. External agencies were also set up: the Commission on Industrial Relations, the British Overseas Trade Board, the Pay Board and the Price Commission and the British Library. The Labour Government of 1974 continued the process of creating 'non-departmental' agencies with the Health and Safety Executive and the Arbitration and Conciliation Advisory Service. The process of creating accountable units was also applied to commercial activities in government and the

Royal Mint, the Royal Ordnance Factories, HMSO, and the Supplies Division of the Property Services Agency were put on a 'trading fund' basis instead of being financed by annual votes and appropriations.

The Civil Service Department

In giving an account of itself to the Expenditure Committee in 1976, the CSD described its responsibilities for personnel management and administrative efficiency as complying with the Fulton recommendations. It pointed out that 25 per cent of the posts in the Department were filled by interchange from the Service generally, though its evidence did not mention whether these were the personnel and management experts that Fulton had suggested and it made no reference at all to senior appointments from outside the Service. It also did not refer to the absence of a planning unit in the Department but pointed to the planning carried out by the Permanent Secretary's management group consisting of the Permanent Secretary, the Deputy Secretaries and the Principal Establishment and Finance Officers. It did not explain how this top management group, supported by a central division which was mainly engaged in co-ordinating CSD activities, internal manpower control, providing a secretariat for management groups and communicating with other departments, could undertake the research into management innovation outside the Service which Fulton thought would make it a model of progress. The CSD said it paid particular attention to all appointments to Under Secretary and saw to it that those with potential for Deputy and Permanent Secretary were given the widest possible experience outside their departments. Otherwise, it said, the relationship of the CSD to other departments was one of partnership. In management services, there had been a move to greater self reliance in departments while the CSD built up its competence in specialist techniques. In personnel management, each department had the main responsibility for its own staff with the CSD co-ordinating departmental thinking and offering advice and guidance where possible. There was no response to the Fulton recommendations that it should call departments to account for any failure to apply new management methods or send in its own staff to investigate and reorganize them.

The National Staff side of the Civil Service complained at length and in detail to the Expenditure Committee about the lack of authority of the CSD in personnel management.[8] It said that Fulton had been ambiguous about the relationship of the CSD to departments but the CSD had taken a less positive role than was necessary. It chose to proceed by persuasion and accepted that departments had an ultimate and over-riding responsibility as employers, a concept to which the staff side did not subscribe. A career service involved central management: civil servants were employed in departments and not by them. A system in which there was central control of recruitment and initial posting but then discharged subsequent career progression to departmental authority did not afford sufficient protection for the concept of a career service. The staff side gave examples of difficulties arising from the lack of power of the CSD: departments would not operate arrangements to equalize promotion prospects; they were reluctant to accept transfers from other departments and to release people wishing to transfer; they were slow in introducing new appraisal procedures and career interviews and there was difficulty in introducing uniform reporting standards. The staff side concluded that the CSD should have the authority to lay down a mandatory framework within which departments and line managers would work. The basis of the relationship should be the delegation of central authority to departments 'rather than the present system of attempting to proceed on the basis of securing a consensus among a confederation of largely autonomous and sometimes self-willed organizations'.[9] The staff side pointed out that this relationship had been achieved for the management of the careers of top people in the Service in the open structure.

The theme of the powerlessness of the CSD was developed in a different way by Lord Crowther-Hunt.[10] Referring to the CSD as a 'very considerable disappointment', he pointed out that the staff of the department had never matched the Fulton specifications: they were almost entirely from the old pay and management side of the Treasury and included 1,400 members of the Administration Group and only 140 members of the Professional, Scientific and Technical Groups. Moreover, the four management service divisions – the focal centre for efficiency in the Civil Service – were headed by an Under Secretary, included 5 or 6 people at Assistant Secretary level, and employed only 100 staff. In contrast, the Cabinet Office which, he said, was largely concerned with secretarial and minute-taking services for the Cabinet and Cabinet committees, employed 600 including 3 Permanent Secretaries, 5 Deputy Secretaries and 8 Under Secretaries. This number included the staff of the Central Statistical Office. Not surprisingly, the CSD had an unduly limited concept of its role and did not appear to see itself as the spearhead of the Whitehall drive for departmental efficiency: it could enter a department only by invitation and its findings were advisory. Ministers who had been in charge of the CSD had never mastered its manifold problems he said, perhaps partly because there was no political reputation to be made there. The department should have as much power in its fields of efficiency and manpower as the Treasury had to control departmental expenditure.

The Expenditure Committee considered whether the CSD should

remain as it was or be reorganized. The first witness to discuss the question was Sir John Hunt, Secretary of the Cabinet.[11] He said that the case for setting up the CSD at the time was overwhelming. There was a feeling that the Treasury 'had done the Civil Service on the cheap', that insufficient attention had been paid to personnel management, that the load on the Chancellor was too great and that a separate department was needed to push through the Fulton reforms. The CSD had ensured that much more attention was paid to management as distinct from policy advice, but the separation of total expenditure in the Treasury from manpower expenditure in the CSD was always a little illogical and there was a risk of aspects of efficiency falling down the middle between the two departments. In the early days of the department, the people concerned with manpower and efficiency were the old Treasury people and they knew their opposite numbers in the Treasury public expenditure divisions but this was a wasting asset. In addition, the 'clout' of the CSD depended upon the immediate post-Fulton dynamism and a department could not exist for ever on the basis of one report. He had long thought that there was a case for combining expenditure and manpower in a 'bureau of the budget'.

This would create the difficulty of separating responsibility for public expenditure from the management of the economy but this objection was likely to weaken as economic policy was becoming increasingly a matter of argument going wider than the Treasury and as the growing burdens on the Chancellor made it difficult for him to give enough time to public expenditure. Sir John Hunt saw three options: to put the Treasury public expenditure divisions into the CSD, leaving the Treasury as a Ministry of Finance; to put the CSD management services back into the Treasury or to leave arrangements as they were but make them work better.

Mr Edward Heath[12] favoured an arrangement in which one minister dealt with public expenditure, including some of the CSD's responsibilities for pay and personnel, and the Chancellor dealt with taxation. Any proposal to put the greater part of the CSD into the Treasury he regarded as gravely reactionary: it would depress Civil Service morale and create an enormously large and cumbersome Treasury.

Sir Harold Wilson[13] thought that there was now a very strong case for a merger of the CSD and the expenditure side of the Treasury though he was very much against transferring any part of the CSD back to the Treasury. Lord Diamond,[14] a former Financial Secretary to the Treasury, was opposed to the withdrawal of public expenditure from the Treasury: the management of expenditure was one of the most important tools the Chancellor had in carrying out his task. He favoured the transfer back to the Treasury of the control of manpower expenditure so as to give it control of all expenditure. Sir Samuel

Goldman[15] of the Treasury, took a similar view but thought that now the CSD had settled down, further disturbance would have to be very clearly justified.

On the basis of little more evidence than this, the Expenditure Committee came to the conclusion 'that reconstruction at the centre is imperative'.[16] It said that the CSD appeared from the evidence to have lost its original drive and to have been handicapped by its ambivalent relationship with the Treasury and the inadequacy of its own powers. 'We do not believe that the CSD in its present form has a prominent part to play at the centre of government.'[17] The Committee thought that the separation of control of expenditure from responsibility for efficiency was indefensible: unless these functions were combined there could be no effective control of the Civil Service. The relationship between the Treasury and the CSD was not adequately considered by Fulton, indeed that report had not recognized the possibility that problems might arise. The Expenditure Committee considered that a department's expenditure as a whole could not be divorced from the efficient use of manpower and the CSD did not have enough leverage over departments. The realistic dialogue was between departments and the Treasury, with the CSD reduced to rubber-stamping and to translating the agreed policy into manpower. It considered that the impotence of the CSD accounted for the disappointing performance of its management services and staff inspection. Unless responsibility for manpower and efficiency were combined with responsibility for expenditure there would be no inducement for departments to accept central management services and staff inspection. The close collaboration between the CSD and the Treasury was easy to achieve in the early days of their division into two departments but was now becoming increasingly difficult. The Committee therefore concluded that responsibility for efficiency and for the control of expenditure should be vested in a single central department. The question then was whether the public expenditure side of the Treasury could be put into the CSD to form a new department of expenditure and manpower control or the entire responsibility for efficiency should be put back in the Treasury. The Committee thought that the removal of public expenditure from the Treasury would be an irresponsible act: it would seriously interfere with the management of the economy. The solution must therefore be to transfer the responsibility for efficiency from the CSD to the Treasury, leaving personnel management, appointments, recruitment, training, pay and pensions in the CSD.

The observations and conclusions of the Expenditure Committee on the future of the functions discharged by the CSD were fairly superficial and not supported by extensive evidence. A committee of MPs, unsupported by any research or investigatory staff, is not a suitable body for making detailed recommendations about important and complex questions of organization. In coming to its conclusions it relied heavily on the observations of a few witnesses and it was not able to test their views by any research in the field. It is true that few of its witnesses had a good word for the CSD. The CSD had failed to be the thrusting, energetic vehicle for reform and modernization envisaged by Fulton. Its management of the Civil Service College had been deplorably inept, it had done little to reform the career structure of the Service and it had not established its authority in either personnel management or efficiency services. On the other hand, it had greatly improved training and human resource management and had tried, by persuasion and advice, to improve management practices in the Service.

The problems of the CSD lay far deeper than the Expenditure Committee probed. Some of these problems arise from the fact that for fifty years the British Civil Service has had a unique internal management function based on 'the establishment concept'. This is discussed more fully in Chapter 8, but here we need only note that this concept covers control of manpower numbers, an advisory service on efficiency, and personnel management (e.g. training and welfare) activities.

The control of numbers was mandatory and very rigorously applied; the efficiency service, though technically competent, was purely advisory and the personnel management side was very poorly developed (except for future top people). The CSD took over this tripartite function for the whole Civil Service and concentrated heavily on improving personnel management. It was therefore faced with the inherent contradiction of applying a long established authoritarian style of manpower control and a new supportive style of personnel development simultaneously.

Secondly, it was faced with the question of departmental autonomy, once the numbers of staff had been agreed. It felt obliged, given the responsibilities of departmental ministers, to apply its functional authority for both personnel management and efficiency as a service rather than as mandatory. This view was reinforced by the personal nature of the accountability of the Permanent Secretary of a department as Accounting Officer. In respect of personnel management, it was unnecessarily timid. The Accounting Officer is already required to manage his department within mandatory personnel management rules drawn up and supervised by the CSD, exercising functional authority in this field. The staff unions were quite right to point out that the CSD had not used its powers to equalize personnel management practices in departments. When we come to efficiency and, in particular, Fulton's ideas that the CSD should call departments to account for failure to use management techniques and to put its own

63

experts into departments to investigate their organization and management, clearly there could be a conflict between the public accountability of the Minister and the Permanent Secretary and their responsibility to follow the requirements of the CSD. In these circumstances, the CSD was probably obliged to act in an advisory role.

If the ability of Parliament to examine the efficiency of departments was strengthened by reforms in our system of state audit (see Chapter 9) the position would be different. A department would then be more likely to employ the CSD's efficiency services before the situation deteriorated to the point where it was likely to be censured by the Public Accounts Committee and the CSD would gain in acceptability as a centre of expertise in efficiency. There might still be occasional cases in which the CSD should impose an efficiency audit or reorganization on a department, but these would have to be discussed and agreed at Ministerial level.

Under these arrangements, the CSD could be strengthened without any change in its position in central management. The argument then turns on whether it is sensible to separate expenditure control from manpower control and whether manpower control and personnel management are compatible in one department. The few, but very distinguished, witnesses to the Expenditure Committee all thought that manpower and expenditure control should be combined. The former Prime Ministers favoured their combination in the CSD while others thought that they should be in the Treasury. Putting them in the Treasury would centralize power in a body which many feel is too powerful anyway and where decision-making is widely criticized for secrecy and inflexibility. It would add to the burdens of a Chancellor who many feel to be over-burdened already. Putting them in the CSD would split the management of the economy and taxation from public expenditure planning and control with potentially adverse effects. Another dimension is added to this problem by the proposal adopted by the Labour Party to establish a planning commission at the centre of government to draw up long term national plans for economic and industrial development which would be bound to involve public expenditure.

In the author's view, there is little point in reorganizing the CSD and the Treasury without a thorough examination of the present and future roles of both these departments, the Inland Revenue, the Customs and Excise Department and the organizational implications of a national plan, if it is ever introduced. Piece-meal reorganization on the basis of a superficial study of part of the problem is likely to be temporary and disruptive. The first step should be to re-define the role of the CSD on the lines described above and to increase its expertise by bringing in to it managers with experience in organizations outside the Civil Service.

The Government's response on this question was that it was a matter for the Prime Minister, that he had not reached any view on it and he would continue to study the issues involved. To date, Prime Ministers have not made any statement on the matter.

Accountable Units

Fulton's call for managerial accountability in the Civil Service and, in particular, the creation of 'accountable units' in departments involved major changes in organization structure, personnel management, planning systems and control of information in the Service. Here we shall deal only with the implications for organization structure. These were the replacement of parallel by integrated hierarchies, the formation of centres within departments to which authority could be delegated and for which performance could be measured and the assessment of the feasibility and value of hiving off functions of departments to autonomous bodies outside the Civil Service.

Under the heading 'Refinement of Hierarchies' the evidence of the CSD to the Expenditure Committee consisted of one very short paragraph. It said that the initiative in this area must rest with departments to mould their organization to their own needs; studies of different kinds of hierarchy had been carried out in departments and some changes had been made. For instance, the Ministry of Public Buildings and Works (now in effect the Property Services Agency) had introduced a new structure in 1969 consisting of directorates responsible for the whole of particular programmes in which the top posts were open to members of all disciplines.

The idea of combining professional and administrative staff in integrated hierarchies was one of the first of Fulton's recommendations to be buried by the Civil Service. This was apparent from a CSD survey on 'the hierarchical organization of a number of government departments' produced in 1970[18] and submitted to the Expenditure Committee by the Institution of Professional Civil Servants. This survey covered ten departments where parallel hierarchies existed. Fulton's recommendation, interpreted as calling for integrated hierarchies in almost every situation, was very strongly rejected. Some integration had taken place – in the MPBW, the then Ministry of Housing and Local Government and the Prison Department (where the headquarters divisions had been completely integrated and the parallel hierarchies abolished as a result of a study by a management review team which included CSD staff and outside consultants). Progress in this field had been made long before Fulton took up the subject, the CSD said. The conclusion of the survey was that parallel hierarchies were best suited to work where a statutory duty was laid on an officer of a particular speciality such that he should be seen to stand apart from the central administration of the department; where the work had a high degree of technicality or a high political/legislative content such that there were large areas of the work *into which the specialist could not be expected to penetrate* (my italics) and where a specialist service supported a number of divisions and it was impracticable to disperse it. In addition, parallel hierarchies were favoured where a specialist group was very small and where differences in pay and grading were sufficiently marked to cause friction and resentment if staff were grouped in a single hierarchy. This survey was the end of any general attempt to find ways of combining professional and administrative staff despite the overwhelming evidence, based on field research by its Consultancy Group, which Fulton had produced to show the inefficiency and frustration caused by the insistence on organizing specialists in separate advisory groups.

The evidence of the Institution of Professional Civil Servants (IPCS) to the Expenditure Committee on this question was highly critical.[19] It pointed out that the CSD survey gave no consideration to the ways in which the specialist could contribute his experience and expertise directly to the process of providing policy advice at the highest levels, nor to ways in which specialists could effectively manage and have overall control of technological projects. No attempt was made to examine in detail the problem of working relationships in the key area of financial responsibility and control. 'The pre-Fulton attitude on the role of the specialist remains firmly entrenched.'[20] It said that few significant developments in integration had taken place since 1970, despite the major restructuring of Government departments that had taken place. The IPCS said that the reorganization of the MPBW in 1969, quoted by the CSD as an example of integration, brought professional and administrative hierarchies together under a single Director of Works at Under Secretary level but nothing was done to integrate the structure below that level – and that was still broadly the position in late 1976. It is interesting that some integration had been introduced in the part of the Property Services Agency (PSA) providing works services to the Post Office in 1975 to ensure that the client was given a full service and because the work was carried out on a repayment basis and the financial control arrangements were different from other activities. This suggests that the introduction of repayment can, as its supporters argue, lead to a clarification of accountability. Elsewhere in the PSA project management was widely used but secretariat and projects staff were not fully integrated and decisions still had to be referred upward through separate chains of command which met only at the Director of Works level. Most of the inefficiencies of parallel hierarchies which had been described by the IPCS to Fulton still remained in this area. The Matthew/Skillington report on design in government building of 1974[21] had said 'the fundamental difference between the PSA and other organizations concerned with large building programmes arises from an assumption that, while the design and management of individual buildings lies properly in the province of professionals, many parts of the total process of obtaining buildings (e.g. taking clients' instructions, planning and managing building programmes, allocation of professional resources, budgeting, cost control etc.) are not considered primarily a professional responsibility and are therefore taken out of the professional sphere of control, into the hierarchy of administration'. The report went on to point out that it was the successful development of these very functions that had characterized the success of British architectural practice in the last twenty-five years and that this country was highly respected for the expertise in establishing and controlling large building programmes developed by its architects and quantity surveyors. The organization of the PSA limited professional development and this had an effect on the recruitment of high quality staff: 'high quality architects will only be attracted to an organization that clearly gives maximum opportunities for the development of total professional skills'. The argument that such factors as the size of programmes demanded an administrative top-hamper into which the professional could break only by abandoning his professional skills was unacceptable. The contrary was true – the bigger the programme the more essential it was that professionals should be at the highest level. The professional should be in direct contact with the client. 'We consider that the role of the architect should no longer be artificially restricted in the way we describe.' As a result of this report, the Secretary of State for the Environment announced that a multi-disciplinary Design Office would be set up in the PSA but it transpired that the department had in mind an office without its own administrative functions for contracts and secretariat work.

The Rayner Report on defence procurement,[22] which led to the establishment of the Defence Procurement Executive, specifically recommended accountable units of management aimed at 'getting away from the existence of parallel hierarchies' and so more sharply focussing responsibility and recommended the establishment of project managers 'with full executive responsibility' including responsibility for contracts and finance. The IPCS showed that in the Executive as set up financial and contractual control remained 'brigaded separately under administrative officers who report direct to each of the Systems Controllers'[23] and financial management in the Controllerates continued in many ways as a parallel hierarchy to project management. Finance staff in the administrative hierarchy exercised the power to concur or otherwise in expenditure proposals on projects which had been approved and where the level of spending was within the project managers' delegated powers. In at least one directorate both the finance staff and the project manager were shown as discharging the vote holder functions so that financial responsibility and authority were not clearly brought together and the role of the project manager was imprecise.

In evidence to the Expenditure Committee, the Department of Health and Social Security[24] said that its organization was based on each profession being organized separately with professional and administrative divisions set up to cover the same policy areas. This arrangement had been deliberately chosen because specialists could not combine sufficient specialist skill and the experience and skill of the administrator; because separate specialists could be seen by their colleagues outside the department as representing their professions' viewpoint in government and because most specialists preferred to stay with the work for which they had been trained. Nevertheless, the department recognized that in some circumstances integrated divisions were the best answer and a number had been introduced. The question of whether to change the structure of the department's building divisions was under consideration. The Department of the Environment, on the other hand[25] claimed to have made much progress in bringing specialists into management, including the creation of integrated hierarchies in two of its divisions. A study of HM Customs and Excise,[26] also quoted in evidence to the Committee, had brought together administrative functions with the specialist functions of the Officers of Customs and Excise and the Waterguard.

The response by the Civil Service to the argument that it would generally be more effective to organize integrated teams of specialists and administrators to deal with technical management activities, rather than to construct separate and parallel units in which administrators exercise control and specialists provide advice, was surprising. It is strange to anybody unfamiliar with the lengths to which the British Civil Service will go to preserve the primacy of the lay administrator that the proposition should be a cause of argument. The concept is unique to this one institution and all independent studies show it to be a mistake. The Fulton Report produced hard evidence from its Consultancy Group that the practice was grossly inefficient; the Rayner report criticized it; the Matthew/Skillington report condemned it. In the few areas in which it has been replaced by integrated forms of organization the change has been for the better and there has been no move to change back. The CSD, however, has never acknowledged that there is anything wrong with parallel hierarchies and has simply refused to answer criticisms of the concept. That it could indicate its enthusiasm for accountable units of management and then nod approval while departments created 'project managers' with no responsibility for contractual arrangements, for financial control or for administrative support shows its lack of power, or will, to make fundamental changes in this matter.

On the questions of hiving off functions of government to bodies outside departments and of creating accountable units within them, the Civil Service produced a variety of responses in the ten years after Fulton. Most of the developments were very modest and few of them went far in the directions proposed by Fulton. Hiving off had the attraction to Ministers of appearing to reduce the number of civil servants, always a sensitive issue. The creation of the Manpower Services Commission, for example, appeared to reduce the Civil Service by some 18,000 posts and obscured its growth elsewhere. Some functions of central government were placed in such agencies as the Civil Aviation Authority, the Health and Safety Commission and the Advisory, Conciliation and Arbitration Service. On the other hand, the Prices and Incomes Board and the Industrial Reconstruction Corporation were abolished, many think mistakenly. The CSD told the Expenditure Committee that extensive consideration had been given to hiving off. The idea was found to have limited application because there were few commercial or self-financing activities in central government and in other areas the requirements of public financial control limited managerial independence. There were difficulties in removing from Ministerial responsibility work which had a high policy content or significant discretionary authority in relation to individual citizens.

Hiving off was strongly opposed[27] by the Civil Service clerical and executive unions, on the grounds of its adverse effect on staff morale. They said to the Expenditure Committee that the threat of hiving off caused feelings of insecurity in the staff concerned and the action itself caused dislocation, and, most important, the loss of career opportunities. Promotion prospects were invariably poorer in a small hived-off body than in a large department. Even the Manpower Services Commission, employing 18,000, could not provide the promotion and development structure of its parent department (Employment). Staff in it regarded the withdrawal of their Civil Service status as an act of bad faith since they had joined the Service as a career (they regained their Civil Service status in 1975).

Apart from the creation of 'agencies', a number of new government functions were given to hived-off organizations which in former times would probably have been taken on by departments, e.g. the Countryside Commission and the Equal Opportunities Commission. The

69

failure to persevere with hiving off was, however, probably due more to a change in political attitudes than to any intrinsic difficulty in constructing them. After 1969 more and more criticism became heard of the growth, and the lack of public accountability of 'quasi-autonomous non-governmental organizations', Quangos, of which about two thousand appear to exist. These are public bodies, usually carrying out functions under legislation, usually in receipt of public funds and invariably outside direct Parliamentary scrutiny. From the middle 1970s MPs frequently complained about the proliferation of these bodies. The tide of Parliamentary opinion had swung away from the emphasis on managerial efficiency which hiving off was supposed to bring and towards an emphasis on surveillance and scrutiny.

There was some development of the idea of accountable units within departments, usually in the form of 'agencies'. We have seen that, as a result of the reorganization of government, the Defence Procurement Executive (DPE) in the Department of Defence and the Property Services Agency (PSA) in the Department of the Environment were set up in 1971. The DPE combined equipment-buying and support for civil aerospace activities of the Ministries of Defence and of Aviation Supply. This organization was headed by a chief executive who was an accounting officer for the staff and research and development votes (i.e. the purchasing agency was to be responsible for the spending and not the user of the equipment or the customer for the research). Four of his subordinate Controllers of weapons systems were accounting officers for the expenditure votes until 1977 when these were transferred to the chief executive. Within the organization there were to be project managers with full responsibility for the specialists assigned to them. There was something of a break with establishments conventions in that the organization was to be 'largely autonomous' in personnel management matters. However, in spite of a lucid analysis of what had been wrong with defence procurement in the past (fragmentation of responsibility, duplication of effort, lack of clear accountability, lack of cost awareness, lack of professionalism) the solution still appeared to dodge the problem of integrating specialist and administrative staff. In fact, it appeared to create a parallel hierarchy of specialists (four controllers of weapons systems and a controller of research and development) and administrators (a Secretary and controllers of 'policy', finance, personnel and sales). The roles of secretary and the Controller of Finance were described in familiar administrative terms. The Secretary was to provide 'the rounded advice of a senior civil servant' and was to advise on 'the reconciliation of procurement policies with the broader requirements of government policy and accountability'. The Controller of Policy was to relieve the systems controllers of the detailed work in thinking through policies, procedures and methods. In other words, specialists were to be confined to specialist matters.

The Institution of Professional Civil Servants said in evidence to the Expenditure Committee[28] that there was pressure to dismantle the DPE and return its finance, personnel and management services functions to the Ministry of Defence, thus ending its existence as a separate part of the Ministry.

The PSA was set up to provide, equip and maintain government buildings and manage government property. It employs 50,000 staff and is headed by a chief executive who is an accounting officer and who has direct access to the Secretary of State. Some 30 per cent of its services are charged to its customers, mainly to the Post Office, and the rest are provided on an 'allied service' basis, with some of them falling on its vote and others on the votes of customer departments. The PSA had adopted an integrated management structure at the top of its organization with posts above Under Secretary open to any specialism and combining policy, financial and executive control,[29] though we have seen that this approach to organization is not general in the agency. Within the PSA there is some approach to an accountable unit as envisaged by Fulton: its Supplies Division operates a trading fund, charging other parts of the PSA for the goods and services it provides. It has been set a financial objective and in future will produce regular trading accounts and other performance indicators, e.g. it will produce comparisons of its prices with those of other organizations. Within the division, it is proposed that the performance of individual operating units will be assessed through a system of budget centres and commodity accounts. As the provider of government accommodation, the PSA has much more in common with the Civil Service Department than with the rest of Environment. It would make sense to constitute it as an agency of the CSD. The Civil Service Department has set up two agencies within its own organization: a Central Computer Agency and a Civil Service Catering Organization. They appear to be little more than re-named divisions, though the Computer Agency combines activities previously carried out in several departments.

Throughout virtually all of these experiments in establishing accountable units, the Service seems not to have understood that changes in structure were only one step on the way to managerial accountability and that it would never be achieved without new planning and control systems to produce the information on objectives, costs, standards and outputs which would enable managers to be held accountable for their performance. This problem is discussed in Chapter 7.

The Expenditure Committee, reviewing developments in organization since Fulton, concluded that hiving off was applicable only to limited areas of government and should be approached with caution. Indeed, more attention should be given to developing proper control mechanisms for hived-off bodies. The Committee endorsed the Fulton principle of accountable units within departments – 'the crux of our recommendations for the increased efficiency of the Civil Service. . . . We do not believe that the Fulton proposal of accountable units has been taken sufficiently seriously in the Civil Service'.[30] The government's response to the Committee's report agreed with the need for accountability, agreed that better management information was required to achieve it, said that it would press ahead with developing information systems and said that further progress was unlikely to be fast.

New Forms of Organization

We have seen that one of the results of the new style of government of 1970 was the creation of giant departments: the Department of Trade and Industry, the Department of the Environment and the inclusion in the Foreign and Commonwealth Office of the Ministry of Overseas Development. Though they may have 'reduced interdepartmental conflict and compromise' and 'permitted the management of large programmes within departmental boundaries', there is no evidence to suggest that their existence 'contributed towards the government's overall strategy' or 'permitted the evolution of strategy for clearly defined objectives' or 'facilitated the application of analytic techniques' and they certainly did not 'make possible more effective delegation' or 'offer more direct identification to the community of Ministers for defined functions' – to quote the purposes defined at the time. Mr Heath, in evidence to the Expenditure Committee[31] did think that the amalgamations gave Ministers greater control over their departments. The creation of the DoE, he said, had reduced manpower and thereby reduced the influence of the Civil Service on Ministers. He had also managed to reduce the number in the cabinet to 19 – 'the ambition of reducing the number in Cabinet has been one which many Prime Ministers have held ever since, I think, the beginning of the century'. The purpose of a reduced Cabinet was to make better strategic decisions and at the same time to push matters down to Cabinet committees. An essential part of the change was to delegate to junior Ministers the running of their parts of the department within the Secretary of State's strategy. The problem was, he said, that it was more difficult for these Ministers to make their own political and public positions than if they had independent departments. The tendency was for people and the media still to go to the Secretary of State for the final word, even if the junior Ministers clearly had detailed terms of reference and their own sphere of operations. There was a reluctance to recognize that a junior Minister could have a specific field for which he was responsible. He said that in the past it had always been said that the upper levels of the Civil Service liked to go to the Minister at the top rather than to a junior Minister: there had been a move away from that idea but it needed to be reinforced the whole time.

Mr Wilson, in evidence to the Expenditure Committee,[32] said it was his idea to create a Department of the Environment and Mr Heath had inherited it as government policy. He thought that his merger of Health and Social Services was possibly the wrong step: his civil servants favoured a merger of social services with the Home Office where there was responsibility for children, the urban programme and immigration.

It was clear soon after they were established that it was proving difficult for Cabinet Ministers in charge of the giant departments to avoid personal responsibility in the eyes of Parliament and the public for everything that went on in their departments. In April 1971, Mr John Davies, then Secretary of State at the Department of Trade and Industry, had to make major Parliamentary statements or speeches on four successive days on the Vehicle and General (insurance) affair, the siting of the third London Airport, the future structure of the British Steel Corporation and government policy for dealing with unemployment. Secretaries of State for the Environment were expected to explain decisions on transport, even though there was a junior minister for Transport, and Secretaries of State for Health and Social Security and not Ministers for Health reported on industrial relations in the National Health Service. It was very soon obvious that the Department of Trade and Industry was too much for one Cabinet Minister to handle and the 1974 Labour government broke it up into departments for Trade, Industry and Prices and Consumer Protection. Mr Callaghan, as Prime Minister, broke a department of Transport out of the DoE and also established a Minister for Social Security with Cabinet rank within the Department of Health and Social Security.

Of the giant departments, the DoE seems to have been the most successful and there was adverse comment on the removal of Transport from it. The DHSS combines two very different organizations. Social Security is a highly managerial operation, employing many thousands of staff, running a national network of local and regional offices and processing many millions of transactions according to established rules. The Health side of the department, on the other hand, is a small policy-making body with few direct managerial responsibilities and exists to exercise surveillance over separate regional and area authorities. There have been suggestions that the Department should be divided, but there is a case for closely associating general health policy with policy for social services.

In general, altering the machinery or large-scale organization of government does not seem to make much difference to the performance of departments. Certainly, the ambition of Prime Ministers to reduce the size of the Cabinet does not appear to lead to any noticeable improvement in decision-making. Most Prime Ministers appear to have an inner cabinet of senior Ministers who decide broad policy directions anyway. It would probably be more profitable to concentrate on the way policy options are presented to the Cabinet than on the numbers in it.

We have seen that Mr Heath also tried to improve the strategic decisions of government with a Central Policy Review Staff, which he found useful and which was continued by his successors. Its work is referred to in Chapter 5. Mr Wilson also created a political unit in the Cabinet office apparently to advise him on the developing political situation. In both governments, Ministers were allowed to appoint advisers from outside the Civil Service. In some departments, there were specialist advisers with expertise in their fields (e.g. Professor Abel Smith, Mr Tony Lines, and Professor David Metcalf in the DHSS in 1974–9) and in others there were political advisers whose job was apparently to look out for the party political implications of present or prospective policies and advise the Minister.

While there was a general acceptance of the value of specialist advisers as experts who could offer Ministers practical knowledge of the working of policy from a point of view sympathetic to their politics and some support for their being enough of them to form a Ministerial *Cabinet* in each department as a source of policy advice to balance that of civil servants,[33] there was criticism of the use of political advisers, particularly from back bench MPs on the government side. They saw one of their roles as discerning the political implications of decisions, or prospective decisions, for Ministers and sometimes resented the access to Ministers and to official documents of political advisers who were often young, politically less experienced than many MPs and were suspected of seeking a quick route into politics.

The Expenditure Committee ventured into the contentious field of the relationships of Ministers to Civil Servants and its report attracted much public comment by criticizing the influence of Civil Servants. The Committee observed that all Civil Servants said that they existed solely to serve government and took their policy instructions automatically from Ministers. 'However, many who have been, or who are, Ministers believe that Ministers do not always get the service which it is claimed that they get.'[34] These Ministers were said to consider that on coming into office they found that some Departments had firmly held policy views which were difficult to change. When they were changed, the Department would often try to reinstate its own policies through the passage of time and the erosion of Ministers' political will.

74

It was said that Departments would delay and obstruct a new policy initiative which was not to the liking of a Department. It was argued that the Civil Service was entitled to prevent what was called 'the worst excesses of left or right' in the interests of stable Government policy. In the opinion of the Committee the duties of the Civil Service should be limited to pointing out the possible consequences of any policy but should not include opposing or delaying the policy.

The Committee said that Ministers may wish to change the organization of their departments: to change their advisers, set up accountable units, hive off or consolidate parts of their departments and to decide upon what outside advice they needed. At present these were matters for the Civil Service to decide, with ultimate responsibility resting with the Head of the Civil Service, who is in turn answerable to the Prime Minister. The Committee considered that Permanent Secretaries should be entirely responsive to the wishes of their Minister in relation to the management of the department and should only invoke the ultimate responsibility of the Head of the Civil Service and the Prime Minister in the most extreme circumstances. Ministers should also be able to require Permanent Secretaries to move civil servants with whom they found it difficult to work. The existing practice of a Minister being able to change his Permanent Secretary with the agreement of the Prime Minister should continue.

The Committee believed that special advisers should become an accepted feature of administration and that there should no longer be a limitation of two per Cabinet Minister. Ministers should be free to appoint a *Cabinet* of advisers, including back bench MPs, without executive authority and should have power to change the organization of their departments after consultation with the Permanent Secretary and the trade unions.

The Government's response to these ideas was that the Committee had misunderstood the powers of civil servants: the Prime Minister decided machinery of government questions. Ministers could make changes in the management of their departments if they wished, with the concurrence of the Treasury and the CSD if there were financial, economic, manpower or efficiency implications and Ministers were always consulted about senior appointments. The rule of two special advisers per Minister was not immutable.

It was clear from the proceedings of the Committee that MPs were concerned about the power of Civil Servants over Ministers. There were allegations that departments had thwarted the wishes of Ministers and eleven Labour MPs supported an unsuccessful amendment to the Committee's report[35] which attacked 'the self-anointed superiority' of civil servants, accused them of as seeing themselves as politicians writ large, as relegating Ministers to the second division by a variety of devices and as arrogating to themselves power that properly belonged to the people and their representatives. The amendment said that Labour governments seeking to alter society had more difficulty with civil servants than Conservative governments, though even Conservative governments came unstuck when they wanted to change society in a radical direction. It accused officials of the Department of Industry of frustrating interventionist industrial policies and some of those in the Department of Trade as being totally out of sympathy with a positive trade policy (i.e. import controls) and with industrial democracy. It called for less secrecy and new weapons to enable Ministers to take on the Civil Service, such as more political appointments, and it called for improved powers of Parliamentary scrutiny of the Executive.

Technology and Organization

The future organization of departments will be influenced by the effects of the massive advances in data processing and transmission which have hardly begun. Today there are nearly 600 computer installations in government, 180 of them used in administrative (as distinct from scientific and technical) areas of work. In the field of administrative computing, there are over 600 management staff, 1,800 staff operating the machines and 7,600 staff engaged in data preparation. The computer operation at Newcastle engaged on social security transactions is among the largest in the world. The job vacancy-matching system, CAPITAL, used by the Employment Services Agency, is exceptionally advanced in concept and design and the Land Registry's system won an award in 1975 for the computer application which had most benefited society. The government has pioneered such very large on-line (immediate response) systems as the Police National Computer project and a system for managing RAF stores. Most Government payments are made by computer and Value Added Tax operations were designed around computers.

So far, computers have been used mainly to mechanize repetitive clerical work or to handle large scale transaction processing or for processing scientific or engineering data. New applications will continue in these fields and will be extended, with the development of powerful mini- and micro-processors, into smaller scale operations – smaller batches of routine work and engineering design, for example. Simple case work and the application of case law, regulations and settled practice will also be partially or completely automated. At the same time, computers will increasingly be used in support of policy making and planning in departments. On the whole, in this area the Civil Service appears to have made less progress than large-scale industry, probably because of the lack of familiarity the highest levels of Civil

Service administration with the potential use of computers and their low valuation of quantitative analysis. One area in which the computer is extensively used for policy work is economic forecasting where for some years the Treasury has used a computer-based model for assessing the impact of many assumptions and variables on the course of the economy in the medium term. There are clearly many other policy areas – the allocation of health care resources, programmes for the inner cities, transportation studies, fiscal planning, anti-poverty programmes where the effects of many interrelated variable factors can most easily be examined by the use of model building and simulation on computers. There will also be a growing requirement for the interchange of data between departments: e.g. between the DHSS and Inland Revenue, which together account for much of the volume of cash transactions between central government and the public and which both require declarations of income and personal circumstances from individuals

The impact of these developments on departmental organizations is likely to become significant within the next decade. Computers, and particularly micro-processors, are likely severely to disrupt executive and clerical hierarchies: clerical staffs and their executive managers may be reduced in numbers and the organizational 'pyramid' will be flattened. Data processing staffs will increase and their most expert members will be as important to departments as the most senior administrators. A Longer Term Review of Administrative Computing in Central Government carried out by a CSD Committee in 1978 drew attention to the inability of the Civil Service to construct organizational and pay arrangements which adequately recognized the importance of data processing specialists. At the time of the review there was a shortage of 15 per cent of highly technical and project management staff in this field and it was foreseen to reach 50 per cent by 1981 if no action was taken. For years, the Civil Service had suffered a high loss of trained computer staff. The review report pointed out that in 1969 special allowances had been paid to programmers to offset higher pay outside the Service and in 1974 a 'functional specialism' was set up for computer staff within the Administration Group, though this had not obviously led to any substantial improvement in the career arrangements for such staff. Insufficient recognition had been given to the value of data processing experience for general duties, the highly technical expert was in a disadvantageous position in career terms and more use could be made of skilled computer staff who were not in the Administration Group. In the coming five years, the report said, when important new installations were to be set up or replaced and the technology would advance, over a third of the Service's senior project management staff were due to retire, including two-thirds of those at Assistant Secretary level. Exceptional arrangements in personnel management, career development and deployment were essential for highly qualified specialists in data processing and there should be no barriers to the employment in highly specialized posts in administrative computing of staff from other occupational groups or to recruitment from outside. There was a particular need for competent project managers, who did not fit neatly into structural or management arrangements for particular groups of staff: early action had to be taken to identify and develop staff with the potential to manage projects from within any occupational group.

This alarming review showed precisely what Fulton had foreseen: the class structure of the Civil Service cannot stand up to rapid technological change. Fulton's solution was to abolish the class structure, so as to free movement from one skilled group to another. The review, having been carried out by administrators, did not recognize that solution but proposed yet more *ad hoc* palliatives.

The organization structure of departments will not be able to stand up to these changes, either. In industry and commerce, data-processing staffs (and the closely associated operational research specialists) have all the non-hierarchical features of specialist and innovatory groups. In the Civil Service, however, administrative computers are the province of the executive grades – markedly hierarchical in structure, non-specialist and primarily organized to manage accounts, casework and clerical operations. Though the attempt is made to fit these grade levels to computer work – Executive Officer programmer, HEO and SEO systems analyst – such arrangements are under considerable strain. Rigid gradings often do not reflect the contribution of different individuals to a computer team: a good programmer may very well be ready to take the lead on the design of advanced systems long before the fifteen years or so that he might have to wait for promotion to SEO. A programming/systems team on a large computer installation (perhaps twenty or thirty strong) may well require an internal organizational form that conflicts with the neat pyramid which the department requires to provide an orderly career progression for its middle management: it may require more SEOs and HEOs for example, or a disproportionate number of Principals.

From industrial experience, we may expect data processing groups to become powerful nodal points in departments, indispensable to their functioning. We can expect large groups of staff engaged on data preparation, verification and coding; groups of skilled staff operating the computer; small clerical hierarchies handling exceptional cases; loosely organized systems design, analysis and research groups of programmers, systems analysts, social scientists, statisticians, engineers, accountants, managers and administrators assembling and reforming in constantly changing and adapting teams. Such teams will be engaged on studies ranging from the maintenance and updating of current accounting routines to the construction of enormously complex models of the transaction – processing and information requirements of pro-posed policies and legislation. In future the data processing implications of a change of policy will become increasingly important and the data-processing facility is likely to develop into a 'corporate staff' with substantial functional authority over the heads of operating divisions.

In spite of all the ferment of ideas on the machinery of government and the internal organization of departments in the last ten years, permanent changes have been few. Giant departments have come and mostly gone. Hiving off has been enthusiastically advocated by poli-ticians, considered by the Civil Service, tried in a couple of areas and then enthusiastically attacked by politicians.

In one area, the Fulton idea of an accountable unit appears to have come to fruition. The Manpower Services Commission, operating employment and training services, appears to have broken out of the administrative mould and to conduct its affairs in a managerial style. Its annual report and annual review and plan specifies its aims, iden-tifies its strategy in pursuit of those aims and displays its executive programmes and budgets together with measures of output and results in a way which no government organization has before publicly attempted (see Chapter 5). The result is that the policy and operations of the Commission are comprehensible and examinable in the style of accountability which was envisaged by Fulton. Elsewhere there are few accountable units in departments. In fact, the only others which matches the Fulton prescription appears to be the Supplies Division of the PSA and possibly DHSS local offices. Nowhere else do we find budget and responsibility centres with quantified inputs and outputs or other measures of performance, mainly because the information system has never been constructed to support them.

However, there are independent forces in the external environment which will have important effects upon departmental organization. So great is political concern about quangos and so weak the justification for some of them that we may well be moving into a phase of 'hiving on', i.e., the assumption of direct Ministerial control over quango functions.* The increasing Parliamentary concern about public accountability may force departments to introduce accountable units so that their management can be called to account by Parliament. Inte-grated hierarchies will eventually have to be created by departments to

---

* However, the purge of quangos promised by the government in 1979 did not amount to much. A review by Sir Leo Pliatzky reported in January 1980 that 211 of the 1,561 advisory bodies, 30 of 489 executive bodies and 5 of 67 tribunals should be abolished, saving £11·5 million out of a total cost of £5,850 million.

deal with technical/administrative functions as Fulton and other studies have demonstrated. Ministers will increasingly come to depend on political and specialist advisers as a countervailing power to the administrative establishment and back bench MPs will also want to join in, possibly to the point where Ministerial *Cabinets* are formed. Data processing expertise will come to rival administrative expertise and will have to be represented at the highest levels in departments. The increasing technical complexity and inherent incompatibility of the personnel management and management services functions of departments will probably lead to their separation. Greater use will have to be made of multi-disciplinary project teams if departments are to be able to cope with large design construction and data processing projects and complex policy studies and plans. A very rapid growth in the information requirements for management and for public accountability will revolutionize the finance function (see Chapter 6).

The outcome of all these forces, apart from stressing the old administrative style to breaking point, will be to evolve a nucleated pattern of organization of agencies, staff groups, centres, and project teams in place of the rigid scalar hierarchy. There will be nuclei of operational units, some permanent, some assembled for specific projects, with far greater delegation of authority over the resources of manpower and money allocated to them. There will be nuclei of specialist expertise – in management services, financial and budgetary control, planning, data processing, personnel management, the Ministerial *Cabinet*. Within all of them, we can expect a lessening of bureaucratic rigidity, with more highly trained and specialized staff tending to define their own jobs in the course of their work. Such nucleated organizations will demand a very high quality of management at all levels and the highly developed information and planning systems described in the following chapters.

References

1. *Committee on the Civil Service, Report*, (June 1968), Vol. I, para. 252.
2. ibid., para. 257.
3. ibid., para. 165.
4. ibid., para. 150.
5. HOWELL, D., *A New Style of Government*, Conservative Political Centre, (May 1970).
6. ibid., p. 30.
7. *The Reorganization of Central Government*, (October 1970), Cmnd. 4506.
8. *Expenditure Committee, Eleventh Report*, (July 1977), Vol. II, part I, p. 135.
9. ibid., Vol. II, p. 153.

10. ibid., Vol. III, p. 1104, para. 64.
11. ibid., Vol. II, part II, p. 746.
12. ibid., p. 760.
13. ibid., p. 780.
14. ibid., p. 797.
15. ibid., p. 801.
16. ibid., Vol. I, para. 72.
17. ibid., para. 74.
18. ibid., Vol. II, p. 556.
19. ibid., p. 532.
20. ibid., p. 532.
21. MATTHEW R. H. and SKILLINGTON W. P. D., *Promotion of High Standards of Architectural Design*, PSA, (1974).
22. *Government Organization for Defence Procurement and Civil Aerospace*, Cmnd. 4641, (April 1971).
23. *Expenditure Committee, Eleventh Report*, (July 1977).
24. ibid., p. 389.
25. ibid., p. 280.
26. ibid., Vol. III, p. 852.
27. ibid., Vol. II, p. 494.
28. ibid., Vol. II, p. 536.
29. ibid., Vol. II, p. 285.
30. ibid., Vol. I, para. 94.
31. ibid., Vol. II, p. 760 *et seq.*
32. ibid., Vol. II, p. 780 *et seq.*
33. GARRETT, J. and SHELDON, R., 'Administrative Reform, The Next Steps', *Fabian Tract* 426, (Fabian Society, November 1973).
34. *Expenditure Committee, Eleventh Report*, (July 1977).
35. ibid., Vol. I, p. lxxvii.

V

Planning

A planning system enables an organization to take a long-term view of its future: to evaluate its present standing, to examine prospective developments in its environment, to make strategic choices, to allocate resources and to provide the basis for monitoring its performance.

Most planning systems are built on a series of steps which relate the broad long-term strategic issues facing the organization to detailed short-term programmes of action for management. Generally these steps are:

1 A statement of *aims* – that is, of the purpose and fields of activity of the organization.

2 Based on these aims, the systematic examination and ranking of long-term *strategies* based on the organization's standing in relation to its aims and on the implications of likely political, economic, technical and social changes in its environment in the foreseeable future. Casting the future of the organization forward usually reveals 'gaps' between the aims of the organization and where it is likely to be if present policies continue to be pursued and alternative strategies therefore have to be devised to close these gaps. In large organizations corporate planning staffs are employed to model the likely results of different strategies and to advise on strategic choices. In addition, line managers (and probably before long, worker representatives) participate in the definition of strategy by bringing to bear their experience of the problems and opportunities faced in the day-to-day conduct of the enterprise.

3 The expression of chosen strategies in a long-term (five or ten year) *plan* which sets out, in detail for the first year or two and in outline for succeeding years, specific *objectives* for the organization.

4 The translation of objectives into programmes, projects, budgets and *standards of performance* for managerial units within the organization.

5 The construction of a control system which enables the results achieved to be compared with the objectives.

6 The establishment of formal annual *review* procedures for assessing

results, for rolling forward the plan year by year, reconsidering aims and objectives and for designating managerial accountability.

Formal planning routines on broadly these lines became general practice in large-scale industry from the early 1960s. At about the same time an expenditure planning system, the Public Expenditure Survey (PES) was developed in British central government, for much the same reason – the need to take a forward look over a larger time span than the traditional one-year budget. The PES system, however, concentrated mainly on the allocation of resources to spending programmes and activities (inputs) rather than objectives and results (outputs). This is not surprising, given the instability of aims and objectives in a political environment (particularly in Britain), the inherent difficulties in measuring the results of many government activities (e.g. defence, education, scientific research, social policy) and the administrative rather than managerial tradition of the higher Civil Service in Britain. There has, however, been a more or less constant campaign by a few reformers to shift the emphasis in government expenditure planning from resources and inputs to results and outputs, quoting developments in the United States (see below), which has had some effect on the PES system.

The Public Expenditure Survey

In 1957–8 the Select Committee on Estimates[1] examined and commented very critically on Treasury planning and control of expenditure. It found 'somewhat disturbing' the fact that the Treasury did not sufficiently appreciate the need to review established policies involving expenditure and appeared to lack a constructive approach to the matter. It called for a systematic and regular review of existing policies in terms of their prospective expenditure. It expressed 'grave disquiet' over the extent to which departments under-estimated their expenditures and the willingness with which the Treasury accepted supplementary estimates when the original ones were exceeded.

The Committee also criticized the 'natural tendency, within the present system of estimates and accounts, to concentrate too much attention on the policy and expenditure proposals for the coming financial year with too little regard to the commitments and consequences for future years ... an obsession with annual expenditure can stultify forward planning',[2] and recommended that longer-term forecasts should be carried out in civil departments.

It concluded by recommending that a small independent committee be appointed to report on the theory and practice of Treasury control of expenditure. The government did not accept the Estimates Committee's recommendation for an external committee of inquiry but set up a body led by Lord Plowden under the authority of the Chancellor of the Exchequer, which reported in July 1961.[3]

The Plowden Committee observed that while in some departments (e.g. defence, education) the practice of long term 'forward looks' had become established, in general the traditional system of piecemeal decisions persisted and no criteria existed to permit a rational choice between different kinds of expenditure.

The Committee proposed that in future 'Public expenditure decisions whether they be in defence or education or overseas aid or agriculture or pensions or anything else, should never be taken without consideration of (a) what the country can afford over a period of years having regard to prospective resources and (b) the relative importance of one kind of expenditure against another'.[4] The Committee then recommended that 'Regular surveys should be made of public expenditure as a whole, over a period of years ahead, and in relation in prospective resources; decisions involving substantial future expenditure should be taken in the light of these surveys'.[5]

From 1961 onwards, annual surveys of public expenditure, looking five years ahead, have been prepared broadly on the lines proposed by Plowden. Early each year officials prepare an analysis of existing expenditure plans, programme by programme, and of the scope for changes. This analysis is prepared jointly by the Treasury and other departments on assumptions agreed by Ministers collectively. The work is co-ordinated by the Public Expenditure Survey Committee, on which sit the Principal Finance Officers of the principal spending departments, chaired by the Treasury. The Committee prepares a report for Ministers defining the existing position of spending plans set out in the preceding year as amended by subsequent policy decisions and price changes. It also sets out amendments and additions to plans proposed by departments and the scope for reducing expenditure, changing priorities or redistributing resources between programmes. Decisions on the content of the next year's survey are taken by Ministers in July to October in the light of a Medium Term Assessment of the economy for the planning period produced by the Treasury. Since 1969, the agreed expenditure plans have been published in a White Paper in January or February. This document shows spending proposals for each of fifteen functional sectors of expenditure (such as law and order, defence, health and personal social services) for each of the past five years, for the year of publication and for each of the four following years. This annual review is a planning, not a control, document and focusses on the volume of expenditure, which is therefore expressed in constant 'survey' prices. For most goods and services, survey prices are those which obtained in the autumn of the previous year (for example, the autumn of 1978 for the 1979 survey). For most transfer payments, e.g. social security, survey prices are the average prices assumed to obtain during the current year of the survey. For future years, provision is made for a contingency reserve of unallocated expenditure. The reserve is to cover requirements for increased expenditure which either are not foreseen or cannot be quantified when the White Paper figures are settled. For the later years, when uncertainties are greater, a larger reserve is allowed for (e.g. in the 1979 White Paper the reserve for 1979–80 was £800 million and for 1982–3 it was £2,500 million). The White Paper planning figures are used as the basis for annual supply estimates by departments, for recruiting and now for establishing 'cash limits' (see Chapter 6). Where cash limits operate they provide a ceiling within which expenditure has to be contained. Because departments commonly undershoot their control figures, partly because of the difficulty in forecasting some items and partly because of caution in working the new cash limit system, the actual volume of expenditure has in recent years usually fallen well short of the total volume proposed in the White Paper. In 1967–77 the shortfall was $3\frac{1}{2}$ per cent (over £2 billion) below the planned level; in 1977–78 it was 7 per cent (over £4 billion) below and from 1978–9 to 1982–3 the shortfall was forecast, or planned, to be £2 billion in each year.

Though the first White Paper of 1969 was greeted as a major advance for Parliamentary scrutiny, in the succeeding ten years the Expenditure Committee, which issued a report every year on the White Paper, heavily criticized its form and content in addition to the Government decisions it embodied. The main thrust of the observations of the Expenditure Committee on content was to demand more information from the Treasury. For a number of years, the Committee pressed the Treasury to publish the Medium Term Economic Assessment on which the White Paper is based so that planned public expenditure could be examined in the context of Government forecasts of economic activity. In several reports the Committee requested the presentation of revenue projections alongside plans for public expenditure, so as to be able to relate income to spending and to evaluate changes in taxation as well as changes in benefits, grants and services. Similarly, the Committee urged the publication of 'tax expenditures': revenues foregone by the granting of relief to certain taxpayers, e.g. on mortgage interest repayments and investment expenditure.

The Committee also criticized the differences in structure and price valuation between the annual supply estimates and cash limits and the expenditure plans and complained that it was difficult to relate annual control figures to the longer-term projections. In 1975 and in 1976, in particular, the Committee complained that during the year emergency cuts in forecast expenditure had so disrupted the plans laid out in the

White Paper that year-to-year comparisons were impossible and the projections for later years were suspect. The Expenditure Committee, and other Parliamentary Committees, persistently criticized the absence of any statements of the objectives of particular programmes or measures by which the effectiveness of programmes could be judged or of the results of past programmes.

Over the years, the Treasury has to some extent improved the survey to meet these criticisms. In the Green Paper of 1969, which announced the annual publication of expenditure plans, the government proposed to present receipts from taxation, contributions and other charges for the first three years of the survey because it considered that public expenditure figures might be 'misleading so long as the revenue side was not presented at the same time'. The first White Paper of 1969 presented expenditure and revenue projections on a common price basis, with tax receipts based on tax rates and allowances at the time but this was not repeated in later years.

From 1972 until 1976 the White Papers included another method of providing an economic framework in which spending programmes could be analysed: the 'resources table'. This was constructed on the basis of assumptions about the supply of total resources and the various claims on them. In particular, requirements were specified for investment and the balance of payments over the medium-term and attention was focused on the resources that might become available for public expenditure and private consumption, after meeting those prior claims. Any imbalance between total supply and demand in the projections was eliminated by changing the assumptions about tax yields: taxation was varied in the projections so as to ensure a match between aggregate supply and demand. The projections were arranged to achieve, by the terminal year of the period, desired outcomes for both employment and the balance of payments. However, these arrangements were not suited, in the view of the Treasury,[7] to a situation in which the economy was in a severe state of disequilibrium and the feasibility of achieving the desired outcomes within the period of the plan itself became a major question. Moreover, two assumptions in the resource table calculation were found to be incorrect after 1974: that the historic rate of growth in the economy's productive potential could be extrapolated for the period covered by the projection and that real output would not be significantly affected by inflation. In 1977, the Treasury proposed a new approach to the problem of setting expenditure plans alongside revenue projections and the envisaged rate of economic growth. It would set out in the White Paper 'stylized assumptions' about the annual path of growth and would project revenues at unchanged tax rates; these would be combined with expenditure forecasts and the financial deficit and borrowing by Government. The resulting table would indicate the balance between government revenues and expenditures if the economy developed as assumed. In the 1979 White Paper,[8] the government presented illustrative projections of expenditure and output based on an average earnings growth of 7 per cent to 11 per cent and consequent price increases, productivity growth, monetary growth, competitiveness and Gross Domestic Product. These were promptly criticized by the Expenditure Committee and commentators as unrealistic in that they were too optimistic about the growth of average earnings and consequential changes. In this White Paper, the Treasury also published a valuation of over 75 tax expenditures, setting the cost of child tax allowance and of house mortgage interest relief alongside the expenditures on programmes for social services and housing. This was welcomed by the Expenditure Committee which also asked that more of the remaining 88 tax expenditures should be valued in future. From 1972 onwards, the Treasury responded to the demand for closer links between the five year expenditure programmes and the one-year supply estimates by aligning each class of estimates with its related programme and showing how the figures for each could be reconciled and then combining the new cash limits (see Chapter 6) with the supply estimates.

In addition to all the arguments about the presentation of the White Paper, the Expenditure Committee and others, have always been critical of its purpose. A recurring criticism, again expressed in the Committee's report on the 1979 White Paper, is that the White Paper does not set out the government's plans for the medium term, but a set of arbitrary projections, the purpose of which is to draw attention to the constraints on policy.[9] A reader of the White Paper has no idea whether the Government considers it can overcome these constraints, or what it proposes to do about them or how public expenditure fits into any overall economic strategy. The commentary provided in the 1979 White Paper emphasized that the alternative projections were neither predictions nor expressions of the Government's intentions. The White Paper is therefore a rather loosely connected set of forecasts or aspirations, rather than a plan, and contains no realistic assessment of economic prospects nor any idea of the options open to the Government in economic or public expenditure policies.

A further criticism, repeated year after year, is that the White Paper is all about inputs and not about outputs: it tells us what we are going to spend, but not what we are going to buy. For virtually every spending programme we have no information on its justification, its objectives, its relationship to the needs of the community at which it is addressed, the past results of the same or similar programmes nor the means by which its efficiency or its effectiveness might be judged. It is as if year after year programmes are sent out into a void from which no response ever comes: we do not know on any regular or systematic basis if urban programmes improve the condition of the urban poor or if various forms of aid to industry are effective or whether a subsidy, or a grant or a tax relief has the greatest impact on some national problem. The Expenditure Committee made this point about the Public Expenditure White Paper soon after it was first published: 'proper discussion of the Government's plans also requires information about the outputs which projected ... expenditures are expected to provide and how this provision relates to policy objectives'.[10] In October 1972, the Expenditure Committee, in a report on *The Relationship of Expenditure to Needs* said 'we have been left in no doubt that the system of information necessary for resource accountability does not at present exist; this means that neither the Government, nor Parliament nor the public can at present be supplied with the material necessary for any systematic discussion or evaluation of priorities'.[11] The report said that the Treasury recognized that an adequate information system on the outputs of spending programmes had not existed and that 'at any rate until recently', Governments had relied mainly on the 'feel' of departments, rather than on an objective system of information. In the absence of information, said the Committee, 'it was impossible to verify whether the planned expenditure had occurred and whether it had been effective. It called for a reform of the survey system so that the analysis of inputs could be matched by the analysis of outputs and discussed examples of areas of expenditure where such an approach could be used: services for the elderly, inter-urban roads, nursery education, prisons. The Treasury, in a note to the Committee, accepted in principle the idea of showing the results of public expenditure but pointed to numerous difficulties.

Programme Budgeting

At the time this discussion was going on, the Conservative administration's 'new style of government' was in full swing and one of its principles was the analysis of outputs or results of spending. The White Paper on the reorganization of government of 1970[12] observed that the Public Expenditure Survey did not provide all the information required by Ministers to balance the claims of competing blocks of public expenditure. It did not call for explicit statements of the objectives of expenditure in a way which would enable a Minister's plans to be tested against general government strategy nor did it embody detailed analysis of existing programmes and of major policy options on them. The government therefore proposed a new system of regular reviews which would provide more and better information, to be designed by its team of businessmen. These would involve a greater emphasis on the definition of objectives and the expression of programmes so far as possible in output terms: the presentation and examination of alternative programmes would be of great importance.

All this emphasis on defining the outputs of spending programmes came from the development of Programme Planning and Budgeting (PPB) in the United States federal government in the 1960s in which there was world-wide interest. PPB, sometimes also called 'output budgeting', is a planning system for public authorities in which expenditures are displayed in a way which relates them to policy objectives and which enables assessments to be made of their results, or impact on the client community. It is underpinned by extensive analysis of the costs and benefits of alternative routes to those objectives. Adopting it involves major changes from traditional government practices in costing, accounting, forecasting, and policy research and presentation.

PPB was developed at the RAND Corporation, a Californian research institute, and applied at the US Department of Defence from 1961 by Defence Secretary Robert McNamara when he arrived there and found conflict and competition for resources between the three armed services, each of which appeared to have different objectives and perceptions of the threat to national security. President Johnson required its use generally in the US federal government from 1965. In the form of output budgeting, it was applied in the British Ministry of Defence in the mid-1960s and, experimentally, in a few civil departments in the late 1960s and early 1970s. PPB was fully described in the author's 'Management of Government' (Pelican, 1972). Its main elements are briefly set out here to provide a background to recent developments in planning and control in the Civil Service.

1 The Classification of Accounts

Traditionally, the accounts for government departments have been set out according to the requirements of the supply procedure of estimates and votes (see Chapter 6). These have been classified according to input, or subject of expenditure – e.g. wages and salaries, accommodation costs, the cost of facilities. This is a convenient form of presentation for auditing but useless for policy-making and the assessment of objectives and results. In contrast, PPB involves the classification of expenditures into programmes, or categories which display the aims of the expenditure and sets out not the inputs, or items which are to be purchased, but the outputs or the purpose to which the spending is to be directed. An example to this kind of display is given by the 1978 Review and Plan of the Manpower Services Commission.

MANPOWER SERVICES COMMISSION

Programme	Aims	Output (in 1977/78)	Estimated Costs (in 1977/78)
ESD Statistics and Labour Market Intelligence	(1)To provide statistics and labour market intelligence to assist Government. MSC and others to increase their understanding of labour market to monitor changes and to make informed decisions on manpower policy; (2) to provide information for monitoring, review and analysis of ES performance.	Wide range of information of various kinds. Includes counts of unemployed and vacancies.	£7·1m
TOPS	To offer training to adults who are unemployed or are re-entering the labour market or wish to change jobs.	98,964 training courses completed.	£194m
Industry Directorate	(1) Through ITBs and other industry training organizations to obtain the provision of adequate training of appropriate quality by industry to meet the training needs of industry; (2) to influence the amount, direction and quality of training towards skills of importance from a national point of view; to see that other national manpower priorities are taken into account and that due regard is given to the interest of individual workers.	Various: mainly changes in policies and performance of training in industry, but including also training supported by special measures and by key training grants.	£89·4m
Direct Training Services	To provide support to employers in appropriate cases in improving the skill and efficiency of their labour force.	Sponsored training in skillcentres: 4,200. Mobile Instructors: 4,000. Instructor training: 2,000. TWI: 24,000 supervisors and 600 training officers attended courses. International Trade Procedures: 2,250.	£3·3m revenue: £584,000

Manpower Services Commission—*continued*

Programme	Aims	Output (in 1977/78)	Estimated Costs (in 1977/78)
TSD Development and Research	To improve the efficiency and effectiveness of training.	Various: including development projects, surveys, research and publications.	About £1m
Special Programmes	To improve the ability of the individual to respond to employment opportunities; to provide a constructive alternative to prolonged unemployment, in particular to provide work preparation and work experience (through YOP) or temporary employment (STEP); to provide particular assistance to those hardest hit by unemployment, especially the disadvantaged and the long term unemployed.	YOP: aim to provide 234,000 young people with opportunities in first full year and employment for 8,000 adults as managers and supervisors. STEP: target of 25,000 temporary jobs at any one time.	£155m in first full year. £68m in first full year.
Corporate Services	To provide resources to operating divisions in accordance with agreed plans and budgets; to promote cost consciousness, cost effectiveness and improvement of staff productivity throughout MSC; to develop financial and manpower control systems; to ensure MSC expenditure is properly accounted for; to contribute to strategic and operational planning and evaluation of the programmes of operating divisions.	(Not created in 1977/78).	
Manpower Intelligence and Planning	To assist all parts of the MSC to develop and implement appropriate, professionally competent, effective and efficient manpower policies and plans and to help develop the MSC's role as an authority on manpower matters.	Various: including professional advice, policy studies, statistics and labour market analyses.	Staff: £467,000. External research: £493,000. Action research on socially disadvantaged: £37,000.

Manpower Services Commission—*continued*

Programme	Aims	Output (in 1977/78)	Estimated Costs (in 1977/78)
General Placing Service	To help people choose and obtain the right jobs and help employers recruit the right people as quickly as possible.	£1·61m placings.	£51·2m.
Services for Training	To advise potential trainees of training opportunities, to recruit sufficient numbers of trainees to meet requirements agreed with TSD and to assist trainees to find suitable jobs on completion of training.	152,090 applications for training taken.	£5·4m.
CAPITAL	To implement a total on-line computerized vacancy matching system.	12,398 placings for 6 months from Oct. 1977 (first 6 months of full operation).	£1·3m.
Other Direct ESD Activities	(1) To ensure operational efficiency and accuracy of statistical returns and protection of UB and SA funds; to uphold requirements of Race Relations and Sex Discrimination Acts; to provide information on employment legislation; to administer schemes to reduce unemployment; (2) to provide a Local Advisory Service to employers.	N/A.	£5·7m.
Careers and Occupational Information Centre (COIC)	To provide up-to-date information service including materials and advice about content, training requirements and prospects of occupations for the benefit of the public, of schools and of those who give careers advice.	284 new items of literature and audio-visual material. Sales: £85,000 worth.	£800,000.
Professional and Executive Recruitment (PER)	To provide a recruitment service for employers seeking staff at professional and executive level fully recovering costs and to provide services to enable job seekers to help themselves in job search.	8,800 candidates placed earning total revenue of £3·25m. 3,750 entered TOPS training.	£5·9m of which £2·7m on supportive and advisory services.

Manpower Services Commission—*continued*

Programme	Aims	Output (in 1977/78)	Estimated Costs (in 1977/78)
Services for Disabled People	(1) To help disabled people find and keep jobs best suited to their aptitudes and capabilities and to help them settle into work as quickly and smoothly as possible; (2) to administer the registration and quota provisions of the Disabled Persons (Employment Act) 1944 and to advise on development of policies on employment of disabled people.	52,000 placings into open employment (excluding self-service placings in Jobcentres); 2,000 into sheltered employment.	£13·8m.
Rehabilitation	(1) To provide an employment rehabilitation service to assess and prepare people who after injury, illness or unemployment want to enter or re-enter employment; (2) To provide financial support to local authorities or voluntary organizations providing an employment rehabilitation service for the blind, spastics or mentally ill.	15,000 ERC courses undertaken. 650 courses undertaken.	£10·86m. £0·56m.
Occupational Guidance	To assist people who are considering a change in occupation or the choice of an occupation on entry or re-entry into employment to make realistic decisions about the careers and jobs suited to their abilities, aspirations and circumstances.	54,107 first interviews; 4,442 subsequent interviews; 2,189 job studies.	£2·76m.
Services to Geographical Mobility	To promote desirable geographical mobility to meet the needs of workers in industry.	Employment Transfer Scheme: 28,211 moves. Job Search Scheme; 13,152 interviews.	£14m.
Sheltered Employment	To provide sheltered employment for those who by the nature of their disability are unable to work either temporarily or permanently in ordinary employment.	13,269 people in sheltered employment at 31.3.78.	£29·7m.

This display of programmes by the MSC was accompanied by a narrative describing the developments under way in each programme and how the programmes fitted into the Commission's development strategy and by tables showing estimated expenditure on each programme from 1978-9 to 1983-4; estimated staff members engaged on each programme to 1984 and rates of increase in expenditure and staff over the period.

2 The Planning Stage

Having developed this framework for organizing planning data, PPB starts with a statement, by the top decision-making authority in the organization, of its purpose and aims. The policy aims of government departments are often more complex and diffuse than those of commercial organizations and have rarely been put in writing. They usually have to be distilled from legislation and regulations, Ministerial statements, discussion documents and White Papers and the proceedings of commissions of enquiry and Parliamentary Committees. These policy aims are related to the programme structure by a planning staff (see below). This involves grouping expenditures into functions and subsidiary programmes. Thus, one function of government is, in White Paper terms, 'Industrial Innovation'. Within this, there is a programme category 'General Industrial Research and Development' which divides into a number of programmes of which one is 'support for microelectronics and microprocessors' which could in turn be divided into such individual programme elements as a project to develop a microprocessor application to factory stock and materials control. In some areas, it may also be necessary to identify programmes aimed at particular 'client groups': low-income families, pre-school children, sufferers from kidney disease.

The development of a hierarchy of programmes provides the basis for examining the weight of expenditure currently given to one aim compared with another; it is possible to examine which activities contribute to more than one aim or which appear to be unrelated to any aim and an examination can begin to be made of the relationship between the programmes of the department and other departments or external agencies.

The next step is the specification of community needs and performance criteria which will allow the formulation of specific and quantified objectives for programmes and elements and the assessment of their impact. Thus, aim: 'to reduce unemployment among school leavers'; objective: 'to provide employment or a place in full time education or training for all school leavers by the summer of 1981'. An objective should be measurable. It should state the quantity (and the quality, if possible) of benefit that is being aimed at and the period in which it is to be provided. In many areas of government activity it is possible to specify such objectives as improvements in health, primary education standards, levels of income, housing and employment, improvements in industrial performance. In others, such as cultural and higher educational provision, research and development, social provision and defence it may be impossible to construct indicators of ultimate benefit but only such 'intermediate' objectives as the volume of service to be provided.

The final step in the planning stage is the definition of issues: the identification of key policy areas which require analysis in depth if policies are to reflect the aims of the organization, to link with government strategy and to enable Ministers to make rational choices between competing ends.

3 Programming

Programming consists of defining, analysing and ranking alternative methods of allocating resources so as to achieve the specified objectives. Programme analysis usually starts with a definition of the 'base case' – what is the total public programme currently being addressed to the satisfaction of a particular community need? What result is this programme achieving? If present social and economic trends continue over the next five years where then will the present programme stand in relation to the need?

Diverging from the base case, the programme-analysis staff generate an array of alternative approaches that are potentially available to meet policy objectives. The examination of alternatives involves attempting to quantify the probable results and the costs of a manageable number of potential approaches to satisfying community needs by using analytical techniques, of which cost-benefit or cost-effectiveness analysis are the best known. Programme analyses result in the presentation of a number of programme choices to the political decision maker. For each programme, a 'balance sheet' of costs and benefits and quantative factors are presented. The politician has to evaluate and compare programmes, assessing their relative worth against political and economic constraints, the government's strategy and his judgement of priorities and decide upon the programmes to be implemented.

When programme decisions have been taken each programme is costed in much greater detail and is translated into a multi-year (usually three or five) plan showing the estimated costs and results of each year of programme implementation and supported by a programme memorandum which describes in detail:

(a)   the strategic and analytical justification for the programme

(b) year-by-year indicators of cost and achievement and acceptable limits of variance

(c) how the programme will be funded

(d) who will be responsible for the management of the programme and its activities

(e) the requirements for special skills or staff training

(f) relationships with allied programmes in other departments or institutions

(g) key issues yet unresolved

(h) the procedure for reviewing the programme.

4 Budgeting

Financial authority has now to be sought from the Legislature for the first year's expenditures on the department's programmes. In some cases, financial estimates are presented in programme form (and it would be most useful for the Legislature if they were) but more usually programmes have to be recast in the form of inputs (wages, accommodation, capital costs) for sanction and audit by a reclassification routine called a 'crosswalk'.

Once the budget is approved, the plan becomes a management instruction and the programmes are put into operation. Where a programme is the responsibility of a single managerial unit it is possible to specify the accountability for its management. Problems arise, however, where several units contribute to a programme. In this case, it has been proposed that programmes be reclassified by another crosswalk so as to coincide with the management structure of departments, divisions and branches. The attempt was made in the US federal government to break such programmes into modules which fitted into the management structure, but this has proved difficult in practice. Is many cases it is better to adjust the programme and/or the management structures of departments so as to achieve the best possible match.

5 Review

Every year the multi-year plan and its constituent programmes are reviewed and rolled forward another year. Ideally, information on programme expenditures and results is produced during the course of the year so that operations can be tracked by programme, by estimate and by organizational unit, and thus the performance of the programme, the spend against the authorized estimate and, where possible, the efficiency of the managing or contributing units, can be monitored. In some cases the feedback of results is rapid (benefits issued, transport improved, families housed), but very often the lag between the expenditure and even intermediate objectives (roads constructed, probation officer training placed provided) runs to years and the lag between the expenditure and the final objectives (improvements in health, the reduction in traffic accidents or of delinquency) may run to decades. In the long-lag programmes, *ad hoc* research studies into the current state of progress have to take the place of a running review and evaluation of results.

After being introduced by President Johnson in 1965, most US Federal agencies had applied PPB by 1970. It appeared to be a very promising development because of the need to find a method of rationalizing the involvement of many US government agencies in single areas of expenditure (e.g. 28 Federal agencies still dispense aid for education) and to provide a consistent procedure for the evaluation of programmes. It had the advantage (a contrast with Britain) of being introduced into a Civil Service with long-established systems of management accounting, budgetary control and efficiency measurement as a result of the Hoover Commission of 1945 and the Budget Accounting Act of 1950 which had required agencies to produce cost data for each organizational unit ('performance budgeting'). Agencies therefore already had a foundation of internal cost and performance data and a number of managers who were familiar with using it.

However, the enthusiasm for PPB waned after 1975. Congressional committees still required agencies to argue for their funds in traditional form; much of the programme analysis was suspect; the problem of making the programme structure coincide with the managerial structure raised great difficulty and both officials and politicians saw PPB as a passing fashion. Mr Samuel Cohn, the top permanent official of the Bureau of the Budget in 1967, said ten years later: 'that system was excellent, sensible and ought to be done, but I think it fell on its face because (the Johnson administration) tried to push it off too fast, on every agency at once. It was too advanced for the clerks who had to do the work. And the top managers, the appointees brought in from outside, in many cases leave government just about the time they've learned their way around'.[13]

Nevertheless, PPB is credited with a number of achievements in the USA and Canada. It obliged departments and agencies to examine their fundamental aims and purposes. It introduced an awareness of the value of analysis into the decision-making processes of government. The preparation of analytical studies prior to policy formulation have come to form part of the regular operating routine of senior managers. The quality of information – on objectives, output, effectiveness and impact – has been markedly improved. As a result of the PPB approach, the US Federal Budget is a document far more illuminating on what the government is doing, and why, than anything produced by the government in Britain.

After the election of President Carter in 1976 there was a revival of

97

interest in a variation of PPB called 'zero-base budgeting' which had been considered and abandoned nearly ten years earlier. From time to time this procedure has been suggested for Britain, mainly by Conservative politicians. Proponents of zero-base budgeting argue that instead of accepting or even considering the base case, departments should be required to justify the need for every existing programme by assuming the base is zero and analysing every programme as if it were about to be created. This would oblige politicians and officials to focus on the basic purposes of expenditures rather than on the additional expenditures for which they were seeking authorization. In 1977 President Carter's administration said that this procedure would be the key vehicle for government planning: 'requiring every activity that spends taxpayers' money to re-justify itself annually'. It was claimed that President Carter had successfully introduced it into the State Government in Georgia in 1972, whence it had spread into other state and local governments. After the announcement there was an immediate rush by Washington officials to sign up for courses on how to fill out zero-base budgeting forms for the Office of Management and Budget.[14] Zero-base budgeting seems likely to go the way of PPB, only more rapidly. Implementing it would place an impossible analytical load on departments, involving an exhaustive review of legislation and other Ministerial commitments as well as of expenditure and much of it would be redundant or produced only in self-defence. A more sensible routine would seem to be to produce a programme-based planning routine annually with periodic detailed reviews of individual programmes such as were produced until recently by departments in Britain through the PAR procedure (see below).

Fulton on Planning

The Fulton Committee commented upon the 'crowding out' of long-term thinking and planning in departments by the more immediate demands arising from the Parliamentary and public responsibilities of Ministers. It concluded that 'a department's responsibility for major long-term policy planning should be clearly allocated to a planning and research unit'. A planning unit should be equipped to assemble and analyse research information and 'its main task should be to identify and study the problems and needs of the future and the possible means to meet them; it should also be its function to see that day-to-day policy decisions are taken with as full a recognition as possible of their likely implications for the future'.[15] The Committee thought that planning units should be staffed by younger generation Civil Service managers and outside experts on short-term contracts and should be headed by Senior Policy Advisers. Though these advisers should be lower in status then the Permanent Secretaries who head departments they should have direct access to Ministers on questions of long-term planning. In some cases Policy Advisers might be personally appointed by Ministers but usually they would be career civil servants.

Fulton's Management Consultancy Group had earlier drawn the attention of the Committee to the need for planning units, which it saw as concerned not only with studies of long-term policy but also with providing a planning system for the management of department operations. 'Such units would be engaged on preparing "scenarios" of the department's situation in future years, identifying the likely policy needs and the associated demands for resources. On this basis the allocation of resources can be planned and can be adjusted to meet changing situations, programmes of work can be initiated and objectives set for various parts of the organization'.[16] Significantly, the Management Consultancy Group then went on to suggest systems of objective setting, control and accountability. The Fulton Committee saw planning as concentrating upon research into the definition of long-term policy objectives; the Consultancy Group's planning units were seen as doing not only this but becoming deeply involved in new accounting and information systems and the definition of management programmes.

Developments in the 1970s

In the reorganization of government in 1970, the new administration established the Central Policy Review Staff (CPRS) a policy research unit in the Cabinet Office, and introduced Programme Analysis Review (PAR) a procedure for evaluating individual policies and programmes as part of the annual public expenditure survey.

The CPRS described its work to the Expenditure Committee in 1976.[17] Its main task was to offer advice to Ministers collectively which would help them to relate their policies and decisions to the Government's strategy as a whole. The unit usually had sixteen to nineteen members, half career civil servants and half from outside the Service: the average length of stay was two years. It had five main activities. First, it carried out strategy reviews – at about six monthly intervals it attempted to take stock of the problems facing the Government and presented a report on objectives, constraints, gaps in government strategy and emerging problems. Secondly, it carried out major studies, a few of which were published, e.g. on *Energy Conservation* (1974) and *The Future of the British Car Industry* (1975). At the end of 1976 studies of British overseas representation, the Heavy Electrical Industry and the relationships between social policies were being carried out. Thirdly, it was involved in departmental policy reviews. It helped to select issues for Programme Analysis Reviews by departments and to monitor the results. Fourthly, it prepared briefs for Ministers. Fifthly, it provided a central focus for co-ordinating science and technology policies.

It is difficult to tell what effect the CPRS has had on government policy-making, since most of its work is not published. The report by its first director, Lord Rothschild, on the management of government research and development was of very high quality and should be of lasting benefit. Its report on the car industry, produced with outside consultants, was a penetrating study of the problems of the industry. It has also produced useful reports on energy conservation and social policy. It suffered considerably, however, for allowing itself to be used as a management consultancy operation in a study of British overseas representation. This study was concerned with the scale and scope of Britain's representation overseas given the country's reduced role in world affairs. On this issue it made some acute comments but the staff who carried out the study also delivered themselves of some fairly superficial observations on a wide variety of second-order matters such as entertainment and accommodation which gave its critics much useful material. A policy research body does not have the competence to handle managerial enquiries of this kind and this study would have been better handled by a more appropriately qualified team. The secretiveness of the CPRS has been criticized, for example by Lord Crowther Hunt,[18] who has also commented adversely on the brief periods of service of its members, on the inexperience of the outsiders who have worked for it, on its failure to co-ordinate the planning operations of departments and its failure to tackle the long-range problems likely to face departments.

PAR was produced by the Civil Service and the Conservative government's team of business men as a response to the concepts of issue analysis and programme memoranda in PPB systems. The PAR procedure involved detailed analysis of the policy options in a particular area of expenditure, with subjects selected so as to cover some ten or twelve major expenditure programmes each year. The evidence of the Civil Service Department to the Expenditure Committee said no more than this, but the CPRS volunteered the information that PARs were part of a regular annual stocktaking and that they 'concentrated on assessing the effectiveness of particular departmental activities in addition to their intended objectives, and on examining whether the objectives were soundly based'.[19] In this context, the CPRS probably meant 'aims' rather than 'objectives' because it is clear that very few departments have specified quantified objectives for their activities. Governments have always maintained that PARs are internal working documents and none have ever been published. The authors of an OECD report on educational development in Britain (see below) were allowed to see PARs on higher education and schools expenditure and said that they were 'excellently reasoned', though the report was critical of policy research and planning in the Department of Education and Science. The House of Commons Expenditure Committee which considered policy-making in the DES was refused sight of these PARs and called for publication in future (with no result). It is a measure of the enveloping secrecy of British government and its deadening effect on informed debate in public that departments' evaluations of their own programmes are treated as official secrets and too dangerous to expose to comment. By 1979 the general view in Whitehall was that PARs were no longer useful and in answer to a Parliamentary question by the author in November 1979 the Treasury said that no more would take place. Effort would now be concentrated on the efficiency studies being carried out with the help of Sir Derek Rayner.

It is clear that the development of policy research and planning systems in departments since the Fulton Report has been piecemeal and uneven and without clear central direction. In its 'Response to Fulton' produced for the Expenditure Committee,[20] the CSD distinguished three main fields of planning in departments. These were:

(a) 'the provision of information and data as an input to inter-departmental and "central" planning: this heading which includes, for example, the preparation of the Public Expenditure Survey (PES), vote and manpower estimates, participation in inter-departmental reviews of policy, and contribution to economic forecasting, is outside the scope of the Fulton proposals.
(b) 'the review of departmental policies to analyse their costs and benefits: work under this heading may take the form of prior analysis of policy options, or of review of existing policies and the arrangements and procedures for carrying them out.
(c) 'the management of resources: work under this heading includes assessment and allocation of financial and manpower resources in the light of the outcome of policy reviews and to reflect decisions on priorities.'

The CSD went on to say that the Fulton proposals for planning units seemed to be concerned only with the second of these functions. It said that policy divisions in departments were normally responsible for analysing policy options and reviewing the operation of current policies. Departments had strengthened their planning machinery in recent years, particularly as a result of the PAR procedure.

Though it is true that Fulton's observations on planning were almost entirely about policy research and evaluation rather than the operation of a departmental planning system, it was somewhat narrow to refer to them as if they had no connection with Fulton's subsequent recommendations for accountable management. There were also no grounds for inferring that Fulton's planning units would not have been involved in public expenditure surveys or 'central' planning. In addition, the CSD's division of planning into three distinct activities – providing information for a central body, reviewing policies and allocating resources – is unrecognizable as a description of a working planning process. As we have seen, these activities should slot together in a logical sequence from setting long-term aims to fixing short-term financial and manpower budgets. On this evidence, the CSD had learned very little about comprehensive planning systems in the decade since Fulton.

The CSD went on to dismiss Fulton's concept of a Senior Policy Adviser, heading a policy planning unit. It said that it was difficult to see advisers operating separately from normal policy analysis and planning work (which was part of the normal duties of administrators) and to see how the concept of an adviser, standing apart from normal divisional responsibilities, could be reconciled with Fulton's requirements for accountability and organizational effectiveness. It had been generally judged, said the CSD, that strengthening the machinery for planning would meet Fulton's aims without changing the existing accountabilities of Permanent Secretaries in the field of policy advice. This should ensure that a Minister had adequate policy advice available to him from his senior officials and that his department was fully alive to outside advice and opinion.

What this implied was that the Civil Service still clung to the pre-Fulton idea that policy research and planning is best seen as a part of the work of generalist administrators rather than a specialist function in itself. It is difficult to imagine any other organization taking this view. Its purpose is to keep the responsibility for policy advice in the administrative hierarchy. However, our administrative hierarchy is particularly ill-suited to quantitative and research-based analysis by education and experience and is primarily tuned to its political environment and not to social and technological developments. If policy divisions integrated specialist and administrative skills there might be an argument for the CSD position.

The weaknesses of the administrative approach to policy formulation has been well illustrated by several commentaries on its operation in the Department of Education and Science. The OECD report of 1975 on Educational Strategy in England and Wales[21] observed that policy formulation in the DES seemed to be characterized by attempts to minimize the degree of controversiality in the planning process and its results; to reduce possible alternatives to matters of choice in resource allocation and to understate as much as possible the full role of the government in the determination of the future course of educational policy and even minimize it in the eyes of the general public. The planning process was closed, excluding public hearings or participation and, though bold in its attempt to tackle the problem of resource allocation between educational sectors, paid little attention to the responses required from education to broad changes in Britain's economy and society. In effect, the OECD report criticized the DES for being inward looking, passive and concerned simply to allocate funds to what it saw as developing needs rather than to examine the role which planning for education could play in the general social development of the country. One of the OECD examiners, Professor Frankel, pointed out that the British attitude of 'leaving well enough alone' was an acceptable philosophy provided what exists *is* well enough and is not on the path to getting worse. He observed that for a bureaucracy not to express its judgement in a certain area is no proof of neutrality, since it involves implicit support for the existing policy, or permits the continued absence of any policy.[22] These criticisms were precisely what one would expect of an organization which made policy evaluation and planning a part-time occupation for administrators.

When Sir William Pile, then Permanent Secretary of the DES, gave evidence to the Expenditure Committee on this matter in 1976, he put the department's attitude very clearly. Departmental planning was not carried out by a separate organization: 'the whole essence of it is that it is simply the officials of the Department with their thinking caps on'. The Departmental Planning Organization was very small (the numbers were in single figures) ... 'There are only a handful of people who are concerned with planning in this context; otherwise everybody else does a day's work at the counter, as it were, dealing with their ordinary business and then becomes a planner for half a day'.[23] He thought that if you put people into back rooms they plan unrealistically ... 'you get into the flabby type of futurological day-dreaming'. As to keeping informed about educational opinion: 'there is hardly anybody at this table who could not at this moment write a little essay giving very accurately the aims and objectives of virtually every interest group in the country'.[24] As to educational research: 'the great thing about research is that a part of it is rubbish and another part (I will not be specific about the proportions) leads nowhere and is really rather indifferent; it is, I am afraid, exceptional to find a piece of research that really hits the nail on the head ...'.[25]

The Expenditure Committee, in its report published in 1976, recommended that the planning staff in the DES should include specialists in sufficient number to provide adequate background material for policy groups; that broad educational objectives should be kept under review; that the DES should adopt a more positive attitude to educational research and that DES planning should be more open.

Planning in the DES was also described by Lord Crowther Hunt, a former Minister in the Department, in his evidence to the Expenditure Committee during their enquiry into the Civil Service in 1977.[26] He said that the Department was ill-equipped and ill-organized for the important task of long-range planning. The Departmental Planning Organization was a network of committees of senior administrators, served by a planning unit as a supporting secretariat. These arrangements were the very antithesis of what was recommended by Fulton: they placed planning as something to be done by those mainly engaged in day-to-day operational and administrative questions. The second fault, he said, was in the composition of the planning unit. A Fulton-type unit would have consisted of education experts, perhaps led by a Professor of Education with a status not inferior to that of the Permanent Secretary and including educational psychologists, economists and sociologists. The DES unit consisted of traditional administrative Civil Servants, led by an Under Secretary, each of whom did a two to three year stint in the unit. In the 15 months he was in the Department, three individuals had filled the Under Secretary job – 'hardly a recipe for being able to develop an awareness of new educational thinking, let alone being able to contribute to it'.[27] Lord Crowther Hunt observed that there was not a single psychologist or sociologist in the Department. He repeated the OECD's criticisms of DES planning as secretive, passive – simply responding to trends – and failing to consider education in society. He described the Department's failure to consider fully the issues surrounding the demand for teachers and planning the provision of places in higher education. Lord Crowther Hunt's examples bear out the criticisms of Civil Service planning that Fulton had made in the first place and point to the possible penalties we pay for inadequate formal planning arrangements at least in one department: one of the few where the planning process has been even partly opened to public view.

The Department of the Environment described its policy planning arrangements to the Expenditure Committee.[28] A top management Policy and Management Group met weekly and was served by a Central Policy and Planning Unit (CPPU) headed by an Under Secretary. The CPPU co-ordinated the advice of functional directorates, organized the drafting of reports on subjects which spanned several directorates, provided a secretariat for working parties, produced contingency plans, liaised with the Central Policy Review Staff and co-ordinated contributions to Programme Analysis Reviews, tracked the progress of legislation and co-ordinated the Department's interests in Energy Conservation. Policy research appeared to be the responsibility of separate directorates, some of which carried out cost-benefit analysis (e.g. on highways) and others measured performance against objective criteria. The CPPU did not sound much like Fulton's policy planning units, appearing to be somewhat low powered and not well placed to carry out reviews of overall environmental policy. There was an operational research unit in the DOE's Directorate of Management Services, under a Senior Principal Scientific Officer, which carried out modelling of, for example, alternative policies for housing finance and priorities in pollution control.

The Department of Health and Social Security[29] described in outline a new planning system for the National Health Service introduced in 1977. It appeared to be similar to the system proposed for the new health authority structure of 1974. Health authorities were required to produce strategic plans setting out policies, objectives and strategies for at least 10 years ahead and operational plans defining action to be taken during the next three years. The planning cycle begins with the issue of guidelines by the Department setting out national policies, objectives and strategies and resource assumptions for the years ahead. In March 1977 their guidelines were set out in a consultative document on priorities for health and personal social services. The cycle ends with a review by the Department of health authorities' plans to ensure that they are in line with central policies and objectives and that agreed objectives expressed in earlier plans have been met.

A new planning system was also described by HM Customs and Excise.[30] All costs in the Department are allocated to functions (e.g. VAT control). Every year managers estimate their manpower and other resource requirements for the next five financial years and headquarters directorates make 'development forecasts' which state their aims and objectives. The objectives are ranked to show working priorities and are grouped into 'essential' and 'desirable'. The resource estimates are tested against the development forecasts, are approved by senior management and, after acceptance by the CSD and the Treasury, are fed into the Supply Estimates. After up-dating, they are used in the next Public Expenditure Survey. The resource requirements estimates and the development forecasts provide the basis on which the Department's Corporate Management Group, consisting of the Chairman and the two Deputy Chairmen, consider whether the resources of the Department are being directed appropriately towards the operational objectives of the Department, what changes are necessary and whether any aspects of the Department's work or its policies require particular attention from the Group. This system and that in the Manpower Services Commission appears to be the closest any department has come to an integrated management planning and control system. It may be significant that they have been developed in organizations with a preponderance of Executive grades and make an interesting contrast with the administrative approach to planning of the Department of Education and Science.

The interest in PPB in Whitehall in 1970 resulted in a request by the

Treasury for departments to produce objectives and programme structures, which many did. The results were compiled in a 'Yellow Book' but were not used for management and were discontinued. Reasons given by departments for discontinuing the production of programme budgets included the extent of spending by outside agencies, the difficulty of measuring outputs and the difficulty of allocating staff costs to programmes.

Within departments, the recommendation by Fulton for long term policy planning produced some widely differing responses. One department (Defence) adopted PPB for its internal management processes while another (DES) produced a PPB-type planning structure and then reverted to traditional administrative style arrangements. The Home Office developed PPB for use by police forces[31] and a simple corporate-planning procedure for its Prison Department[32] in 1970 though very little has been heard of either since. One department (DOE) developed analytical systems for individual policy areas without fitting them into a long term plan. Three departments designed full blown management planning and control systems stretching from overall objectives down to action programmes for management (DHSS, Customs and Excise, Manpower Services Commission).

The concept of planning units in departments was also interpreted very differently from one department to another. The Foreign Office, the DHSS and the Ministry of Defence have each had some such unit since the 1960s. In 1980 a survey by E. J. Razzell[33] showed that there were at least eight different kinds of units in departments which could be said to have some kind of planning role. Razzell categorizes them as:

1 co-ordinating policy
2 acting as 'guardian' of the planning system – providing guidelines and timetables
3 advising line management and policy units
4 developing strategies
5 policy formulating, e.g. where research, or a long-term view, is required
6 gathering intelligence
7 reconciling conflicting claims on resources
8 forecasting.

Razzell shows that few units have developed close contacts with outside authorities; that there is limited evidence of contributions to new thinking in the field; that 'the capacity to use quantitative techniques is not uniformly present'; that, in general, outsiders have not been recruited and that the turnover of staff varies from one-and-a-half to three years in post. He finds little evidence of direction from the Treasury or CSD or Cabinet office in the work of these units and that the heads do not have *any* formal right of access direct to Ministers, though some do have access to Permanent Secretaries. Planning unit heads reported that they were caused problems by political and organizational change, by the involvement of several departments in the pursuit of policy objectives, by the impact of public expenditure cuts and by the difficulty of finding top quality staff. 'Mention was also made of the attitudes of senior officials, some of whom did not take planning seriously or found it difficult to think in corporate terms.' Razzell refers to the conventional wisdom about planning in Whitehall, that planning is the responsibility of policy divisions and a central unit should only provide support and advisory services. 'The idea,' he says, 'of a planning unit head having unrestricted access to a Minister is anathema.'

Meanwhile, the Civil Service Department set out its policy in the planning field in a way which tried to show that expenditure planning, policy review and resource allocation were three distinct activities and the Treasury tinkered with the structure of the public expenditure survey instead of developing it into a national planning system for public expenditure. Ministerial autonomy in this field has meant that there is no facility for comprehensive government policy planning or performance measurement. Above all, there is a wholly inadequate basis for Parliamentary and public discussion of the purposes, justification and results of public expenditure plans. If we take the one-year supply estimates and the five-year public expenditure plans for any function of government and compare it with the ideal planning system set out at the beginning of this chapter we can see how great this inadequacy is. Health expenditures are a good example.

1 Supply Estimates, 1978-9 Programme 11.1 HEALTH
The Supply Estimates for health cover an expenditure of £5 billion. This programme is broken down into eight sections: Hospital and Community Health Programmes (£4·2 billion); Family Practitioners (£1·2 billion); Departmental hospitals (£15 million); Training (£34 million); Laboratory and Vaccine services (£16 million); Administrative services (£17 million); Other Health Services (£24 million) and NHS contributions (−£619 million).

Each section is broken down into a few subsections: e.g. Hospital and Community Health into current and capital advances to health authorities and contributions to local authorities and the Family Practitioner section is broken down into payments to doctors, dentists, opticians and for pharmaceutical services. For these two items there is no further subdivision of hundreds of millions of pounds in expenditure. On the other hand, the training programme goes so far as to separately identify the travelling expenses of persons attending courses and a grant to the Midwife Teachers Training College.

2   The Public Expenditure Survey 1979-80 to 1982-3
Programme 11 HEALTH

The five-year survey for health expenditures breaks down annual spending into Capital (hospitals and community health services and other) and Current (hospitals and community health services, family practitioners and other) for each year from 1973–4 to 1982–3 with no finer division at all. These expenditures are supported by tables showing selected health outputs for 1975, 1976, 1977, A few of them relate to the spending programmes, e.g. general practitioner list size, length of stay in hospitals, outpatient attendances, but most, e.g. statistics on geriatric care, mental health and obstetrics, courses of optical treatment, health visitor cases, do not. In addition, there are other tables of widely varying relevance to the expenditure programmes: population forecasts by age group to 1983; estimated health expenditure per head in England 1976–7; spending compared with plan for the past two years, spending on family practitioner services for the last year, the present year and next year and a brief bibliography of health statistics and reports. This supporting statistical data is of very little help in evaluating the benefits or purposes of choices in health spending and the whole display clearly falls a long way short of being any kind of plan for the nation's health care.

By comparison, the US Federal Budget published in January 1978 displayed twenty health programmes (e.g. occupational health, medicare, medicaid, health research) for fiscal 1976, 1977, 1978 and 1979. It showed the spending agencies and intermediary organizations which were accountable for the expenditure and it identified twenty-six 'beneficiary groups' (e.g. crippled children, the mentally ill, alcohol abusers). It was accompanied by a volume of special analyses setting out thirty statistical and narrative descriptions of major health care questions, many of them related to the spending programmes (e.g. outlays by type of medical research, hospital construction by type, medicare costs and benefits) and useful information on health care provision by state, by social group, racial group and disease category. A further volume of the budget *Issues '78* set out background information on programme decisions and policy issues which had been reflected in the budget, including a number of health issues. The Federal budget thus provides some basis for legislative scrutiny and public debate on health policies and issues while our supply estimates and public expenditure white paper do more to confuse than enlighten and are ludicrously inadequate as a source of information.

Clearly, a number of reforms are urgently required in the presentation of our public expenditure budgets and forecasts if they are to be useful for planning and review. A simple first step would be to cast the annual estimates and the five-year forecasts in the same form and detail: in that way the development of any programme can be examined over the planning period. Next, an analysis is required for every major programme or programme category which shows:

1 the department or agency responsible for it
2 the aims of that department or agency
3 the aims and annual objectives of each programme
4 the manpower and financial resources to be devoted to the programme
5 indications of programme efficiency, i.e. the past, present and proposed cost per unit of service provided
6 measures of programme effectiveness, i.e. the past, present and proposed results of each programme in relation to its objectives
7 programme analysis reviews for selected programmes showing their relationship to government policy, their justification and rationale and the alternatives that had been considered.

For many spending programmes much of this information already exists and the technical difficulty of collating it are being reduced by the use of data processing systems. One of the first tasks of the new departmentally-related committees of the House of Commons must be to require departments to set about producing information in this form.

References

1. 1957–8 Treasury Control of Expenditure, *Select Committee on Estimates, Sixth Report*, (July 1958), RC 254.
2. ibid., para. 23.
3. *Committee on the Control of Public Expenditure, Report*, (July 1961), Cmnd. 1432.
4. ibid., para. 7.
5. ibid., para. 12.
6. *Public Expenditure: A New Presentation*, (April 1969).
7. Expenditure Committee, *Memoranda on the Control of Public Expenditure*, (February 1978), HC 196.
8. *The Government's Expenditure Plans*, (January 1979), Cmnd. 4017.
9. *Expenditure Committee, Fourth Report*, (1979-80) HC 237.
10. *Expenditure Committee, Third Report*, (1970–71), HC 549, para. 43.
11. *Expenditure Committee, Eighth Report*, (1971–2), HC 515, para. 8.
12. *The Reorganization of Central Government*, (October 1970), Cmnd. 4506.
13. 'Zero Based Budget ABCs', *Washington Post*, (April 18, 1977).
14. ibid.
15. *Committee on the Civil Service, Report*, (June 1968), Vol. I, para. 173.
16. ibid., Vol. II, para. 364.
17. *Expenditure Committee, Eleventh Report*, (July 1977), Vol. II, para. 603.

18. ibid., Vol. III, p. 1102.
19. ibid., Vol. II, p. 605.
20. ibid., Vol. II, p. 25.
21. *Educational Strategy in England and Wales*, OECD, (Paris, 1975).
22. ibid., p. 62.
23. *Expenditure Committee, Tenth Report*, (1975–6), HC 621, p. 120.
24. ibid., p. 29.
25. ibid., p. 116.
26. *Expenditure Committee, Eleventh Report*, (July 1977), p. 1090.
27. ibid., p. 1118.
28. ibid., p. 276.
29. ibid., p. 349.
30. ibid., p. 864.
31. WASSERMAN, G. J., 'PPB in the Police Service in England and Wales', *O & M Bulletin*, (November 1970), p. 197.
32. GARRETT, J. and WALKER, S. D., 'Management Review – A Case Study from Prison Department', *O & M Bulletin*, (September 1970), p. 133.
33. RAZZELL, E. J., 'Planning in Whitehall-Is it Possible?-Will it Survive?' *Long Range Planning*, February 1980.

VI

Control

To the manager, control means the collection, analysis, comparison and distribution of information to permit the performance of the organization and its constituent parts to be regularly compared with pre-determined standards so that action can be taken when the variance between achievement and standard exceeds acceptable limits. The aim of control information technology is to provide the organization with a nervous system which enables it to perceive and react to internal and external events in time to correct deviations from plan. An effective control system requires, first, a strategic plan which expresses policy decisions about the allocation of resources in, and the results that are required from, the enterprise as a whole and its major managerial sub-units; secondly, information so organized that the disposition of resources can be expressed as budgets and standards and subsequent performance can be measured against them; thirdly, arrangements which establish the accountability of managers for results.

The last chapter was concerned with strategic planning in a Civil Service context. In this the requirement for control information is discussed and in the next, managerial accountability.

The concept of control has dominated management thinking from the earliest days of 'scientific management' over seventy years ago. In recent years, the study of self-regulating control systems has achieved recognition as the new sub-science of cybernetics.

The first control systems in industry were developed from attempts to describe and measure manual operations in manufacturing industry by the use of procedures called 'Taylorism' at the turn of the century, after F. W. Taylor 'the father of scientific management', and later called time and motion study and in recent years, work study. By studying and timing the activities and the movement of materials in manufacturing processes the work study practitioner can describe the most efficient sequence of movements and the best layout of the work place, write instructions describing the 'standard method' and establish the 'standard time' for each process. From such data it is customary to

111

establish productive capacity, output targets for units and whole factories, production plans and costs and production control systems to enable performance to be monitored. Similar systems for clerical work measurement were developed in the 1920s and in 1922 there was a very important advance in control technology with the publication of the first work on budgetary control.

Budgetary control has the object of comparing actual income and expenditure with forecast or budgeted income and expenditure under headings which permit the analysis of the efficiency of the various units in an organization. It involves organizing financial information in such a way as to identify managerial responsibility for costs, expenditure and revenues; to provide a basis for the formulation of plans, and to permit the identification of deviations from plans in the course of their operation. An additional level of financial control is provided by 'standard costing'. This involves pre-determination of the costs of labour and material (and sometimes overhead costs) of performing a task by the standard method at a stated level of output and facilitates analysis of the reasons for departures from standard. It also provides a cost model which can be used to show the effect of changing such variables as materials and processes. 'Management accounting' is a generic term for the arrangement and presentation of accounting data for use in these systems of short-term planning and control.

The development of electronic data processing has permitted new advances in control systems, particularly towards cybernetic or self-regulating systems. For example, modern inventory-control systems are designed to minimize both the cost of stock-holding and the risk of being out of stock by balancing forecast demand for individual items, optimum re-order quantities, the lead-time for replenishment and inventory management cost. Cybernetic systems are widely used to hold many variables in balance in flow-production industries (e.g. refining, milling), transport industries and retailing. In addition to these control systems based on data internal to the firm (costs, productivity, work-load) it is possible, with the improved availability of information, to develop indicators relating to the firm's external standing: share of market, inter-firm comparisons. It has therefore become the practice, in large commercial organizations, to design a system of key indicators derived from the corporate plan of the enterprise to track the performance of operational units, divisions, subsidiaries and the enterprise as a whole. These often relate to profit on capital employed and sales; sales in relation to fixed assets and stocks; market share; output per employee and such 'social' indicators as absenteeism and labour turnover. The objective of such a control system is to enable each manager to assess the performance of his unit in key areas of its activity, to correct deviations from plan and to roll plans forward each year, to relate the performance of his unit to the objectives of the organization as a whole and to establish his accountability for results. Management controls of this type are essentially positive: they are concerned to enable managers to attain pre-set objectives within allocated resources, to enable managers to assess and decide upon priorities and continuously to monitor performance. In contrast to these forms of management control, control in public administration has been mainly directed to negative ends, to stop unauthorized expenditure by prior sanctions and post-accounting. Primarily, this kind of control is concerned with regularity – that is, to ensure that accounts are kept correctly, that all spending is for authorized purposes and that the mis-application of funds is prevented. This has led to the development of elaborate book-keeping routines in government and to restrictions on the delegation of authority to line managers to authorize expenditure, but to relatively little attention being paid to the measurement of performance or the construction of performance indicators for departments or agencies.

It is also worth noting here that many politicians use the word 'control' in quite another way. There is much talk in Parliament of controlling public expenditure and complaints that it is 'out of control'. Used in this way control means neither monitoring the effectiveness nor the regularity of spending but simply reducing it either directly or by appeals for prudence and good housekeeping.

Financial Control in the Civil Service

The machinery for exercising regularity control is provided by the supply procedure, an arrangement by which Parliament authorizes those cash payments by government departments which have to be voted annually. Every October, the Treasury asks departments to compile estimates of proposed expenditure for the financial year beginning in the following April. By the end of November Finance Divisions have aggregated the estimates of the branches and divisions in their departments and send these to the Treasury. Between December and January, the Treasury and the spending departments discuss the estimates, referring disputed points to Ministers. In February and March the agreed estimates are published and presented to the House of Commons. In July or August, the Appropriation Act is passed which authorizes the expenditure of the estimated sums, now known as 'votes'. Because by this time nearly one-third of the year to which the estimates relate has already passed, a 'vote on account' is made by the House before the beginning of the financial year authorizing the next few months' expenditure. Supplementary estimates for new services to be provided by the government are presented in June or July and supplementary estimates required because of an overspend or an original underestimate are presented in November and the following February.

During the year, expenditures take place usually on the authority of the Department's Principal Finance Officer and are recorded by his Accounts Branch. Annual Appropriation Accounts show the actual spending on each vote and are published in the January following the end of the financial year. The Permanent Secretary in a department is its Accounting Officer and is held personally answerable for its expenditure by our state audit machinery (see Chapter 9). A significant number of individual items of expenditure have to be referred back to the Treasury for approval during the year except where the Treasury has delegated authority to the department.

There have been some important developments in the form and content of the supply procedure in recent years. In 1973, as a result of pressure from House of Commons' Select Committees, the Treasury announced[1] a revision of the form of the estimates to align their structure with that of the public expenditure survey, i.e. in programme form. We have seen in the last chapter that this change has not been particularly useful because the few individual programmes which are shown in the estimates are not shown in the published survey but are lost in huge programme categories. In 1973 and 1974 there was concern in the Treasury and in Parliament about the size of the supplementary estimates which the government had been obliged to present to Parliament because or runaway inflation. It was clear that a revised system was needed for monitoring the flow of spending. The Treasury undertook a study of the problem[2] and by March 1975 the Financial Information Systems project had produced a system based on quarterly or monthly 'profiles' of expenditure estimated in advance with which actual spending could be compared, distinguishing price from volume changes and projecting changes forward. The new arrangements were tried out in the Home Office in 1976 and were generally introduced in departments in the 1977–8 financial year.

In April 1976 the Treasury introduced a new cash limits system. Because of rapid inflation the estimates provided an increasingly inaccurate indication of the amount of money likely to be spent in a year. The Treasury therefore proposed to issue, at the time of the budget, a statement on cash limits for departments: fixed 'rations' of cash for blocks of expenditure which included an allowance for inflation. Cash limits covered about 60 per cent of central government expenditure and excluded areas of expenditure determined by demand: e.g. social security and unemployment benefit. Cash limits, unlike estimates, were not presented to Parliament for approval. The problems caused by cash limits in respect of staffing are discussed in Chapter 8. It has also been found that cash limits create difficulties for departments with large and rapidly changing capital expenditure programmes (e.g. Defence) which run over from one year to another.

In August 1978, the Expenditure Committee complained about the proliferation of different forms of government accounting. By this time there were not only the supply procedure, cash limits and the public expenditure survey, all on different price bases, but the government had also extended the use of trading accounts (in departmental bodies which received part of their finance from votes and part from other sources, e.g. the Export Credits Guarantee Department) and trading funds (in public bodies which produced profit and loss accounts – e.g. the Royal Mint). The Treasury met this complaint with proposals[3] to align the structure of the supply procedure with cash limits and to set out expenditures which were not cash limited into separate estimates. It also proposed to present supply estimates on the same price basis as that used to set cash limits, namely estimated out-turn prices including forecast pay and price changes during the year ahead. The Expenditure Committee welcomed these proposals as improving Parliamentary scrutiny but observed two possible disadvantages in them. First, though the new arrangements would provide for prospective inflation they would not show what that provision was. If the allowance for inflation were too small, there would be cuts in real expenditure upon which the House of Commons had not been consulted. If the allowances were too large the House would unintentionally allow Departments more scope for increased real expenditure. Secondly, the new arrangements might institutionalize the expected inflation by removing Treasury pressure on departments to operate economically and allowing cost increases to be accepted without question. The Committee required that the inflation forecasts used in cash limits should be shown explicitly for cash estimate and should be an objective figure and not a political target and that estimates showed price and volume changes. The Treasury introduced a new form of cash limited estimates in March 1979.

It is clear that the supply procedure, even after recent improvements, is still a cash control, rather than a management control, system. As the report of the Expenditure Committee on the Civil Service said in 1977: 'it was designed simply to ensure the Parliamentary control of funds and it provides no information about the performance of individual divisions and units'.[4] The estimates are not linked to policies, nor to organizational units in departments, nor to any volumes of output which would show value for money. Lord Armstrong, in evidence to the Committee, described management accounting in the Civil Service as 'pretty embryonic' and the head of the Government Accountancy Service, Mr K. J. Sharp, said that it obviously left 'some scope for improvement'. Mr Sharp admitted that he had not been consulted on the form and value of government accounting, which was fundamentally a question for the Treasury to answer.[5] The Treasury's attitude, in the words of the Committee, was 'predictably conservative'. The Committee concluded that a change in the system of accounts would outweigh any disadvantages: 'the supply procedure should not be adhered to because it has always been there. It is anachronistic, if not obsolete, that the accounts that Parliament is presented with simply do not correspond to the realities of public expenditure and that as an instrument of control they are useless'.[6] Much the same had been said by the Procedure Committee in 1969 and the Expenditure Committee in 1972.

The government, in reply to the report, said that 'the development of systems designed to provide the necessary basis for sound decision-taking, effective control and the assessment of performance needs much care and uses up scarce skilled resources; further progress is unlikely to be fast',[7] and that any attempt to expand the supply estimates to incorporate further information would make them unmanageable. The Comptroller and Auditor General, in his observations on the Expenditure Committee report said that he considered that 'a reconstruction of the Parliamentary estimates and accounts designed to reflect more closely the internal accounting and management control structure of departments could not be widely achieved without jeopardizing clarity'[8]. This from an official whose job, at least in theory, is to act as an agent of Parliamentary scrutiny.

The Public Accounts Committee, in a later report,[9] referred to the importance of the development of management information systems, including measures of performance and output wherever possible and trusted that the Comptroller and the Treasury would continue to promote these aspects of accountability in all departments.

In its response to the government observations on its Civil Service report, the Committee repeated its conviction that 'measurements of productivity should be part of the control information made available to Parliament'[10] and again called for a reform in government accounting. In 1978 the Procedure Committee,[11] virtually repeating its complaints of a decade earlier, observed that the financial information presented to Parliament was inadequate for effective budgetary control and called for a thorough review of the accounts, statistical analyses and regular reports presented to the House with a view to improving the means of Parliamentary scrutiny. So far, the government has not acted on this request.

Criticisms of financial control in the Civil Service have not been limited to the system but has included those who operate it. In the late 1950s the Estimates Committee commented on the exclusion of technically qualified officials from the discussion of expenditure proposals: 'laymen may be examining proposals by laymen, while the technical officers who initiated the proposals and who really understand the details, remain behind the scenes'.[12] Fulton's Management Consultancy Group made a similar criticism in its comments upon the relationships between specialists and administrators. It noted that financial responsibility lay almost exclusively with administrators, while technically qualified specialists acted purely in an advisory role: 'On the question of financial control, administrators did not have the technical competence properly to challenge the specialists except on obvious or relatively trivial points . . . in industry, managers with specialist backgrounds are very often entrusted with the expenditure of funds without having their decisions under continuous scrutiny by laymen. There is no evidence that this leads to unwarranted expenditure.'[13] The control of expenditure therefore tends to take the form of pointed questions by laymen upon expenditure decisions which are increasingly taken by specialists on technical cases. Inevitably, the laymen ask questions about the peripheral matters which they can understand.

One of the objectives of the reforms in personnel management proposed by Fulton was to create a general management cadre in the Service with a technical and accountancy background who were capable of operating modern control systems. Fulton commented very critically on the absence of accountants in management jobs in the Service. There were only 309 accountants in the Service, none paid more than the Assistant Secretary level, and only six at that level. Those that were employed were used mainly on the examination of external commercial accounts, e.g. to monitor overheads and profits on government contracts and, less frequently, on cost accounting. They were not seen as a cadre for the highest managerial posts. Fulton's Consultancy Group said: 'to the outside observer, the most striking feature of the Professional Accountant Class in the Civil Service is the severe limitation on the prospects for advancement and the very low status of its members when compared with accountants outside'.[14] It concluded that the skills of the modern management accountant appeared to be increasingly needed in top level policy areas of the Service. These skills were concerned with the evaluation of policy in financial terms, cost-benefit analysis, establishing budgets and analysing the causes of variances from them and producing financial information for efficiency measurement and planning. The response of the Civil Service to this criticism was to commission a report (Melville-Burney) on the use of accountants in the Service which led to the creation of a Government Accountancy Service under a head of profession appointed from outside and to the encouragement of more civil servants to train as accountants. The effect on the quality of financial information was slight, except in the few cases where trading funds were introduced and supported by management accounting systems.

Establishments Control

As we saw from Chapter 4, every department has an establishments function, usually headed by a Principal Establishments Officer (PEO). These divisions are concerned with personnel management, efficiency studies and the control of staff numbers.

The Treasury circular of 1920 which defined the status of the Principal Establishments Officer laid down that the consent of the Prime Minister was required to the appointment or removal of a PEO. The PEO is his department's representative in most dealings with the central establishments authority, the CSD, and has a special status. Though usually an Under Secretary, he normally answers directly to the Permanent Secretary in respect of his work. Departmental management services (formerly Organization and Methods, 'O & M') branches are usually under the control of Establishments Officers. In addition to undertaking efficiency exercises, Establishments Divisions also vet and sanction requests for accommodation, equipment, typing, duplicating and reprographic services. As Fulton's Management Consultancy Group said: 'The Establishments Division is the means by which a Department checks its own growth in internal costs, which are mainly those of manpower. All requests for more staff and more equipment go to it and, in addition, it mounts O & M investigations into procedures and Staff Inspections into numbers and grades employed.'[15]

The control of complements (the number and grades of staff allowed) is applied by the scrutiny and vetting of annual forecasts of staff numbers, by the authorization of new posts, upgradings and promotions during the year and by *ad hoc* examination of the numbers and grades of posts. All this work is in turn under the scrutiny of the Civil Service Department and results in extreme centralization of authority in staff matters. Each year the major units of a department submit to the Establishments Division their estimates of staff requirements for the following year. The Establishments Division will have an idea of what increase the complementing side of the Civil Service Department will tolerate and will use this as a guide when vetting unit estimates. It will then enter into a debate with the Civil Service Department on its bid for staff for the whole department, having to trade off a requested increase in one section or in one class of staff against another according to the central department's view of priorities and the Cabinet's ruling on the permissible overall percentage increase, or the required decrease, in the number of civil servants. The result is the imposition of a 'manpower ceiling' on departments above which they may not recruit and is now reinforced by cash limits. During the year political or economic pressure may build up to provoke the imposition of an across-the-board cut in complements which the Civil Service Department shares out among departments. Hitherto these have very rarely been cuts in actual numbers because departments may have strengths (numbers actually in post) well below their complements (numbers to which they are entitled); even if they are up to strength the cut in complement will often be effected by delays in recruiting. In 1979, however, the new Conservative administration announced that it wanted, in addition to an immediate 3 per cent cut in complements, departments to prepare plans for 5 per cent, 10 per cent and 20 per cent reductions in costs on the basis of inviting Ministers to assign priorities to the work of their departments.

Apart from their annual review of complements, Establishments Divisions mount *ad hoc* investigations, by staff inspectors, of the staffing of individual posts or sections. Staff inspectors, who are HEOs or SEOs posted to the work in the normal course of their careers, typically investigate the need for any new post which a division applies to create and also have a regular programme of working through the department to check on the numbers of staff required to handle current work and whether the posts at each level are correctly graded. There are also teams of Civil Service Department staff inspectors who carry out central inspections.

This powerful machinery of control over staff numbers reflects the intense Parliamentary interest in the number of civil servants in contrast to its interest in expenditure. It has been crudely effective in holding down the numbers employed in the Civil Service in relation to the volume of work which has been loaded on to departments by Parliament. On the other hand, establishments control in the Civil Service has a number of weaknesses. First, it so dominates the work of establishments divisions that positive aspects of personnel work – planning, improving job content, career development – tend to have a low priority. Secondly, the annual estimating routine, with its emphasis on cutting back the numbers requested, has led either to inflated bids in the first place or to arbitrary decisions on where cuts shall be made. Thirdly, a procedure which has concentrated on numbers rather than cost leads to costly ways of substituting for numbers – overtime working, the employment of temporary typists and contract staff – though where cash limits apply this effect may be reduced. Fourthly, the cutbacks tend to be indiscriminate and regardless of the potential value of different types of staff – Fulton's Management Consultancy Group commented upon 'long-term diseconomies (which) may arise from a departmental decision to reduce the numbers of staff whose work could lead to increase efficiency and resultant savings'[16] and quoted training and management services as examples of this effect. This observation was again borne out by the disproportionately heavy cuts which fell on the Civil Service College in the expenditure reduction campaigns of 1975 and 1979. Fifthly, establishments control suffers from the same negativism as financial control in the Civil Service – it is control by overall limitation of increase, by minute scrutiny of cases and by foray, rather than control by the continuing analysis of cost and benefit, fitted into 'a systematic review of the relative priorities and continuing justification of departmental activities and thus of the staff needed'.[17] Sixthly, both establishments and financial control in the Civil Service are too centralized, moving initiative and authority from the level of the individual manager, who, being close to the point where the cost is incurred, is in a far better position to do something about controlling it.

The Information Requirement

The management of organizations in public administration requires information organized in three general categories (as the New York Bureau of Municipal Research pointed out as long ago as 1907):[18]

1 For submission to the Legislature for appropriation and statutory audit so as to demonstrate the *regularity* or propriety of expenditure. This category of information has to be arranged in a way which shows the personal responsibility of officials ('accounting officers' in British government departments) and which allows expenditures on particular items – e.g. wages and salaries, superannuation, accommodation – to be checked by an auditor. It is provided in Britain by the supply procedure of estimates, votes and appropriation accounts described above.

2 For making policy decisions on the allocation of resources; for long-term planning and for evaluating the impact of policies and spending programmes on the communities at which they are aimed. Information in this category has to be organized on the basis of output or objective of expenditure and by programme, as described in the last chapter. Its purpose is to assist in the definition of policy objectives, to enable choices to be made between programmes on the basis of analyses of cost and benefit and to enable the subsequent effectiveness (that is, the relationship of output to objective) of a department to be measured. Its main value is to assist long-term decision-making by the Cabinet, by Ministers and the top management of a department and it is important for proper Parliamentary and public scrutiny of departmental policy. This information is not generally available in Britain.

3 For budgetary and other forms of short-term, usually annual, control; for setting staff levels, measuring line management performance and identifying managerial accountability. Information in this category

has to be organized on the basis of the structure of management responsibility within a department, that is by division, branch, section and project: the 'accountable units' proposed by the Fulton Committee. Its purpose is to enable the *efficiency* of the department to be measured (that is, the input/output ratio: the cost per transaction, per benefit issued or other unit of service) and is primarily designed to assist short-term decision-making at middle and lower management levels in departments. This kind of information is at present not published by departments, though it exists in some areas of relatively easily quantified work such as Social Security offices, the Inland Revenue and some research establishments. Work in this field in the Civil Service comes under the general heading of 'performance measurement'.

Performance Measurement

To measure the efficiency of a unit of organization we need to know its total costs, its capacity for handling work and its actual work output. Until recently, it was not possible to determine the total cost of even large units of government organization because the structure of the accounting data assembled for the supply procedure did not coincide with the organization structure of departments. In addition, some important costs were not carried on the votes of the user departments at all but were provided as a common or 'allied' service on the votes of the departments providing the service. Thus, the costs of space and utilities were attributed to the Property Services Agency in the Department of the Environment and printing and stationery to HMSO, with the result that departments which incurred such costs were not responsible for them and the departments which were responsible for them had little real influence over the demand for them. The recommendations of the Fulton Committee on accountable management and the necessity for the attribution of costs to departmental units has led to increasing attention being given to the principle of 'repayment' or 'charging-out' by service departments to users. HMSO and the Central Computer Agency are about to charge departments for their services though most services, e.g. those of the Property Services Agency, Central Office of Information and the Civil Service Department are still accounted for on an allied service basis. Charging-out is most worthwhile when the service being charged for is well defined; when it is fairly easy, within a reasonable period, to establish that performance is satisfactory and when a relatively simple or generally acceptable method can be devised for establishing the level of charge to be made. It is least effective when the costs of a service are difficult to allocate between users; when the extra costs of book-keeping and attribution are greater than any possible benefit or

121

when the cost of a service is best controlled centrally and by specialists.

Having established as fully as possible the total costs of a unit's existence we have to try to establish a measure of its capacity for work and its workload. Most departments include large areas of measurable work: in clerical and executive units, data processing units, groups handling other fairly routine transactions, research and construction projects and so on. A higher administrative and policy levels, simple work measurement procedures are not relevant but there are reporting and evaluation techniques, such as management by objectives (see Chapter 7) which can be applied. The conventional view, however, has been that senior officials need not be greatly concerned with efficiency since this was a matter for a department's Establishments and Finance Divisions and since 'policy' was different from 'management' there was no need to plan and control policy activities. This has been one reason why the top management of departments has not seen the construction of management information and control systems as having a very high priority.

Work on developing performance measures appears to have been undertaken in several departments under the leadership of the Civil Service Department in the early 1970s and from time to time progress reports appeared[19] on developments in areas of clerical work, maintenance and vehicle testing. After about 1972 progress in this field appears to have come virtually to a halt, except in the Department of Health and Social Service and the Inland Revenue. Some officials indicate that this was due to union opposition to work measurement and it is true that labour relations in the Service started to go sour around this time and the unions became less co-operative (see Chapter 8). Probably equally important is that progress on the Fulton reforms petered out almost everywhere in the Service around this time: administrators generally felt that change had gone far enough and understood or cared little about performance measurement, political interest was low and Ministers were not concerned about the subject. The few officials who were interested in performance measurement were also faced with a technical problem: it was often not possible to establish the total cost of an organization against which to assess its output. As one of them wrote shortly before the campaign was called off: 'performance indicators based on total cost are the ideal as this is the only way of showing the utilization of total resources in a single term. . . . In the Civil Service there are, however, considerable difficulties in using total cost as the measure of input because the vote accounting system does not enable the costs relating to particular inputs to be readily isolated.'[20]

The fact that the supply procedure did not provide an adequate cost basis to measure the performance or efficiency of managerial units within departments was pointed out by Fulton. It was also observed in a report by a team who carried out the first 'management review' of a government department – Prison Department – in the late 1960s.[21] That team proposed new accounting arrangements so as to establish the actual cost of running the department and its major units. Ten years later, the May Report on the United Kingdom Prison Services said: 'any organization as large as the Home Office Prison Department requires an effective, if not elaborate, system of financial control and budgeting. We cannot say that we have found that it possesses such a system. As we see it, all organizations of any sophistication should have a reliable view of comparative unit costs of their operation and be capable of developing financial controls which enhance efficiency and managerial performance.'[22] The May Report went on to say that Prison Department accounts were primarily based on the model of Parliamentary votes: 'although it does discharge its accounting responsibilities to Parliament, it is not capable of delivering more than general or rudimentary information about operating costs. We were surprised to learn, for example, that the Home Office was unable to tell us how much each prison costs to run each year'.[23] The Administration officers in prisons proposed to the May Committee that there should be sweeping changes in estimating and control procedures – but the Home Office were reluctant to accept that such an approach had merit. The May Committee concluded that managers in the department should be made accountable for the money they spent and recommended improvements in financial information for management which they saw as achievable at relatively little cost.

The Treasury has consistently refused to reform the supply procedure so as to enable it to be developed into the basis for a control system for management and for a more effective system for Parliamentary scrutiny. As a result, performance or efficiency measurement has developed in the Civil Service only slowly and in a piecemeal way despite the studies initiated by the management services divisions of the CSD in several departments.

Work on measuring local office activities had been undertaken in the Social Security side of DHSS long before Fulton gave impetus to the idea and it continues to the present day. After Fulton, the DHSS system become known as Participative Management and was accompanied by a reorganization of management structures so as to establish a line of accountable management from a local office, through regional offices to headquarters. Every line manager is provided with a management guide specifying the results for which he is held accountable. On an annual cycle, managers set performance standards for particular tasks, agree on priority areas for improvement, produce action plans and examine results in formal performance reviews. This procedure is supported by a management information system which enables the regular monitoring of resource utilization and performance, provides control information on a daily or weekly basis for local offices and at longer intervals for regions and headquarters and is the basis for annual manpower budgeting. The management information system was introduced throughout the Social Security organization in late 1974 and performance indicators and targets have been produced for most of the work of local offices. Regional directors can compare at four-weekly intervals the manpower utilization, work done and performance (e.g., error rates) in each of their local offices. In their evidence to the Expenditure Committee, DHSS officials produced examples of 'best', 'worst' and average performances in regional organizations for processing claims to sickness benefit, retirement pensions, postal claims for supplementary benefit, supplementary benefit visits and percentage errors in payment of sickness and supplementary benefit.[24] Further development of this system is planned to relate resource utilization, productivity and performance so as to provide regional directors with measures of efficiency, indicators of effectiveness and arrangements for quality assessment: e.g. the quality of service given to the public at reception points, in dealing with correspondence and telephone enquiries and the standard of investigations of claims to benefit. Quality assessment will be integrated with performance indicators in a comprehensive control system which is extremely advanced in concept and probably as good as any control system ever attempted in commercial organizations.*

The Inland Revenue and Customs and Excise have also produced key performance indicators, e.g., the cost/yield ratios of tax systems, for many years. Studies have been carried out in the Inland Revenue of the possibility of developing such other measures as staff numbers/taxpayers and revenue costs/total income subject to tax but both of these are considered unreliable as performance indicators and it has been decided to refine cost/yield ratios and supplement them with other output measures.[25] Performance measurement is also long-established in parts of the Ministry of Defence and, in recent years, some work in this field has been carried out in the Department of Employment. Performance measurement in the non-industrial Civil Service has not developed much outside these departments. It is not surprising that the DHSS, Customs and Inland Revenue have made the running because more than any others they are engaged on processing easily definable transactions in large volumes and relatively few performance

---

* The further development of the DHSS management information system was described by Mr R. S. Matthews in *Management Services in Government* (August 1979).

indicators can be used in many local offices. In addition, they have always been strongly managerial, rather than administrative in style.

This style is also typical of the US Federal Government, where performance measurement goes back to the 1930s. The measurement system there now covers 1·9 million staff in 279 departments and agencies, some 67 per cent of the federal civilian workforce, and showed an average annual increase in productivity of 1·3 per cent from the base year 1967 to 1975. Under the annual Joint Financial Management Improvement Programmes (JFMIP), which were initiated by Presidential Order in 1949, every bureau has to produce for its 'priority areas', quantitative indicators for measuring performance, improvement goals and evaluations of past performance.

In the 1976 Report to the President and Congress of the JFMIP (which is managed jointly by the Office of Management and Budget, the General Accounting Office, the Treasury and the Civil Service Commission) it was reported that productivity measures produced by the scheme had been valuable in:

1 setting specific goals for management
2 budget justification: for many years there has been a requirement that agencies submit productivity improvement data in support of annual budget estimates. 'The use of productivity data and specific goals can contribute to better projections of resource needs and the review by others of those needs'[26]
3 cost reduction and organizational improvement: productivity indices are necessary for measuring the results of management action to reduce costs, material consumption and staffing requirements, and the effects of capital investment
4 control of operations: productivity measures can be combined with budget and cost figures, staffing levels and levels of investment to develop a control system for the management of government operations
5 improvement motivation: productivity measures can be an objective means for rewarding performance, as a basis for productivity bargaining or as part of a management by objectives programme (see Chapter 7)
6 accountability: measures of efficiency provide one source of defining and reviewing the results for which managers can be held accountable.

All of these benefits could follow from the widespread use of performance measurement in the British Civil Service: the key to increasing its use would be, as in the federal government, to incorporate it into the annual budget process. If departments in Britain were obliged to submit efficiency (and effectiveness) measures and the results of current and past programmes along with their estimates there would be a rapid change in attitude to control systems and much greater interest in their development. Such a change in budgeting does not always work: in the federal government departmental and agency managers have been discouraged by lack of recognition for productivity improvements and arbitrary cuts in budgets imposed on them by budget reviewers regardless of the productivity figures. Since the usual practice in British government is to go for arbitrary across-the-board cuts at times of financial difficulty anyway, the existence of performance measures might increase the rationality with which such decisions are made and applied. Certainly, if accountability is to mean anything, senior officials must be provided with information which enables them to take a view on the efficiency with which their subordinates deploy their staff and to assess the manpower effects of new demands placed upon the organization. The value of control information goes beyond simply measuring and improving efficiency: reliable performance indicators can provide the basis for planning future manpower needs and for substantiating claims for more staff, for identifying bottlenecks in the production process and directing attention to points where managerial action is needed, for enabling managers to plan and organize the flow of work and to evaluate their own performance.

The report on the Civil Service by the Expenditure Committee recommended that the productivity indices which existed should be published and that more research should be carried out on measuring performance. The government's reply to this recommendation said that the productivity indices produced by the US Federal Government were not accurate measures of management or staff efficiency but were primarily of value as trend indicators and such indices had to be interpreted with extreme care (ignoring the fact that the US Government and Congress had thought it worthwhile to persevere with them for twenty years). The government thought that indices were most relevant to manpower-intensive areas such as social security payment and tax collection but in general it did not believe that 'the production and publication of a comprehensive and linked series of productivity indices would justify their cost'.[27]

Building a Data Base

Government departments need to create a central reservoir of information, or data base, from which reports and analyses can be streamed off to meet the requirements of Parliament and different levels of departmental management. Parliamentary Committees, Ministers, top officials and planners require detailed information on the effectiveness and impacts of departmental programmes, generalized statements of trends in efficiency and indications of the progress of spending against authorization. Middle management requires effectiveness measures for the programmes they manage and performance indicators for the units under their control; junior management require in addition to performance indicators, a rapid feedback on capacities, unit costs, work loads, operational bottlenecks and day-to-day outputs. The construction of a data base for all these requirements poses a number of problems. On the input side, all costs have to be classified by spending programme or service; by organizational unit and by item bought. Therefore, every expenditure has to be coded:

1 'subjectively': that is by reference to the nature of the goods or services purchased or the obligations discharged, Subjective classification groups, for example, all payroll expenses, all equipment expenses, all expenses of travelling, accommodation, postage
2 'objectively': that is according to the purpose for which it is incurred, or by programme. Objective classification groups, for example, all construction programme costs, all training programme costs, all research programme costs
3 by organization unit: for example research establishment, local office, regional office, headquarters division or directorate
4 by accounting period in which the transaction took place.

Using such a coding arrangement and data processing facilities, costs can rapidly be cross-analysed and summarized to meet the needs of each function and level of management.

On the output side, measurements of volumes of work have to be classified by organizational unit and spending has to be 'profiled' against budget estimates to keep track of over-or-under-spending. More difficult, external measures have to be recorded and analysed: social and economic indicators which can be attached to programmes to indicate their results and effectiveness. Examples of these indicators are those relating to levels of unemployment and the availability of skills, poverty levels and social and housing conditions in different groups of the population, death and disease rates, investment levels, trade performance. Some are regularly published, e.g. by the Central Statistical Office, the DHSS and the Department of Employment while others can be established only by *ad hoc* survey. In addition, the accounting and statistical structure has to be connected to the organization structure of departments so that managerial and public accountability can be reviewed and monitored. This question is discussed in the next chapter.

In spite of all the work on improved accounting practices carried out in the Treasury and other departments in the last decade, we are still a long way from such an 'integrated' data base in government. Much of the information which is required exists and in some places the system is being developed: in Social Security, for example, and in the National

Health Service it will exist when the planning system proposed as part of the reorganization in 1974 is completed. Elsewhere, we have a supply procedure which displays individual items of expenditure, and which sets out cash expenditures in a variety of programme categories; a public expenditure survey which sets out projected expenditures in larger categories and a variety of trading accounts for quasi-commercial activities. For most government activities we have no measures of productivity and for nearly all activities we have no measures of effectiveness which can be directly attached to spending programmes. The methodology exists to organize a data base and to fill in most of the missing numbers. There appears to be little interest in doing so in the Civil Service, though one would think that Civil Service managers would be keen to develop new control systems in the interest of better management. The impetus for this development will have to come from Parliament, for no reform could do more to enable it to regain some of its lost power over the Executive.

References

1. 'Revision of the form of the Supply Estimates', *Expenditure Committee, Eighth Report*, (May 1973), HC 209.
2. BUTLER and ALDRED, 'The Financial Information Systems Project', *Management Services in Government*, (May 1977), p. 77.
3.
4. 'The Civil Service', *Expenditure Committee, Eleventh Report*, (July 1977), Vol. I, para. 98.
5. ibid., Vol. I, para. 99.
6. ibid., Vol. I, para. 100.
7. *Government Observations on the Eleventh Report from the Expenditure Committee*, (March 1978), Cmnd. 7117, para. 48.
8. *Observations by the Comptroller and Auditor General on the Eleventh Report from the Expenditure Committee*, (1978), HC 318, para. 7(ii).
9. *Committee of Public Accounts*, Session 1978-9, (March 1979), HC 232, para. 27
10. 'Response to the Government Observations on the Committee Report on the Civil Service', *Expenditure Committee, Twelfth Report*, (July 1978), para. 16.
11. Procedure Committee.
12. 'Treasury Control of Expenditure', *Select Committee on Estimates*, Sixth Report, (July 1958), para. 48.
13. *Committee on the Civil Service Report*, (June 1968), Vol II, para. 202.
14. ibid., Vol. II, para. 132.
15. ibid., Vol. II, para. 210.
16. ibid., Vol. II, para. 217.
17. ibid., Vol. II, para. 218.
18. SCHULTZE, C. L., *The Politics and Economics of Public Spending*, (Brookings Institution, Washington DC 1968), p. 9.

19. HOLBROW, J., 'Progress with Performance Measurement', *O & M Bulletin*, (November 1971), p. 223.
20. ibid., p. 227.
21. GARRETT, J. and WALKER, S. D., 'Management Review of the Prison Department', *O & M Bulletin*, (September 1970), p. 139.
22. *Committee of Enquiry into the United Kingdom Prison Services*, (October 1979), Cmnd. 7673, para. 534.
23. ibid., para. 535.
24. *Expenditure Committee, Eleventh Report*, (July 1977), Vol. II, p. 404.
25. *Board of Inland Revenue, 121st Report*, (February 1979), Cmnd. 7473, p. 12.
26. 'Productivity Programmes in the Federal Government', *Joint Financial Management Improvement Program*, Vol. 1976, p. 95.
27. 'Government Observations on the Committee's Report on the Civil Service', *Expenditure Committee, Twelfth Report*, (July 1978), para. 16

VII
Accountable
and
Efficient Management

An accountable manager is one to whom specific authority over part of an organization's resources has been delegated and who is required to answer for the results he has obtained from the deployment of those resources. Accountability implies the delegation to managers of authority over money and manpower; a form of organization in which managers can be made responsible for the activities of sub-units; a strategic planning framework in which the objectives of those managers can be related to corporate objectives; an arrangement of control information so that progress towards the attainment of those objectives can be monitored and a procedural system for securing managerial commitment to unit objectives and for reviewing results.

The Fulton Committee emphasized the importance of accountable management in developing the new managerial style it proposed. It also considered that its proposals in this field would improve standards of management in the Service only if they were accompanied by new arrangements for the audit of efficiency and the application of the best available management techniques.[1] It therefore coupled its proposals on accountable management with recommendations for improvements in the efficiency services ('management services') available within departments and provided by the Civil Service Department.

The concepts of accountable management have spread fairly generally throughout large-scale industrial organizations since they were first developed at General Motors in the 1920s. The General Motors system has been described by Peter Drucker as 'the development of the maximum of independent command at the lowest possible level and the development of an objective yardstick to measure performance in these commands'.[2] Such a system of accountability implies the greatest possible delegation of operating authority to middle and junior management while top management concentrates on overall planning and control including the monitoring of performance at lower levels and supervision of the supply of competent general managers for 'accountable units'. These units are 'cost' or 'budget' centres around which control of information is organized so as to demonstrate the results of the performance of their activities.

A system of accountable management usually calls for the construction of a complex infrastructure, particularly when it is applied in public administration. In addition to the division of the organization into the appropriate units, a comprehensive system of planning and control information has to be devised to link the units together, to ensure they pursue compatible objectives and to permit the specification of the accountability of the managers who run them. The organization has to have a performance appraisal procedure for setting and reviewing management objectives and should have a participative management style which involves managers and staff in the discussion of objectives and encourages managers to feel that they can use their initiative and the authority delegated to them. It also has to have the means for identifying and developing a supply of competent middle managers to whom authority can be safely delegated. Schemes of accountable management are prone to failure because of inadequacies in their infrastructure, particularly when they are developed to their fullest extent in conglomerate organizations in which the organization is constituted as a number of almost autonomous units. On the other hand, they can produce a rapidly-reacting, adaptable, cost- and results-conscious enterprise with a minimum of bureaucratic rules and regulations and an active and self-reliant management style.

The Fulton Committee defined accountability as 'holding individuals and units responsible for performance measured as objectively as possible' and recommended that 'the principles of accountable management should be applied to the work of departments'.[3] An accountable unit was defined as a unit of organization for which output could be measured against costs or other criteria and where individual managers could be held personally responsible for their performance. Such units would be mainly those handling a flow of regular transactions (such as supplies, stores, local offices and a wide range of other executive activities) for which measures of performance could be calculated. In areas of administrative work different considerations would have to apply. Here, output could not usually be measured because it consisted of reviewing policy and considering complicated cases, because of the unpredictable demands that arose from the Minister's responsibility to Parliament and because of the importance of consultation, negotiation and the preparation of legislation. In these areas, the principle to be applied was 'management by objective': heads of branches should agree with their superiors and subordinates the tasks assigned, relative priorities and dates for completion and regularly review progress. The effectiveness of the branch and the contribution of its individual members could then be more objectively assessed.

In making these recommendations, the Fulton Committee failed to deal with several important problems which arise in trying to implement managerial accountability in public administration. It did not fully consider whether in the public service it was possible to allow the delegation of authority over money and manpower to individual managers on a scale which enables accountability to work in industry or even whether full authority over costs lay within departments. It did not adequately explain how the internal accountability of individual managers could be reconciled with the public accountability of Ministers and Accounting Officers. It only briefly discussed the problems of designing and implementing the planning and control systems required to support accountable management. It developed a proposal by its Management Consultancy Group that research programmes should be undertaken in departments into the scope for delegation and the measurement of managerial effectiveness into a major principle of accountability without fully considering the implications. The Consultancy Group said that experiments in delegation would establish to what extent it was possible to set up within departments 'budget centres' for which costs and outputs could be measured and 'responsibility centres' to which costs could be allocated but for which only deadlines and priorities could be specified.[4]

It is clear that in the Civil Service the scope for delegation is affected by the conventions of public accountability, the highly centralized arrangements for the control of spending by the Treasury and of manpower and pay by the Civil Service Department and the need for equity and consistency in the treatment of cases (though there has always been extensive delegation in the field of casework). The personal responsibility of a Minister to Parliament for the actions of his department has been held to be a basic principle of the constitution.[5] One result has been that 'the fear of involving Ministers in having to account for operations of which they can have no first-hand knowledge leads officials to excessive caution and secrecy, to insistence on passing decisions up to levels far higher than their merits warrant and to consequent delay. Thus the practical application of the theory of Ministerial responsibility, to the point where delegation of authority is actively opposed, has brought managerial inefficiency without any compensating benefits in the term of greater accountability.'[6]

The theory of Ministerial responsibility has often been called into question in recent years. It was put to Sir John Hunt, in the hearings of the Expenditure Committee's enquiry into the Civil Service that it was 'really out of date and a bit of a charade'. He replied that 'the concept that because somebody whom the Minister has never heard of, has made a mistake, means that the Minister should resign, is out of date, and rightly so'. Sir John went on to say that a Minister still had a responsibility, which he could not devolve entirely to his Permanent Secretary, for the efficiency and drive of his department.[7] He thought that if civil servants were to be made more accountable in public there was a risk of greater caution because of the fear of exposure and personal criticism. It might also lead to civil servants giving their views publicly, which would be a change in the whole character of the Civil Service.[8]

An Accounting Officer, usually the Permanent Secretary of a department, is personally accountable for the expenditure and receipts of his department under our state audit arrangements (see Chapter 9). In 1920, the Public Accounts Committee asserted that the Accounting Officer's position 'is the foundation of the financial system of the country as far as departmental control is concerned'.[9] In 1978 the Treasury produced a paper on the responsibilities of an Accounting Officer which said that the Public Accounts Committee expected the Accounting Officer 'to satisfy them that the policy approved by Parliament has been carried out with regard to economy and to furnish them with any explanations to the contrary to which their attention has been drawn'. An Accounting Officer should also be ready to state clearly and explicitly, in writing, to his Minister his disagreement with any aspects of a proposal which as Accounting Officer he considers he would have difficulty in defending as a matter of prudent and economical administration before the PAC and to ask for a specific instruction from his Minister on these issues if his advice is not accepted.[10] It is difficult to imagine a greater restraint on delegation within a department than the constitutional position of the Accounting Officer as described by the Treasury.

Managers in departments usually have less control over the demands made upon them than managers in industry. New tasks (wage controls, new taxes, public expenditure cuts) are given to them with the minimum time for preparation. In addition, 'a senior civil servant's duty . . . can often only be defined as dealing with anything which may arise within a certain sphere and sometimes no permanent overriding policy objective may have been laid down'. At lower levels of responsibility, the executive civil servant is operating in a more predictable environment, often applying established legislation to a fairly well-defined client community (farmers, industrialists, claimants for benefit) but still unable to do much to influence the flow of work. Technical and specialist civil servants operating in technical fields (research and development, construction, specifying technical standards) may have a substantial degree of control over their workload but still, typically, have less than in industry. There can also be no discrimination between customers in the interests of efficiency as there can in industry. To the outside world a department has to present a common front. The scope for delegating authority in dealing with 'customers' is therefore often small.

Implicit in the Fulton proposals was the idea that it was possible to construct an 'internal' system of managerial accountability in departments which did not effect the 'external' or public accountability of Accounting Officers and Ministers. Once it was clear that the scope for hiving off was severely limited, the only alternative was to go for the maximum delegation to units or agencies within departments. The logical outcome of this route would have been the division of departments into small central units for policy planning, financial control, personnel management, efficiency audit and Ministerial functions and large executive agencies with responsibility for the management of day-to-day operations with extensive delegated authority over spending and manpower. We have seen in Chapter 4 that this was one of the ideas behind the 1970 'new style of government' and that some departments did develop large executive agencies on these lines (Property Services in Environment, Procurement in Defence). This idea was never fully developed, however, because of a failure fully to explore the scope for delegation and because of the refusal to develop an information system adequate to designate and monitor accountability. This problem was discussed in the last chapter.

Management by Objectives

The crucial problems of delegation and information systems were not resolved when the Civil Service decided to adopt, as the centre piece of its work on accountable management, a procedure for performance appraisal called management by objectives (MBO). MBO was first referred to by Peter Drucker in his book *The Practice of Management* (1954) and was worked up into an elaborate routine which enjoyed great popularity in British industry and commerce in the 1960s. It was proposed by the Fulton Committee as a means of applying principles of accountability to administrative work, though the Civil Service Department chose to try it out almost exclusively in areas of executive work.

MBO involves the production, for every management post, of a full job description; a list of the key tasks involved in doing the job together with a statement of the standard of performance required in each task and a job improvement plan setting out the action required to achieve improvements in performance, the responsibility for taking this action and a deadline for its completion. A manager draws up this documentation and agrees it with his superior. The job improvement plan is reviewed at four- or six-monthly intervals to monitor progress and adjust the plan to any changes that may have taken place in the job. In addition to providing a means of securing increased efficiency, MBO was aimed at encouraging a participative management style, improved communications and consultation procedures and a systematic and regular examination of the purpose of an organizational unit.

The Civil Service Department took up MBO with great enthusiasm from 1968 onwards and by 1974 had installed 45 projects covering over 12,000 managers, representing the most extensive and thorough trial the procedure has ever had. A review of these projects in 1974[11] reported cost savings in seven (later ten) of them and intangible benefits in more than twenty. Typical intangible benefits were more effective planning, clarification of roles and responsibilities, better communications and, in twenty-five projects, improvements in attitudes, morale, job satisfaction, training and the effectiveness of groups. In the six cases of discontinued projects, two reasons for failure stood out: the lack of commitment by superiors and inadequate assistance from advisers on MBO. The most successful projects had been in three main functional areas: the application of law and regulations to individual cases; quasi-commercial work and such support services as accounts, training and stores. In general line management, it had been found that the development of management information systems was an important requirement in advance of MBO and without these systems there had been difficulty in gaining managers' enthusiasm: the need for a common information system for area offices was particularly acute. The review said that the 'top down' approach had proved to be the best: 'the essential first step being the promulgation of a clear statement of the aims of the unit and the identification of the constraints under which it is to operate'[12] and it frequently referred to the need for the commitment of top management if MBO were to be successful: 'unless the head manager can demonstrate clearly that he believes in the worthwhileness of the exercise and that he intends himself to play his full part, his subordinates are unlikely to put real effort and enthusiasm into the often time-consuming and burdensome initial stages'.[13] The outlook for MBO in the Civil Service was promising the report said: as in industrial applications attempts were being made to improve it by simplifying the associated paper work and to move the emphasis towards the managfement team rather than the individual manager. The author of the review, Mr C. J. Hancock of the Civil Service Department, concluded that MBO 'offers the best and most comprehensive vehicle we have yet discovered for the introduction and maintenance of an effective style of management'.[14]

Unfortunately, progress on MBO stopped at about this point. When the Civil Service Department reported to the Expenditure Committee three years later no further MBO schemes had been undertaken and the Department referred to 'drawbacks'. These were said to be that in some cases MBO had proved over-elaborate and costly to install and that staff representatives had been worried by the unfair pressure on individuals caused by aspects of reviewing and recording performance. In evidence to the Expenditure Committee, Mr R. W. L. Wilding of the CSD referred to the pressure on individuals – 'pressure to do more work without getting more pay, that kind of thing'[15] and said that with the staff side the CSD had produced guidelines for Management by Objectives Mark II using the best of MBO but avoiding the pitfalls. These guidelines were issued under the title 'Improving Management Systems' by the National Whitley Council Committee on Management Services. They referred to overzealous or insensitive settings of targets in MBO programmes and defects in their participative aspects primarily in respect of consultation with, and involvement of, junior staff. They laid down procedures for consultation with staff at the beginning of, and throughout, the installation of any performance appraisal scheme and for the review of all existing MBO schemes.

It was clear that MBO had been dropped, in spite of its encouraging success, in favour of the pronouncement of general principles underlying good management. It also seems pretty clear that the information systems in departments were inadequate to support MBO; that many top administrators had not been enthusiastic for what they saw as an aid to executive management, a low-level occupation in their eyes and, fatally, it had been imposed on junior staff in an authoritarian way. Every textbook on MBO, from Drucker onwards, had warned about this danger. S. D. Walker and the author in their paper for the Centre for Administrative Studies on the subject in 1969 had actually proposed MBO as a means of introducing a participative style of management in departments which had hitherto been too mechanistic in style. The blame for this expensive mistake can be laid fairly on top management of the Service who should have been sensitive, at a time of worsening labour relations in the Civil Service, to developing problems of this kind.

The Expenditure Committee and Accountability

The Expenditure Committee was unhappy with progress on the introduction of accountable management since Fulton: 'accountable units have been systematically introduced only in the new agencies, the PSA and the Manpower Services Commission . . . it would appear that there is an element in the civil service opposed to the introduction of accountable management and its implications for the status quo'.[16] The

Committee went on to say that the introduction of accountable units formed the crux of its recommendations for the increased efficiency of the Civil Service: 'without accountable units the system of accounting and controls that we recommend is impracticable. We do not believe the Fulton proposal of accountable units has been taken sufficiently seriously in the Civil Service. We recommend a determined drive to introduce accountable units in all areas of executive work and, where possible, in administrative work.'[17] The Committee linked 'internal' to 'external' accountability: 'accountable management will be effectively driven home if the heads of accountable units, or groups of units, are made publicly accountable for their actions . . . the introduction of publicly accountable heads would require some civil servants to be directly answerable in public to such bodies as Select Committees of the House of Commons'. This would not infringe Ministerial accountability for political decisions, the Committee said. Making civil servants account for their management decisions would be an improvement on 'our nineteenth-century constitutional machinery which might go some way to bridging the gulf, of which complaint is often made, between the people and their administration'.[18] The Committee went on to discuss the implications of accountable management for the accounting methods used by government. It observed that management accounting, i.e. the provision of control information, was being introduced on a haphazard and limited scale and recommended that the accounts presented to Parliament should correspond with accountable units.

The Government's observations on the Committee's report said that the complex and interrelated objectives of government departments limited the opportunities for specifying units with sufficiently discrete tasks to make it sensible to isolate them, to give their managers measurable objectives and control over the resources needed to achieve them. In its reply to the Government's observations, the Expenditure Committee repeated its demand for accounting on the basis of accountable units and refused to believe that this would make the estimates unmanageable. The Committee returned to this question in a later report on Financial Accountability to Parliament published in August 1978.[19] This proposed the replacement of the estimates by an 'expenditure budget' showing expenditure for the preceding year, estimated out-turn for the current year, budgeted expenditure for the forthcoming year and price and volume changes for the forthcoming compared with the current year all organized under vote heads which corresponded with accountable units in departments. The Public Accounts Committee, which could be expected to be keen to advance the cause of Parliamentary scrutiny, produced a report in March 1979 which supported the views of the Comptroller and Auditor General and observed, without ever having appeared to study the question or to have followed the debate on managerial accountability which had been going on for over ten years, that it was neither appropriate nor practicable to attempt to organize or present discrete areas of work as accountable units 'though where this can effectively be done it clearly should be'.[20]

The Civil Service view on this question was neatly put by Sir Frank Cooper, the Permanent Secretary of Defence, in an article in May 1979. He said that 'we do not, and cannot in an annual cash-flow statement, show in any meaningful way to Parliament what we are getting for the money they have granted. That task has to be handled by internal management of the decision-making processes aided by management accounting techniques . . . internal reporting systems supplement the annual accounting to Parliament. They should not, and indeed cannot, be unified into a single structure of so-called accountability.'[21] It was not clear if Sir Frank Cooper saw this internal data as being published alongside the supply estimates as a means of displaying accountability for management performance.

Information for Accountability

We have seen that in the last ten years there have been improvements in the form of government accounts, though these have been almost entirely directed to keeping better track of the amount of public spending, rather than illuminating its purpose. Parliament has never been clear or consistent on what financial information it wants. In the last ten years select committees have called both for information organized on the basis of spending programmes and organized on the basis of accountable units. These two bases can be incompatible. The Treasury[22] has pointed out that very often programmes and organizational units do not coincide. For example, the implementation of a programme may be in the hands of local authorities; a number of units in a department may contribute to implementing a particular programme (e.g., an inner urban programme) or one unit may handle several programmes (e.g., a DHSS local office dealing with a variety of benefits). There may also be difficulties in allocating overheads and common services costs to both programmes and units.

Nevertheless, substantial improvements can be made and are needed as we have seen from Chapters 5 and 6. The most practicable approach at present is probably to continue with programmes as the prime classification of the accounts for both the annual estimates and the five-year spending surveys though with a common degree of programme detail in both and with a statement of objectives for each programme and such measures of output or results as can be provided. The costs of what are, at present, allied services should also be allocated to operational programmes. Where one unit handles one programme, the annual estimate could also specify the cost of the unit and measures of its efficiency. Where programmes cross organizational boundaries, the estimate would have to be accompanied by separate general efficiency measures for the units involved. We would then have a system in which the annual estimates (or expenditure budget) of a department could set out its aims and objectives, its individual programmes and measures of their results. These programmes could then be projected forward in the five-year surveys with reviews of the results of past programmes and issue analyses reviewing selected policies and programmes. Each department's estimates could be accompanied by an analysis of its accountable units and their performance.

Much of the information required for such a comprehensive system of accountability exists in departments already. What does not exist could be built up over a period of years. The House of Commons Procedure Committee called for a thorough review of the financial and statistical information presented to Parliament and suggested that the new Treasury committee and the Public Accounts Committee should together carry it out. It is long overdue.

Management Services and Efficiency Audit

Most large organizations have found it necessary to establish a centre of expertise in management techniques and efficiency studies, an internal management consulting force, usually reporting directly to the Board of directors and with wide-ranging powers to investigate the organization and management of operating units. Such groups (often called management services units) usually consist of a nucleus of specialist accountants, engineers, economists and social scientists and a number of younger managers seconded for particular projects or as part of their career development. The Fulton Committee thought that the maintenance of the highest standards of management in the Civil Service would require machinery of this kind for ensuring that each department kept its organization up to date, conducted regular audits of efficiency and constantly applied the best available methods and techniques to its tasks.[23]

The Civil Service was a pioneer in the development of management services in this country. Soon after its creation in 1919 the Treasury's Establishment Division set up an Investigation Section to carry out improvements in office management, clerical methods and the use of office machines. In 1941 the section became the Oganization and Methods (O & M) Division. This Division was tranferred to the Civil Service Department in 1969 and became its Management Services Divisions. After 1945 most large departments set up their own O & M units, usually within establishments divisions. In addition, we have seen that both the Civil Service Department and individual departments have a group of staff inspectors concerned with seeing that posts are properly graded, that staff numbers are justified and assessing claims for more staff.

Prior to the Fulton Report, the work of O & M units was largely concerned with studies of clerical efficiency. Typical assignments were to review and make recommendations on the organization of small executive/clerical units, on clerical methods, the flow of paper through clerical or technical sections, manual filing systems, recording and reporting procedures. They were usually carried out by an officer at the HEO or SEO level. The narrowness of Civil Service O & M work, its concentration on methods rather than organization, had been criticized by Parliamentary committees long before the Fulton Committee reported. The Select Committee on National Expenditure of 1941 observed that since the establishment of the Investigation Division there had been a failure 'to foster the systematic study of organization as applied to government departments', and it recommended that officers engaged on this work should examine the distribution of functions in departments as well as routine business.[24] The Estimates Committee in 1946–7 made the same point: 'The part played by O & M techniques and knowledge must be that of planning the structure and machinery of government rather than that of attending to its plumbing and maintenance.'[25]

In spite of these observations, O & M work was never generally seen as having any contribution to make to the higher management and organization of departments. The activity was a preserve of the Executive Class and administrators and specialists were rarely engaged on it. It was seen as a low-level 'house-keeping' activity rather than as a means of auditing the efficiency of government. Traditionally, the conduct and management of O & M work was not given to promising administrators but to the executive grades or members of the administrative grades who were near to the end of their careers.

The Fulton Committee made several recommendations on departmental management services units. Its Consultancy Group had found that the Executives who staffed O & M sections usually spent about five years in them and that the Assistant Secretaries to whom these sections ultimately reported served for even shorter periods in this area and had little or no training and no first-hand experience of the work. As others had done before them, they commented on the concentration of O & M units upon clerical methods and procedures: 'We saw no evidence that top-level organization and procedures were ever scrutinized by departmental O & M.'[26] They criticized O & M work in the Service on the grounds of the lack of qualifications of O & M officers – contrasting the generalist HEO with a few weeks' training with the typical management consultant who would normally have a degree of professional qualification at degree level (for instance in accountancy or engineering) and six months' formal training. They saw O & M and the staff-inspection activities of establishment divisions as separated aspects of a common task: the analysis of procedures and the examination of the number and grades of staff required to carry them out. They thought that departmental management services units should be 'empowered, under the direction of top management, to examine any part of the organization of a department', and should be involved in the implementation of their recommendations; that career specialization in the consultancy function should be encouraged and that its direction should be in the hands of officers who had specialized in the work. They thought that there should also be a central management consultancy unit in the Civil Service Department, responsible for consultancy training, research into the development of new techniques, inter-departmental and high-level assignments and reviews of the efficiency of the management of departments as a whole.

The Fulton Committee accepted these proposals and recommended that each department should contain a management services unit with wider responsibilities and functions than had been given to O & M divisions in the past. It thought that there should also be the following operational changes:

(a) there should be efficiency audits involving all aspects of a department's work at all levels, with special attention to studies designed to improve organizational efficiency
(b) the management services unit should be made responsible for promoting the use of the best management techniques
(c) O & M should be combined with staff inspection
(d) management services staff should be drawn from administrators and appropriate specialists, including accountants, and many should have a relevant degree or professional qualification and experience of management in an operating division.

Developments in Management Services

The Expenditure Committee's Report on the Civil Service emphasized the 'central relevance' of management services to the efficiency of the Civil Service and considered them essential to the apparatus of controls it proposed. 'There is still a tendency to give management services insufficient weight – despite the Fulton Report and its stress on efficiency auditing.'[27] It was vital, the Committee wrote, to allow management services staff sufficient power. The Committee found three defects in the system of management services and staff inspection. The relationship of the CSD to departments had not been satisfactorily defined and the sovereignty of departments had seriously inhibited the work of the CSD. The CSD had inadequate powers to implement its proposals. The separation of management services from staff inspection had continued, with a loss of effectiveness. We have seen that the Committee recommended the return of management services functions to the Treasury, so that they would have the authority and 'clout' of the Treasury behind them, and the amalgamation of staff inspection and management services into a mandatory efficiency service.

The CSD's evidence to the Committee said that it had carried out a comprehensive review of management services in the Civil Service in 1969–70. This had found that much good work had been done especially at middle and lower levels but that there was more scope for work on higher-level organization, management information and project control. In large departments management services had been made the responsibility of an Under Secretary. There was close co-operation between management services and staff inspection. Training for senior staff in this field had been improved. From 1972 onwards a programme of management reviews of all major departments had been introduced: these were studies carried out by a team of CSD and departmental staff reporting to a steering committee of senior members of the department and representatives of the CSD chaired by the Permanent Secretary of the department. Management reviews covered all aspects of the efficiency of a department, including its organization structures and its systems for allocating and controlling resources and planning and operations. Six of these reviews had been carried out and two were in progress. The CSD itself had four management services divisions, employing 100 staff headed by an Under Secretary. These divisions provided a service to the twenty-eight small departments who had no management services function of their own; provided specialist skills to all departments; collaborated with departments in management reviews and developed and disseminated information on management techniques. The CSD concluded that progress in management services had been encouraging, though slow in some areas. The most useful developments had been in management review, the design of management information systems and the growing use of operational research (i.e. quantitative) techniques in government.[28]

In its evidence to the Committee the Institution of Professional Civil Servants[29] was particularly concerned that the Civil Service still did not employ staff with professional and specialist qualifications nor with outside experience on management services work. Lord Crowther-Hunt[30] said in his evidence that the CSD had failed to meet the staff specifications laid down by the Fulton Committee: there were too few professionally qualified staff in 'this focal centre of Whitehall management services': this lessened the authority of the CSD in efficiency matters. Moreover the CSD did not see itself as the spearhead of the Whitehall drive for departmental efficiency, but saw itself only in an advisory role.

The Expenditure Committee pursued the question of the power and authority of the CSD's management services. Lord Armstrong told it that the matter had been endlessly debated, but that he considered it had enough power. Mr R. Wilding, of the CSD, said that 'there have been times when we have made proposals to departments which have not been followed through' but he had not been conscious of the lack of ability to make things happen.[31] On the question of the separation of management services from staff inspection, Sir Douglas Allen said that from the early days the first had been seen as advising and encouraging, the second as a control function and the Service felt that things were best left as they were. Mr Wilding said that in recent years there had been a drive to raise the standards of staff inspection and now this had been done there was active consideration being given to combining it with management services. In fact, the two functions had been combined in the departments of Education and Science and Employment and were combined in the central Department of the Environment in the course of the Expenditure Committee's enquiry.

The Committee also considered whether management reviews amounted to the high level audits of efficiency recommended by Fulton. They are certainly at a higher level than any O & M exercise carried out before Fulton: they report to the Permanent Secretary of the client department, the investigating team is led by an Under or Assistant Secretary and they examine the organization, management and operating systems of departments. The account of the review of Customs and Excise provided to the Expenditure Committee said that it had produced a more effective organization by, interestingly enough, given the CSD's opposition to unified grading, unifying the grading of the department from a number of existing career classes and integrating general with specialist hierarchies and strengthening line management in local offices. Mr Wilding of the CSD explained that management reviews did not exist to examine the efficiency or particular blocks of work in departments: this was the responsibility of departments themselves: 'we have not yet attempted in the course of a management review to assess the efficiency with which the department conducts one of its own major blocks of work. We have been more concerned with trying to make sure that it has the kinds of control and the kinds of systems which would enable it to do that for itself.'[32] The Committee criticized the fact that the reviews of the Inland Revenue and Customs and Excise were not concerned with the cost of collecting taxes, despite the ease of measuring it. It concluded that 'a review of organization which does not take efficiency into account at all represents an un-economic and ineffective deployment of resources'.[33] It also considered that the CSD did not have the power to enforce the recommendations contained in the management reviews, mainly because the department under review had the major voice in it: 'current management reviews, substantially by departments of themselves, are weak instruments'.[34]

There is no doubt that the Expenditure Committee showed that Fulton's intentions on efficiency had not been implemented. In spite of many improvements, management services in the CSD and in depart-ments are not sufficiently high in status, and often not sufficiently expert in staff, to act as a positive force for efficiency. The CSD does not carry sufficient weight with departments to require improvements in efficiency. Management reviews, though a very valuable develop-ment, are too reliant on the support of departmental management. The drive for efficiency is to some extent limited by the continuing separa-tion of staff inspection from management services in many departments. It was understandable that the Expenditure Committee would try to give greater emphasis to efficiency by calling for the Treasury to take it over and thus combine the responsibility for efficiency with ex-penditure control. This solution has the disadvantages of further centralizing power in the Treasury and reducing the Civil Service Department to an ineffectual rump. A simpler and more effective step might be for the CSD to give more authority to management services/ staff inspection and the Cabinet to confer reserved mandatory powers on it in the matter of management reviews. A further advantage of trying to keep the Civil Service Department in one piece is that technical advances in management consultancy increasingly call for the combination of efficiency and personnel management skills in assignments aimed at improving the effectiveness of organizations. The growing practice in these assignments is to widen them beyond studies simply of efficiency into studies of the total behaviour of the organiza-tion including staff attitudes and morale, job satisfaction, communi-cations, the perceptions held of the organization by its members, its customers and others with whom it has dealings and its general social environment. This concept has been developed in the US Federal Government in a procedure called 'Total Performance Measurement'.[35] This involves a team of specialists in industrial engineering and the behavioural sciences carrying out attitude surveys among the staff of an agency and its clients and analyses of its productivity and outputs. It is thus possible to observe an organization in three dimensions: its efficiency in handling work, its internal 'health' in terms of employee attitudes and morale and the condition of its external relationships. Management and staff are involved together in reviewing the results and planning improvements. The consideration of attitude and performance data by the staff themselves 'eliminates the punitive threat of the data and stimulates commitment and involvement at all levels of the organization'. The further development of management review on these lines is much more likely to be effective if it is conducted by the Civil Service Department, with its strong personnel management base, rather than by the Treasury, with all its overtones of financial restrictions and cut backs. Any vestige of hope for such a development was ended in December 1979 by the decision of the CSD to reduce management review work as part of its contribution to the cuts in the Civil Service.

References

1. *Committee on the Civil Service, Report,* (June 1968), Cmnd. 3638, Vol. I, para. 163.
2. DRUCKER, P. F., *The Concept of the Corporation,* (Beacon Press, Boston, 1960), p. 32.
3. *Committee on the Civil Service, Report,* (June 1968), op. cit., para. 150.
4. ibid., Vol. II, paras. 372 and 373.
5. ENNIS, R. W., *Accountability,* (Lyon, Grant & Green, 1967), p. 15.
6. HOWELL, D., *The Dilemma of Accountability in Modern Government,* (ed. Smith and Hague, Macmillan, 1971), p. 237.
7. 'The Civil Service', *Expenditure Committee, Eleventh Report,* (July 1977), Vol. II, part II, Q. 1855.
8. ibid., Q. 1856.
9. COOPER, Sir F., 'Some Thoughts on Accountability', *Management Services in Government,* (May 1979), Vol. 34, No. 2, p. 64.
10. *Expenditure Committee, Twelfth Report,* (July 1978), Cmnd. 576, Appendix 3, paras. 4 and 7.
11. HANCOCK, C. J., 'MBO in the Government Service', *Management Services in Government,* (February 1974), Vol. 29, No. 1, p. 16.
12. ibid., p. 22.
13. ibid., p. 20.
14. ibid., p. 26.
15. *Expenditure Committee, Eleventh Report,* (July 1977), Vol. II, p. 92.
16. ibid., Vol. I, para. 93.
17. ibid., Vol. I, para. 24.
18. ibid., Vol. I, para. 95.
19. 'Financial Accountability to Parliament', *Expenditure Committee, Fourteenth Report,* Session 1977–8, HC 661.
20. 'Parliamentary Control of Public Expenditure', *Committee Public Accounts, Third Report,* Session 1977–8, HC 232.
21. COOPER, Sir F., 'Some Thoughts on Accountability', Management Services in Government, (May 1979), p. 64.
22. HC 661, op. cit., p. 124.
23. *Committee on the Civil Service, Report,* (June 1968), Vol. I, para. 163.
24. 'Organization and Control of the Civil Service', *Select Committee on National Expenditure,* 1940–41, *Eighteenth Report,* HC 120, para. 81.
25. 'Organization and Methods and its Effect on the Staffing of Government

Departments', *Select Committee on Estimates*, 1946–7, *Fifth Report*, HC 143, para. 49.
26. *Committee on the Civil Service, Report*, (June 1968), Vol. II, para. 286.
27. *Expenditure Committee, Eleventh Report*, (July 1977), Vol. I, para. 112.
28. ibid., Vol. II, p. 73.
29. ibid., Vol. II, p. 537.
30. ibid., Vol. III, p. 1105.
31. ibid., Vol. I, p. 82.
32. ibid., Vol. I, p. 75.
33. ibid., Vol. I, para. 120.
34. ibid., Vol. I, para. 120.
35. 'Government Productivity', Vol. I, *Joint Financial Management Improvement Programme*, (Washington DC, 1976), p. 110.

VIII

Personnel Management

Personnel management has undergone a revolution in the last thirty years. The growth in complexity of industrial relations practices and of employment legislation and technical advance in the field have meant that today it calls for as great a professionalism as any other function of management. Its employment responsibilities involve recruitment, induction, training, assessment, the development and deployment of skills and manpower planning. Its payment responsibilities involve negotiation, job evaluation and the maintenance of pay structures. Industrial relations responsibilities involve maintaining and developing the machinery for joint consultation, communications and handling disputes and grievances. Welfare responsibilities involve the application of law and regulations, the assessment and improvement of working conditions, the management of staff facilities and personal counselling.

In addition, the personnel managers in most large organizations nowadays see themselves as concerned with the development of the individual, the improvement of the functioning of working groups and the maintenance of organizational 'health'. These concerns have drawn personnel management into staff appraisal, career planning, job enrichment and enlargement, studies of employee attitudes and morale and organizational development. They have involved personnel management in the application of the behavioural sciences to the understanding and development of jobs and organizations and the improvement of the fit between people and jobs. The traditional role of personnel management as a service to line management has changed into a role of actively seeking to influence the management style and behaviour of the organization. Some of the innovations in this field have been little more than passing fads while others have been of lasting value in enabling organizations to adjust to social change, to improve their effectiveness and to comprehend and adjust to the attitudes and values of those who work in them.

147

Establishments Work

Personnel work in the Civil Service has had quite different origins from personnel work in industry. As we have seen from Chapter 6, it has been part of a much wider 'establishments' function concerned with financial control. During and after the First World War, the report of the Select Committee on National Expenditure on financial control, the Haldane Committee on the Machinery of Government, and the Bradbury Committee on the Organization and Staffing of Government Offices considered employment in the Civil Service at a time when there was a strong emphasis on economies in public expenditure. Their reports led in 1920 to the creation of Establishments divisions in the Treasury concerned with staff, pay, recruitment, grading and the use of labour-saving office machinery and of Principal Establishments Officers heading Establishments divisions in departments. The first Principal Establishments Officers were appointed shortly before the Geddes Committee was set up to make recommendations 'for effecting forthwith all possible reductions in the National Expenditure on Supply Services' (1921). Establishments work therefore began as a means of assuring the strictest possible limitations of staff numbers under tight central control. It hardly changed in the following forty-five years and was described by Fulton's Management Consultancy Group as:

1 Work concerned with personnel, including:
(a) A highly developed form of control over the complement of the department (that is, over the numbers and grades of staff employed).
(b) the co-ordination of departmental requirements for manpower, recruitment, postings, promotions, pay and conditions of service, welfare and training.
2 Provision of* accommodation, equipment, typing, duplicating and reprographic services.
3 The encouragement of efficiency by Organization and Methods studies including, in some cases, the installation and operation of automatic data processing.[1]

These functions were discharged in accordance with the direction of the 'pay and management' side of the Treasury until the Fulton Report and of the Civil Service Department thereafter. This central department has responsibility for policy on personnel management and administrative efficiency. In its personnel management and pay divisions it formulates and applies policy on recruitment, training, promotion, postings; terms of service; pay and allowances; grading and occu-

---

* More accurately, control over departmental requirements for. . . .

pational groupings; superannuation, welfare and security. Regulations on these matters are set out in a *Pay and Conditions of Service Code* and an *Establishment Officers Guide.*

Industrial relations are handled by the Whitley machinery for negotiation on pay, benefits, pension arrangements and terms of service which has been in existence for sixty years. The proposal by the Whitley Committee of 1917–18 that there should be a national joint standing council of representatives and employers for the Civil Service, originally strongly opposed by the Treasury, has (until recently) proved to be a model of good labour relations practice. A National Whitley Council was set up in 1919 and later seventy departmental Whitley councils and many hundreds of district, office and works Whitley committees were established on each of which there are an equal number of 'official' and 'staff side' representatives. The Whitley arrangements have provided a means of negotiation and consultation which have enabled Civil Service managers and trade unions to examine staff issues in an informal and co-operative way without direct and public confrontation, but these arrangements have in recent years come under severe strain as a result of pay policies and reductions in public expenditure.

Pay determination in the Civil Service is by another long-established procedure which worked well for many years. The Tomlin Commission of 1929–31 laid down that Civil Service pay should be decided on the basis of 'broad general comparisons' between classes in the Civil Service and outside occupations and should reflect the long term trend in wage levels and in the economic condition of the country. These principles worked reasonably well for twenty years but by 1953 'the system had fallen into total disrepute'.[2] The pay of virtually every main grade had been forced to arbitration because of the inability of the negotiating parties to reach agreement on outside pay rates. In 1953 the Priestley Royal Commission was set up to re-examine the question of Civil Service pay, superannuation and conditions and it reported in 1955. Priestley proposed that the primary principle for determining the pay of civil servants should be fair comparison with the current remuneration of outside staffs employed on broadly comparable work. The government of the day accepted the fair comparison principle and set up the Pay Research Unit (PRU) to establish the facts about pay and conditions in occupations which were comparable to those in the Civil Service. The PRU was established as an independent entity under a Director appointed by the Prime Minister and with staff on three to five year secondments from the Civil Service. At first, the PRU worked on a four to five year cycle but with increasing experience and after the removal of the Post Office from the Civil Service it was able to carry out annual surveys. Until 1967 the PRU related Civil Service pay to current pay outside but in that year the government imposed a six month delay and thereafter Civil Service pay lagged behind outside comparable pay rates. The incomes policies of successive governments then led to a succession of delayed or phased 'catching up' exercises for the Civil Service until in 1973 there was widespread industrial action in the Service. A new agreement on pay was made in late 1974 to take account of the lag between the date of fixing outside rates and the operative date of Civil Service settlements. In 1975 the government would not allow the full uprating required but agreed to do so in 1976 but by then a new incomes policy was in operation and the government unilaterally announced the suspension of pay research. There was further industrial action by civil servants, prolonged in some cases, in 1977 and 1978 until the government announced the reintroduction of pay research and the staging of its findings in 1978. Further industrial action by some groups took place in 1979 because of the way in which the settlement was implemented, particularly for professional staff. We have seen in earlier chapters that this severe deterioration in staff relations in the Service led to difficulties in carrying out a number of Fulton programmes, such as Management by Objectives.

Fulton on Establishments Work

Though Fulton noted that the Civil Service had enjoyed many years of co-operative staff relations and more than a decade of amicable pay settlement arrangements the Committee found a lot to criticize in personnel management in the Civil Service. The Committee's Management Consultancy Group pointed out that the Establishments division was the means by which a department checked its growth in internal costs, which were mainly those of manpower: the fundamental and unifying fact was that establishments work was an aspect of financial control with initiative and ultimate sanction vested in the Treasury.[3] The bureaucratic impersonality of Establishments officers and their staffs was contrasted by the Consultancy Group with the more open and supportive 'human relations' approach then becoming customary in other large organizations. Establishments work appeared to be untouched by developments in personnel work outside the Service: 'In the Establishment area of activity the isolation of the Service was most marked.'[4]

'Establishment Officers . . . apparently prefer to remain remote from the men whose careers they are handling. This cultivation of detachment reflects the emphasis upon equity and impartiality in promotion arrangements; as a result discussion between Establishments Officers and individuals is not only rare but is regarded as inappropriate. This detachment of Establishments Divisions is particularly daunting to new young entrants to the Service'[5] . . . 'It would be difficult to say from what we saw that "Establishments" is generally held in high regard in the Service, either as an area in which to work or as a service to the staff.'[6]

150

The Consultancy Group criticized the Treasury's custom of making across-the-board cuts in staff complements, which it saw as counter-productive. It was critical of the operations and staff inspectors, who were concerned with examining the numbers and grades of staff, considering them to be inadequately trained and to be guided by superficial experience rather than by analysis. It criticized the annual staff-appraisal routine for concentrating upon such subjective factors as initiative, leadership and zeal and for failing to assess in any objective terms an individual's performance in his job. These appraisals were often conducted, or countersigned, by officials who had little idea of what their subordinate's job entailed (that is, administrators who had little first hand knowledge of the work of the executives and specialists on whom they reported). Career planning was largely non-existent – 'we found that much of the movement of staff from job to job arranged by Establishments Officers masqueraded as career planning'.[7] Though this movement was sometimes an inevitable result of the turbulence created by the imposition of new tasks upon the Civil Service, establishments divisions tried to make a virtue of it by seeing all movement as 'broadening' and all specialization as 'narrowing'.

The Consultancy Group also criticized features of promotion arrangements. Many competent officers regularly failed promotion boards because they could not create a good impression in these unnatural circumstances: the Group observed that boards placed emphasis upon 'articulateness in a stress situation'. It also questioned whether the brief conversation on board topical issues which was the content of many board interviews adequately tested the managerial abilities of interviewees; whether the administrators on boards fully understood the qualities required to do executive and specialist jobs; and whether board members were adequately trained. The Group considered that there should be a change of emphasis in promotion procedures so that more weight was given to an officer's performance in his job as assessed by his superiors and rather less to seniority and to the impression he made on a promotion board. The Group also questioned the effectiveness of the procedures after an officer passed a board: the usual practice was to list them in the order of the seniority they held in their existing grade and then usually to promote them in seniority order as each vacancy arose, regardless of their suitability for that particular vacancy.

Other reforms in the personnel field suggested by the Consultancy Group were that annual increments in pay should be based on a review of the officer's performance in the past year: unsatisfactory performance should be marked by the withholding or reduction of an increment while exceptional merit might be recognized by a double increment. Officers who obtained qualifications while in the Service should also be eligible for merit awards. The Group also noticed, and commented on, the inept and wasteful way in which the Service employed many of its young recruits from school. Young executive officers were sometimes confined to routine and undemanding work and many young clerical officers and clerical assistants were grossly underutilized by the jobs they were given. Surveys by the Treasury had shown that half the staff under 40 in these grades considered that their work did not fully employ their capabilities or enable them to develop their potential.

As we have seen from Chapter 2, the Consultancy Group's major recommendation in the personnel field, based on extensive field research, was that all Civil Service career classes should be merged into one unified grading structure, using job evaluation techniques to assess the relative worth of every job in a scale of about seven grades running from Clerical Assistant to Deputy Secretary. In addition to producing crucial improvements in civil service management and expertise and removing the unfairness in the opportunities for specialist staff, the Consultancy Group considered that this reform would simplify the work of the Pay Research Unit.

The Fulton Committee accepted these proposals and, as we have seen, recommended the creation of the Civil Service Department as a centre of expertise in personnel management and efficiency services. It proposed that the Service should devote far more effort to that part of personnel management concerned with understanding and developing the abilities of the individual.

Developments after Fulton

In 1973, widespread discontent and strikes in the Civil Service was a cause of concern to both official and staff sides. The National Whitley Council recognized that pay was the main problem but that there were 'wider issues' which needed to be examined if staff-management relationships were to be improved. The Civil Service Department therefore set up the Wider Issues Review Team of officials 'to identify the factors which increasingly affect the attitudes to work and the sense of satisfaction derived from it of the staff, particularly in the lower and middle grades of the Civil Service', to consider remedies and make recommendations. The team produced an interim report in March 1974 and a final report *Civil Servants and Change* in February 1975.

This very thorough and perceptive report, written in a much more sensitive style than could ever have been produced by an establishments officer before Fulton or before civil servants had dared to strike, considered the image and the changing character of the Service. The stereotype of a civil servant, it said, was a middle aged man in a bowler hat, but two-thirds of the clerical staff were women and a third of all staff (a half in the DHSS) were under 30. Before the war, there had been intense competition to get into the Service from school (in one year 1 in 14 had been accepted) but now new entrants did not regard themselves or the Civil Service as very special. The Civil Service had become regional and local and many members of the lower grades never moved away from their home area and did not naturally associate themselves with the business of government in London. A large proportion of the staff had been brought up in the postwar world and their values and attitudes had been shaped by the security of the welfare state, by changes in the educational system which encouraged a more questioning outlook and by the wider horizons of the television age. The earnings and the social standing of civil servants had declined relative to workers in industrial and manual employment. The success of organized labour in industry had led civil service staff associations to resemble other trade unions, i.e. by taking industrial action.

In addition, 'civil servants feel they have been mucked about a lot in the last five or ten years': successive governments reversed the policies of their predecessors and often changed their own, radically and quickly; departments had frequently been created, merged and abolished; the Service suffered from undermanning; civil servants had been singled out by incomes policies; cuts in public expenditure had led to the deterioration of accommodation and civil service jobs were being dispersed out of London with all the consequent upheaval in people's lives. Large numbers of staff spent their working days in narrowly specialized, repetitive or grinding jobs and many junior staff were better educated and more capable than their daily jobs required.

The team considered that since the Fulton Report, many improvements had been made: between 1968 and 1975 there had been a 30 per cent increase in the number of staff providing personnel services; unified grading had been introduced at the top of the Service and other class structure changes had been made 'so as to remove some of the artificial barriers to advancement' (an interesting admission from a department which then, and now, denied the existence of such barriers). Job reviews (see below) and career interviews had been introduced and, in some departments, career development schemes. Serving staff could join the AT scheme; young specialists could get administrative experience; eligibility for promotion had been standardized and there was more training. However, the lowest grades of staff had not been much affected by these improvements and there was criticism of senior management for being anonymous, remote and indifferent (as Fulton had pointed out five years before). In many places accommodation had become, after pay, the most potent source of dissatisfaction and probably gave rise to more walkouts than other cause.

The report concluded that Ministers should avoid discriminating against the public service in the application of their economic and social policies and should consider the effect of their actions on the staff. A number of job satisfaction projects were under way to improve routine jobs; there were experiments in flexible working hours, covering 75,000 staff, and other improvements in rules and conditions of service and welfare arrangements were in hand; an office improvement programme had been launched and a new agreement had been reached to extend facilities for staff association and trade union representatives. The report set out a programme for improving staff relations for the Civil Service Department: relaxing rules, improving interdepartmental promotion opportunities, improving the style of administration in the treatment of staff as individuals and improving communications. Departments were also encouraged to consider what they could do to enhance the well-being of their staff and examples were given of actions that were being taken by some of them in this field.

The Wider Issues report, though far stronger on diagnosis than on treatment, signalled an important change in personnel management in the Civil Service from the emphasis on financial control inherent in the establishments concept to an emphasis on human relations typical of modern personnel work. It showed a concern, which it hoped would spread to departments, for the working conditions of junior staff (until recent times called 'minor and manipulative grades' in at least one department) who had rarely received any attention before. It was part of a general attempt by the CSD, from around 1972 to 1976 to introduce modern personnel and organizational development practices to Civil Service departments until it was brought to an abrupt halt by the economic crisis and cuts in public expenditure.

The Civil Service acted on a Fulton Committee recommendation that annual staff appraisal interviews should concentrate more on performance in the job and less on personal characteristics by introducing the Job Appraisal Review (JAR) procedure in 1970. This procedure applies to staff up to and including the Assistant Secretary grade and involves an annual interview of the job holder by a line manager, usually the 'countersigning officer' of his annual report, i.e. two grades higher. The discussion focuses on the job which the individual has been doing, the problems encountered in doing it and how job performance can be improved. In some departments, the review results in an 'action sheet' sent to the department's personnel division to help in career planning for the individual concerned, a copy of which is given to the individual. A study of the results of the JAR system by psychologists in the CSD published in 1976[8] was encouraging. A large majority of the appraisers felt that they had greatly benefited from the exercise in that they had been made aware of staff problems and problems related to the work itself about which they had not previously known. Over 70 per cent of appraisees had a favourable opinion of the scheme and half of them thought that it had led to an improvement in work performance, or job satisfaction or both. Communications between staff and supervisors had been improved and many staff appreciated 'knowing where they stood'. Civil Service unions have criticized a lack of enthusiasm in some departments for introducing the JAR scheme and the lack of arrangements for translating information gained in the interview into action for career development.

At about the time of the introduction of the JAR system, the CSD urged departments also to introduce a system of career interviews, concerned with an individual's career development and prospects. In a career interview, the reporting officer considers a subordinate's promotability and long-term prospects and his suitability for, or need for experience in, certain kinds of job in the future. Civil Service unions have strongly criticized the lack of progress in departments of introducing career interviews: in a report in 1976 covering thirty four departments, only five had interview arrangements which they considered satisfactory. Moreover, the unions have strongly objected to the general principle that the interviewee was not told what was in the interview report and have argued for 'open' reporting.

The Civil Service Department told the Expenditure Committee of a number of improvements in career management and planning which it had introduced in response to the Fulton Report: a central personnel record system (PRISM) for improving the match between people and jobs; encouraging departments to devote increased resources to the career management of young Executive Officers; giving particular attention to the development of specialist officers through career development panels and the cross-posting and transfer arrangements described in Chapter 3, and the interchange of staff with outside employments (around twenty or thirty transfers out per year). Again, the unions found much to criticize in the speed at which these systems had been introduced and the lack of uniform progress in departments. The Society of Civil Servants and Civil and Public Services Association wrote, in evidence to the Expenditure Committee: 'It is completely unsatisfactory that agreements negotiated centrally in the field of career development, promotion arrangements, etc should be frustrated in implementation in departments because the role of the CSD is only advisory in these areas. It is surely extremely bad industrial relations practice for management not to be able to ensure that agreements entered into with the unions are implemented throughout the Service.'[9] The Institution of Professional Civil Servants pointed out that the CSD had set up a Science Group Management Committee to advise on the career development of scientists. There was also an interdepartmental committee of representatives from departments' personnel divisions set up to consider the same questions. The views of each had to be processed through the other before being submitted to the committee of Establishment Officers and any change had then to be implemented department by department ... 'it is a good example of bureaucracy run mad!'[10]

As a result of the Fulton Report, the CSD decided to carry out research and development in the field of personnel management and, in particular, to carry out a number of job satisfaction studies. Much of this work was undertaken by its Behavioural Sciences Research Division, set up in October 1970 and disbanded in March 1977 as a result of the economy cuts of that time. In those six years, much important and valuable work was carried out, particularly in trying to improve the jobs and working arrangements of junior civil servants so as to create more worthwhile and satisfying jobs. The disbandment of the research division (the motto of which was 'People Matter – People Differ') was an extremely unfortunate and short-sighted decision and good personnel management in the Civil Service suffered a severe setback as a result.

Dr Edgar Anstey, the director of the BSRD, reviewed its accomplishments in an article in Management Services in Government in February 1977.[11] About one-third of its work had been in recruitment and selection; a third in personnel management and a third in organizational studies. It had assessed the predictive value of the markings given to assistant principals by Final Selection Boards and found them exceptionally accurate (not altogether surprising, given the expectations created by the markings themselves). It had improved the methods of selection for the Executive Officer grade and some specialist grades, had rationalized and improved selection methods for policemen and produced a paper on the techniques of selection interviewing. In the field of personnel management it had carried out work on appraisal interviewing, the identification of training needs and the evaluation of training courses and career interviewing. In the field of organization, it had carried out a dozen consultancy projects on for example, staff wastage in the Bankruptcy and Insolvency Service and the human factors involved in designing and implementing computer systems. After initial difficulties and misunderstandings with staff representatives in the early years of its existence, the BSRD had worked in collaboration with the staff side in a study of job satisfaction among Preventive Staff in Customs and Excise and undertook a study of democratic participation and involvement of staff in the Inland Revenue for the staff side of that department.

In addition, the Job Satisfaction Unit attached to the Personnel Management of the CSD has carried out a number of studies including one of an accounts section of a small department which was suffering a very high level of staff turnover and sickness absence.[12] Individual departments also took an interest in job satisfaction: the DOE undertook studies in a London Office and the Vehicle Licensing Office in Swansea and the Inland Revenue at its office in East Kilbride employing 1,500 clerks. One of the most important of these studies was the 'New Model Office' project in the Department of Health and Social Security.[13] This project began in 1973 with the objectives of improving the service given to the public in DHSS local offices and improving the job satisfaction of staffs in those offices. Work began in the Swansea local office and was followed by further studies in Wallsend and Wakefield. The success of the scheme in evolving new working methods, better training and communications and better relations with the public and Social Service departments led the DHSS regions to apply the scheme in other local offices. The CSD Job Satisfaction Team used the new model office approach in further work at the Swansea Licensing Centre.[14]

From 1973 onwards, the Civil Service began to experiment with flexible working hours which were being increasingly introduced in commercial and industrial offices. The most extensive applications were in the Inland Revenue and the Ministry of Defence (180 schemes in that department by early 1979) and proved popular and successful. Also, as part of the attempt to improve office working conditions at a time of increasing staff dissatisfaction and rising staff turnover, the Civil Service Department decided to do something about the very poor office environments in which many civil servants worked and on which the Fulton Committee commented. The Working Environment Joint Unit, reporting to the CSD and the Property Services Agency, was set up in 1973 to improve office standards according to priorities agreed with the staff side. The Unit produces office accommodation standards and improvement programmes for the 7,000 office buildings used by the Civil Service and has achieved significant improvements in accommodation, notably for the 900 typing pools in use in the Service. In all these ways, the Civil Service has genuinely tried to improve its reputation as an employer and has made an attempt to replace the establishments concept by modern personnel management practices, with some marked successes. However, these changes need goodwill between employer and employed and this goodwill largely evaporated after the middle 1970s with the imposition of staff cuts, the failure to implement pay research findings and after 1977 the imposition of cash limits, a new and indiscriminate system of limiting staff costs which looked like becoming a permanent source of conflict between staff and official sides.

We have seen from Chapter 6 that cash limits were introduced as a means of improving annual financial control. However, their effect was to ration funds to the public service so as to predetermine the possible combinations of numbers employed and salary costs. Arbitrary cash control figures, decided upon by the Cabinet, have not been related in any systematic way to the volume of commitments or functions required to be carried out by the Civil Service. If the cash limit was last year's expenditure plus 10 per cent, any increase in negotiated or pay-researched salaries over that figure would have to be met by a compensatory overall reduction in numbers employed. As the Civil Service unions pointed out: 'we consider the system of cash limits to be a negative, insensitive, short-term means of controlling cash expenditure, which is no substitute for the proper planning and control of resources: a mechanism which cannot be reconciled with effective long-term planning and an ordered scheme of social priorities.'[15] The operation of cash limits depended on the government's forecast of inflation, since this determined the allowable increase in cash for the public service, but these forecasts were notoriously inaccurate and almost always too low because of the government's fear that they might be taken as the base figure for wage claims. This meant that the Civil Service suffered both from the government's unrealistic hopes for inflation and from excessive settlements in the private sector. Furthermore, the cash limit system could mean, in effect, the end of collective bargaining in the Civil Service if the setting of a cash limit in advance of pay negotiations decided the overall amount of money available for pay increases.* The staff side has pointed to the inherent inflexibility of the cash limit system. If it looked as if the cash limit was likely to be exceeded, the volume of expenditure would have to be reduced, which would lead either to the reversal of an agreed policy or the carrying out of policy to reduced standards: a classic example of the means determining the ends. In addition many demand-related transfer payments, such as pensions and social security benefits, are not cash limited but the administrative costs of handling them are. This means that the staff may not exist to administer social welfare schemes which are supposed to be exempt from cash limits. Using cash limits in this way amounts to an abdication of managerial responsibility: the use of an arbitrary across-the-board cut in personnel and services rather than any rational ranking of priorities for spending programmes and management costs.

After the Fulton Report there was a period of about five years in which there was considerable experiment, innovation and advance in personnel management in the Civil Service. This development was slowed down and then virtually halted by deteriorating labour relations in the Service caused by incomes policies and public expenditure cuts. The new ideas of progressive personnel management were overtaken by the old establishments function of cost control and cutbacks. This

---

* For 1980/81 the government undertook not to set cash limits until after the results of pay increases were known.

reversal has had serious implications for the management of the Service, because a strong and resourceful personnel management function is needed more than ever to enable the Service to cope with rapid technological changes in office employment. The coming 'microprocessor revolution' will have a disproportionate impact on office work, on which the Civil Service employs hundreds of thousands of staff. Early applications of microprocessors are likely to be in such fields as registries and record-keeping; 'counter' applications in post offices, tax offices and social security offices; training; information retrieval and processing; project control; attribute matching and selection and client interviewing; all common activities in government offices. The redundancy effects of microprocessor applications have probably been exaggerated, given the results of computer applications in the past two decades, but the effects on recruitment, training and staff management are likely to be very far-reaching and the need for staff and official side collaboration will clearly be very great. In addition, there will be heavy demands upon personnel management to produce staff with new skills to handle the organization and management of Civil Service operations in the era of the microprocessor. Personnel management divisions themselves will have to acquire new skills – in organizational development, for example. Organizational development is a field of growing importance in personnel management and management services outside the Civil Service which seeks to improve the fit between task, organization and people so as to improve the operating effectiveness of organizations. It relies heavily on the workers in an organization being trained and assisted to diagnose the faults in the system in which they work and to design and implement change. Work in this field is taking place in the Civil Service Department and marks a further shift away from the narrow interest in manpower control of the establishments divisions towards the wider concerns of modern personnel management. All this important work could be put at risk by the apparent hostility of politicians and government to the Civil Service at a time when it is most needed to enable the Service to tackle increasingly difficult and complex tasks.

Finally, the current preoccupations with cuts and retrenchment must not prevent the highest levels of Civil Service management from giving a great deal of thought to the future development of worker participation in the Civil Service. The demand for greater disclosure and discussion with trade union representatives will grow in the Civil Service as it has done in private industry. In January 1979, twelve public sector unions, represented by the National Steering Committee Against the Cuts, published a pamphlet *Behind Closed Doors*[16] which said that they were 'seriously concerned about the way in which decisions on how much money to spend on the public services were taken'. 'There is virtually no opportunity for the public, Parliament or trade union representatives to be consulted on the decision-making process' – the Committee proposed that annual reviews of public spending programmes and monthly progress reports should be discussed with the unions representing workers involved in the programmes. These proposals raise important issues of Parliamentary as well as industrial democracy which will become more pressing as the government try to push ahead with programme reductions and redundancies in the public sector.

References

1. *Committee on the Civil Service, Report,* (June 1968), Cmnd. 3638.
2. *Expenditure Committee, Eleventh Report,* (July 1977), Vol. II, p. 150.
3. *Committee on the Civil Service, Report,* (June 1968), Vol. II, para. 210.
4. ibid., para. 229.
5. ibid., para. 245–6.
6. ibid., para. 297.
7. ibid., para. 240.
8. DULEWICZ, FLETCHER and WALKER, 'Job Appraisal Interviews Three Years On', *Management Services in Government,* (August 1976), p. 134.
9. Expenditure Committee, Eleventh Report, (July 1977), Vol. II, p. 502, para. 93.
10. ibid., p. 546, para. 84.
11. ANSTEY, Dr E., BSRD, 'A Valedictory Message', *Management Services in Government,* (February 1977), p. 26.
12. PACE, D. E., 'A Job Satisfaction Approach to a Management Problem', *Management Services in Government,* (November 1975), p. 26.
13. BURDEN, D., ' "The New Model Office" Project in the DHSS', *Management Services in Government,* (February 1976), p. 5.
14. WOOD, M., 'Job Satisfaction at DVLC Swansea', *Management Services in Government,* (August 1979), p. 137.
15. *Expenditure Committee, Eleventh Report,* (July 1977), Vol. II, p. 493, para. 32.
16. 'Behind Closed Doors', *National Steering Committee Against the Cuts,* (January 1979).

IX
Parliament
and
Public Accountability

'Public accountability implies a duty, upon government departments, public agencies and other bodies in receipt of state funds, to publish or provide information about financial administration to the legislature. In addition to this narrow definition of public accountability as financial audit, it would be generally accepted that it should also include a duty upon government to make available, as far as is consonant with national and commercial security and personal privacy, information which would enable the legislature to examine government spending plans, the policies behind them and the objectives and results of those policies.'[1]

An examination of the management of the Civil Service has to consider the extent to which it is publicly accountable. An essential feature of a democratic constitution must be the ability of elected representatives to call Ministers to account for their policies, their actions and their stewardship of public funds and to examine officials on whether they have implemented these policies efficiently and economically. To achieve these ends, there must be effective Parliamentary machinery – a structure for scrutiny – and information systems which display, as far as possible, the objectives, costs and performance of Government departments and other publicly funded organizations. In respect of both structure and systems, the British Parliament is very poorly provided. In general, this has not greatly bothered Parliamentarians because most of them do not see themselves as agents of public accountability in any systematic or regular way. They are often very concerned to call the Executive to account, but usually on an *ad hoc* basis as a result of a government decision which affects their constituents (e.g. the closure of a steel works) or some general issue of the day (e.g. policy on Zimbabwe-Rhodesia). Regular and persistent scrutiny has also been hampered by the tradition (now weakening) of many MPs having outside employment and therefore insufficient time for the lengthy research and briefing that would be required and the virtual absence of research assistants to whom much of this work could be given. The tradition of 'keeping in touch' with the 'real world' by having outside interests in business and the law has meant that MPs have been that much less able to keep in touch with what the government is up to.

There are several other reasons why expert scrutiny by the legislature of the Executive has not strongly developed in Britain. There is, particularly among older Parliamentarians, a dislike of the idea of professionalism in Parliament because of what they see as the risk of a loss of contact with the problems of Party members and constituents and the fear that a professional and specialist MP might be drawn into too close a relationship with the bureaucracy he is supposed to be scrutinizing. There is the fear that an MP equipped wtih a research staff might simply become their mouthpiece as is alleged has happened to some American legislators. There is the power of patronage which tends to subdue MPs of the governing party since their only avenue of advance is into government. There is the simple view that an MP's job when his party is in government is simply to support it and when in opposition simply to oppose the government, whatever the arguments in the case.

It suits the Government and the Civil Service that Parliamentary interest and scrutiny is on an *ad hoc* rather than a systematic basis and therefore governments have usually strongly resisted the creation of effective structures and systems for Parliamentary surveillance. Over the years, there has been a modest improvement in structures by the development of select committees but virtually none in systems: the government, and particularly the Treasury, has seen to it that information on the operations of departments has been hard to assemble and Parliament has not usually persisted with what is thought of as a technical matter.

The result is that the development of the powers of Parliamentary scrutiny have lagged way behind the growth in government. Our Parliament still heavily relies on the debate, written and oral questions and Ministerial statements on the floor of the House of Commons as a means of calling the Executive to account. But these are not adequate means for getting at the truth about the origin and development of policy, the ordering of priorities, the justification for spending, the effectiveness of programmes and the efficiency of management. A well-briefed and articulate Minister can usually conceal more than he reveals in these brief interchanges. It has been clear for a very long time that in order to question, probe and closely examine the work of departments and other public bodies a system of effective investigatory committees is needed, with the power to question Ministers and officials, with access to the information they require and with expert support staff.

162

The Estimates and Expenditure Committees

The case for such committees has been argued from time to time for the past century and with growing force for the past thirty years but lack of sustained interest in Parliament and opposition from Government has meant that progress has been very slow and it was not until late 1979 that a comprehensive committee structure was established.

In the nineteenth century the House of Commons sporadically set up committees to examine estimates of expenditure. In 1848, for example, there were select committees on Army Expenditure, Navy Expenditure and Expenditure and Management of Woods and Forests and in 1849 and 1850 select committees on Army Ordnance Expenditure were appointed. In 1888 the Hartington Committee proposed that a standing committee of seventy members, rather than a committee of the whole House, should examine certain estimates, but this proposal was not accepted.

In 1902 a select committee of the House of Commons was appointed 'to inquire whether any plan can be advantageously adopted for enabling the House, by select committee or otherwise, more effectively to make an examination, not involving criticisms of Policy, into the details of National Expenditure'. This committee on National Expenditure reported in 1903.[2] It considered that 'the examination of estimates by the House of Commons leaves much to be desired'. Estimates were used in practice 'mainly to provide a series of convenient and useful opportunities for the debating of policy and administration, rather than to the criticism and review of financial method and the details of expenditure'. The committee was impressed by the advantages for the purposes of detailed financial scrutiny which were enjoyed by select committees and therefore recommended the establishment of an Estimates Committee, with the same powers as the Public Accounts Committee (see below) including the power to send for witnesses and papers, 'not of a secret character'. The Estimates Committee should examine a class of the estimates for the current year not exceeding one-fourth of the whole, this class having been selected for them by the Public Accounts Committee. The selected estimates should be debated by the House when the Estimates Committee had reported upon them. Increased information should also be afforded to members showing the comparative growth of estimates and a fuller explanation of the reasons for new expenditure.

In July 1905, Winston Churchill, in a debate in the House on the Public Accounts Committee[3] said that all were convinced that the present system of financial control was lax and ineffectual and that no proper scrutiny of the estimates or control of finance was exercised. The contrast between the examination of the accounts for the purposes of audit and the examination of the estimates before the House was deplorable. The consideration of the estimates on supply days had value as occasions for raising grievances and discussing questions of policy, but 'so far as any systematic and scientific examination of the expenditure of the country was concerned, they were a series of farces from beginning to end.' The report of the committee of 1903 ought to have been acted upon, or at any rate publicly considered, he said. The policy of expenditure was a matter for the Cabinet and the House of Commons; the audit of expenditure was adequately dealt with by the Public Accounts Committee and the Treasury; but between these two there was a lacuna or middle ground which he called the 'merit' of expenditure and upon that no control adequately or effectively operated at that time.

In April 1912 Lloyd George, as Chancellor of the Exchequer, proposed that a Select Committee on Estimates should be set up.[4] He referred to the gigantic growth in expenditure, from £71 million in 1872 to £186 million in 1912. This growth had been due to the enormous increase in the cost of battleships, the increased cost of the post office, the new cost of pensions and the need to help local authorities with their obligations for education and sanitation. A committee was needed to examine the question of getting value for the money expended. It was scandalous, he said, that in the previous year the House had authorized the expenditure of £62 million without discussion. The House of Commons had not within living memory exercised any control over expenditure: the clerks of the Treasury were the only check. In every supply debate, members had called for more expenditure: the House had never put itself in the position which every representative of the Treasury had to put himself. The House should establish an Estimates Committee as an experiment on the lines proposed by the committee of 1903. The proposition was attacked by Austen Chamberlain as either useless or 'in the highest degree mischievous': a committee of the kind suggested would lessen the responsibility of ministers for public expenditure and it would be difficult to get any members of standing to devote themselves to that class of work. Earl Winterton thought that very few members were competent to discuss the estimates and the proposal would put an unnecessary burden upon officials. Lloyd George's motion was carried and the Estimate Committee was set up in May 1912 with fifteen members.

The working of the Estimates Committee was reviewed by the Select Committee on Procedure in 1932.[5] It felt bound to say that various attempts to make the Estimates Committee an effective instrument for the control of public expenditure had failed. The Committee had done good work from time to time but the difficulties in their way had arisen from the fact that they were powerless to deal with policy, they did not receive the estimates in time, they had no staff to survey the whole field of public expenditure and that no definite days were allotted for a discussion of their reports in the House. The Procedure Committee recommended that the Estimates Committee be enlarged, that it should consider matters of policy, that it should regularly survey the relation of total public expenditure to the national income and that it should be provided with an independent technical staff adequate for its functions. At least three days should be set aside by the House for a definite consideration of its report. In May 1933 Neville Chamberlain, Chancellor of the Exchequer, in a brief oral answer gave the government's reply to the Procedure Committee's report. The Estimates Committee could not deal with matters of policy without encroaching on the powers of Executive Government, he said. Where questions arose in which policy and administration overlapped, if administration was the predominant factor the government had no objection to the Committee making recommendations, so long as it interpreted its term of reference with discretion. The Committee could not employ a body of technical officers but the Government was willing to place at its disposal several officers from the Treasury who would act as assistants to the Treasury official already attached to the Committee. The Government was in sympathy with the request for opportunities to discuss the reports of the Committee but the matter would have to be considered further.

The Procedure Committee returned to the question in 1946.[6] It discussed the purposes of the Public Accounts Committee and the Estimates Committee: the first was established to ensure financial regularity in expenditure and the second to criticize expenditure on the basis of economy and sound business principle. Though the functions of the two committees were distinct, their subject matter was the same. The Public Accounts Committee worked on the appropriate accounts and the Estimates Committee worked on the estimates, but estimates in one year became appropriation accounts in the following year and for long term schemes and projects involving expenditures over several years the work of the committees overlapped. The Procedure Committee proposed a merger of the functions of both committees into a single Public Expenditure Committee, with sub-committees. The government rejected this proposal.

An important step in the development of select committees was taken in the 1956–7 session with the establishment of a Select Committee on Nationalized Industries which was soon generally accepted as a success. Harold Wilson, in a speech at Stowmarket in July 1964, said that 'we have seen how effective certain select committees – Estimates, Public

Accounts and Nationalized Industries – have been in getting to the heart of some national problems by summoning witnesses, taking evidence and reaching agreed conclusions, cutting right across party controversies. I believe this could be taken further . . .' This echoed the theme of shaking up British institutions – the Civil Service, the City, industrial management – constantly stressed by Mr Wilson at that time. Encouraged by this atmosphere of change and reform, the Procedure Committee of 1964–5 suggested that 'the House should possess a more efficient system of scrutiny of administration'[7] and called for more information to be made available to Parliament on the way government departments carried out their responsibilities so that, when discussing major controversial issues, it could be better informed. It proposed a new structure of specialist sub-committees developed from the Estimates Committee and suggested that these should enquire into how departments carried out their responsibilities and examine estimates and expenditure. The Leader of the House at the time, Mr Bowden, said that the Government opposed these ideas because they were very anxious that such a committee 'should not get into the position where discussion of financial control and keen scrutiny of the expenditure of departments is lost and replaced by policy decisions.'[8] The Estimates Committee tried to go ahead anyway in sessions 1965–6 and 1966–7 and appointed seven sub-committees, e.g. on Economic Affairs and Building and Natural Resources. This development was stopped by the committee being run down in membership so that it could no longer cover all its new subjects.

At the end of 1966 a new Leader of the House, Mr Richard Crossman, declared his enthusiasm for Select Committees and proposed two new ones on an experimental basis: a 'departmental' committee on Agriculture and a 'subject' committee on Science and Technology. A year later, Mr Crossman revealed that 'our original intention was that a departmental committee should spend one session on each department and then move on'[9] and then announced that the Agriculture Committee would be wound up. He thought that the subject committee on Science and Technology was different and satisfied a very important need and should survive. The Agriculture committee fought hard to remain in existence and was finally abolished by an order to report in early 1969. Concurrently, two other departmental committees – on Education and Science and Overseas Aid – were established and so were other subject committees – on Race Relations and Immigration (1968) and Scottish Affairs (1969).

In July 1969 the Procedure Committee produced a report on the 'Scrutiny of Public Expenditure and Administration'[10] in which it returned to the ideas it had set out in its report in the 1964–5 session. It recommended that the Estimates Committee should become a Select Committee on Expenditure with eight 'functional' sub-committees, each assisted by expert staff, but went much further than its earlier report by proposing Parliamentary examination of the management methods being adopted by departments to implement policies and strategies behind public expenditure programmes. It also suggested that Parliament should be able to assess the efficiency with which departments set and realized their objectives. These recommendations mirrored the Fulton recommendations of the previous year on 'accountable and efficient management' in the Civil Service and its proposals that departments should adopt new management methods for setting objectives and planning.

The government's reply to the 1969 report said that it was going to review the whole committee system, but this review was not completed before it lost office. The new Conservative government brought out a Green Paper, 'Select Committees of the House of Commons' in October 1970.[11] It recommended an Expenditure Committee with seven subcommittees (General; Defence and External Affairs; Environment; Trade and Industry; Education; Arts and Home Office; Social Services and Employment) and with the right to question Ministers on their policies, to scrutinize public expenditure programmes and projections and to enquire into departmental administration. The Green Paper proposed that the departmental Education and Overseas Aid Select Committees should be wound up and that the subject Select Committees on Science and Technology, Race Relations, Nationalized Industries and Scottish Affairs should continue 'for the remainder of this Parliament'. The Green Paper said that this scheme would mean that the House of Commons would have the opportunity of watching the Expenditure and specialist committees in operation side by side and at a later stage would be able to decide in the light of practical experience whether to deploy more of its Select Committee resources in the one direction or the other. The Government's proposals were accepted and the Expenditure Committee began work in early 1971. Later on, the government gave way to pressure and reappointed the Overseas Aid Committee in February 1973 as a subject, rather than a departmental, select committee. The Select Committee on Procedure in session 1970–71 meanwhile proposed an enlargement of the Expenditure Committee to enable the formation of a sub-committee on Taxation and Finance which might develop 'into an independent Select Committee on Taxation and Economic Affairs'.[12] The Treasury opposed this proposal, which was repeated in the Procedure Committee's report in the following session, though the government did set up select committees to examine corporation tax, a proposed tax credit scheme and a proposed wealth tax.

The Expenditure Committee reviewed its work in a report in session

1971–2.[13] It proposed that its sub-committees should report direct to the House, instead of through the full Expenditure Committee; that adequate time be allowed for debating its reports and that departmental observations on its reports should be issued within two months. The Government's views[14] on this report were large dismissive: it did not approve direct reporting, there was no promise of further debating time and there was no promise to issue departmental replies in a fixed time but departments should always do their best 'to reply expeditiously'. In 1972–3 the Expenditure Committee proposed an investigation into the desirability of an amalgamation of the Public Accounts Committee and the Expenditure Committee – a repeat of the request made in 1946. At other times the Expenditure Committee had deplored the fact that it had no specialist support staff of its own. The Leader of the House (Mr Prior) accepted no specific proposals to strengthen it though he did say that the government was concerned that it 'should be able to develop in a way which would provide a stronger, more effective and more co-ordinated instrument of Parliamentary scrutiny'.[15]

After the elections of February and October 1974 the demands for greater Parliamentary scrutiny over government policy and spending increased in strength and frequency. The Leader of the House of the earlier part of the period (Mr Ted Short, now Lord Glenmara) was sympathetic and in June 1976 the government approved the setting up of a special Select Committee on Procedure 'to consider the practice and procedure of the House in relation to public business and to make recommendations for the more effective performance of its functions'. This committee reported in July 1978 (see below). Meanwhile, Parliamentary interest in increasing the power of the House of Commons over the Executive was running at a very high level. Nearly 400 MPs signed a motion calling for a select committee on foreign affairs in the 1977–8 session and in the same session there was a trial of strength between the Select Committee on Nationalized Industries and the British Steel Corporation over the release of information about the BSC's financial position which led to the chairman of BSC being ordered to appear before the Committee. There was a row over the right of a select committee to demand the appearance before them of the Minister they wanted to question on government aid to Chrysler Limited and the Crown Agents affair was held to show how inadequate Parliamentary powers of scrutiny were in practice.

A powerful case for a greater independence of Parliament from the Executive was made in the report on House of Commons Administration[16] prepared by a committee under Mr Arthur Bottomley, MP, which recommended the formation of a House of Commons Commission with control of its own budget and an end to the arrangement whereby the Treasury and Civil Service Department were responsible for Parliamentary staff. In July 1977, the Expenditure Committee's report on the Civil Service[17] included a section on 'Parliamentary Surveillance' which recommended a new system of backbench committees specifically related to the departments of state and backed by an adequate specialist staff.

What this short history of over one hundred years of Estimates and Expenditure Committees shows is the unwillingness, until very recently, of either the House of Commons or the Government to take them seriously. Parliamentary concern has been sporadic and unsustained and governments have been allowed to fob Parliament off with grudging and half-baked reforms. This history certainly gives the lie to the idea of some prominent Parliamentarians that the House of Commons is vigilant and alert in its scrutiny of the Executive. Every decade or so, the Procedure or other Select Committee has proposed a system for the regular and systematic examination of expenditure and the policies which justify it and on every occasion, until 1979, the government has rejected the proposal and the House of Commons has let the matter drop.

The Expenditure Committee, which could have been developed into a powerful system of Parliamentary scrutiny and was intended to do so, was not generally effective. The reasons for its failures may illustrate the dangers which may lie ahead for its successor committees which were set up in the Autumn of 1979.

The Procedure Committee of 1968–9, which recommended the establishment of the Expenditure Committee, proposed that it should:

(a) study the expenditure projections for the department or departments in its field, compare them with those for previous years and report on any major variations or important changes of policy and on the progress made by departments towards clarifying their general objectives and priorities.

(b) examine in as much detail as possible the implications in terms of public expenditure of the policy objectives chosen by Ministers and assess the success of the departments in attaining them.

(c) enquire into departmental administration, including effectiveness of management.

These terms of reference implied a very great increase in the power of the Legislature to call the Executive to account. They also implied revolutionary changes in the amount and scope of the information provided by government departments. The Committee believed that departments could, and would, provide such information as a result of the recent acceptance of the Fulton Report by the Government. We have seen that one of the main results of the full implementation of the Fulton

Report would have been the construction of new systems of departmental planning, policy analysis and performance measurement. There were to be policy planning units producing analytical studies of the operation of policies; units of accountable management and management by objectives. The Procedure Committee referred to accountable units as facilitating the enquiries of the proposed Expenditure Committee. It also referred to the development of programme budgeting, a subject on which it took evidence, and recommended that the Treasury take steps to replace, or complement, the supply procedure of estimates, votes and appropriation accounts with an accounting system organized in a programme budgeting form. The essence of programme budgeting, as we have seen from Chapter 5, is the statement of objectives and the production of measures of output and effectiveness for each programme.

When the Procedure Committee reported in 1969 it appeared that very rapid development was about to take place in the management processes of departments and in the availability of information about departmental plans, policies and management. Fulton's accountable units would have produced a stream of new information about the efficiency of departments and Fulton's planning units, operating programme budgeting systems, would have produced a stream of new information about the effectiveness of departmental policies. Unfortunately, as we have seen in earlier chapters, the Fulton proposals were never fully implemented and most of the information never appeared. The Expenditure Committee could not carry out its terms of reference without it. The Committee could, however, have used its terms of reference to oblige departments to produce the information. It could have based its enquiries on the spending programmes set out in the annual Public Expenditure White Papers and continually demanded more information about the details of specific programmes, their objectives, their justification, the priorities between programmes and the results of past programmes. Instead, the sub-committees of the Expenditure Committee (with the exception of the General Sub-Committee) usually undertook one-off studies of issues of the day: overseas accommodation for diplomats; Gibraltar; house improvement grants; milk production; police recruitment and wastage; wages and conditions of African workers in British firms in South Africa. Many of these studies have been very valuable and have shed light in many dark corners but they have not left any time for what was intended to be their main task: the examination of departmental objectives and priorities, efficiency and effectiveness.* Moreover, if the Expenditure Committee were to have undertaken this task, it was clear that each of its sub-committees would

---

* In 1974, the Committee resolved that its sub-committees would review selected expenditure programmes each year. Two such studies were carried out in 1977–78.

require a specialist staff of analysts, researchers and experts. In its last year, before its replacement by the new departmentally-related system, the Expenditure Committee employed about thirteen administrative staff and about fifteen part-time specialist advisers. Its General Sub-Committee which 'shadowed' the Treasury, the Inland Revenue, Customs and Excise, the Civil Service Department, HMSO, the Central Office of Information and sundry other bodies had one clerk and one very part-time adviser to match the authority and expertise of these powerful departments.

In a report on its work from 1974 to early 1979,[18] the Expenditure Committee said that its fifty-three reports had, in several cases, given rise to action by departments though it had not been able to develop its surveillance of Government policies and spending programmes as it would have liked. This was because the Public Expenditure White Paper had not included a presentation of objectives and measures of effectiveness of individual programmes and because the Committee had not had sufficient specialist staff properly to examine, nor to call departments properly to account for policies and programmes. The Committee also drew attention to the inordinate delays which had occurred before the government had replied to many of its reports, hence forestalling proper debate by the House (only about one in five of the reports were ever debated, anyway). The time between a report by the Committee and the publication of the government's observations on it was usually about six months, but in some cases it had been as long as a year (the reports on accident and emergency services, 1975; New Towns, 1975; Private Practice in the NHS, 1972; Wages and Conditions of South African Workers, 1974) or, in one case 32 months (Postgraduate Education, 1973). The government observations themselves, though occasionally promising action, usually went no further than agreeing with some recommendations and promising to keep the matter under review. As the author of a study of the Expenditure Committee has said 'Government inaction following Expenditure Committee reports is common, government action is rare. Some criticism for this state of affairs must rest with the Committee itself. It does not help matters by choosing to study broad issues, often only indirectly related to public spending, the nature of which encourages vague recommendations and does not leave sufficient concrete points with which to prod departments into action.'[19]

We shall see, below, that the Procedure Committee of 1978 tried to design a new committee expenditure system which would avoid the most obvious weaknesses of the old system but Parliament and the government will have to take the new arrangements much more seriously than in the past if it is to represent any improvement.

171

The Public Accounts Committee and State Audit

Prior to 1802, government accounts were presented by the Commissioners of Audit to the Treasury. In that year an arrangement was introduced whereby annual accounts were presented by the Treasury to Parliament but these accounts simply showed issues from the Exchequer and Parliament still had no means of checking whether the money it had voted had actually been spent on the purpose for which it had been voted. Then in 1832 the first appropriation accounts, comparing actual expenditure with the sums which had been appropriated by vote, were produced for the Navy and Victualling Broads and this system was extended to the Army in 1847. In 1857 the Select Committee on Public Monies recommended that the system should be extended to the civil and revenue departments and all such accounts should be submitted annually to a committee of the House of Commons nominated by the Speaker. Meanwhile, in 1834 the old office of Auditor of the Exchequer was abolished and its functions transferred to the Comptroller of the Exchequer who, for the first time, was established as independent of the Executive. His job was to ensure that all money that was issued was used for prescribed purposes.

In 1861 a standing order was passed which instituted the Public Accounts Committee (PAC), in 1866 the Exchequer and Audit Act was passed which produced a uniform system of accounting and in 1869 the first complete accounts of the public service were laid before Parliament. The 1866 Act also combined the functions of Comptroller of the Exchequer and the Commissioners of Audit in the post of Comptroller and Auditor General (CAG) at the head of the Exchequer and Audit Department (EAD). The EAD has over 600 staff who examine accounts and the accounting procedures of departments. On receipt of the appropriation accounts the CAG certifies them as satisfactory or 'subject to the observations in my report'. The accounts he certifies and the reports he makes are submitted by the CAG to the PAC. This committee formally examines each appropriation account, but in fact concentrates its attention on those matters on which the CAG has made observations. In pursuing these matters, the PAC may call before it the Accounting Officers of departments. The appointment as Accounting Officer implies a responsibility to appear personally before the PAC because he signs the accounts and accepts responsibility for them, though in law the Accounting Officer is simply someone who certifies the accounts. The reports of the committee are published and the Treasury's views on the reports are published in a Treasury minute. Both reports and minutes are presented to the House of Commons and are usually debated on one day per session. In the next round, the Committee can examine officials on the Treasury minute and report again.

The establishment of the PAC, the CAG and the EAD established the British system of state audit whereby the House of Commons could ensure that the money which it had voted was spent on the objects for which it was intended. This 'great scheme of reform'[20] has continued, virtually unaltered, for 120 years. Throughout the years, these arrangements have been held to be one of the glories of our constitution and the means by which an elected Parliament effectively controls the spending of the government bureaucracy. The PAC is often referred to as the senior committee of the House and its chairman is always a respected senior backbencher, often a former Minister. Only in the last ten years or so has the value of the PAC/CAG system been called into question, first by a scholar, Dr Normanton, outside Parliament and later inside Parliament. Gradually, a campaign for the reform of the system has built up since 1975 until in 1979 the government felt obliged to propose a thorough review of the Exchequer and Audit Act and its machinery.

The first weakness of the system is the extent to which it is independent of the Executive, the expenditure of which it is charged with auditing. There is no doubt that the CAG was intended to be responsible to the House of Commons alone. There are innumerable references to this responsibility throughout the century and more that the office has existed. Gladstone, in moving the motion of 1861, establishing the PAC, said that the object of the committee would be 'to revise (i.e. review) the accounts of public expenditure after they had gone through the process of examination in the hands of the executive government'. The 1866 Act firmly established the CAG as the servant of Parliament: 'every appropriation account shall be examined by the Comptroller and Auditor General on behalf of the House of Commons'. The vital phrase 'on behalf of the House of Commons' was repeated in the 1921 Exchequer and Audit Act which brought additional categories of accounts within the audit. Speaking in the second reading debate in August 1921 the Chancellor of the Exchequer said that the accounts were audited 'officially and formally on behalf of this House, so that the responsibility over them through its officer, the Auditor General is, as it were, signalized by statute'.[21] Over the years the CAG has often been referred to as 'an officer of the House, independent of the Treasury' (Lloyd George, as Chancellor, 12 April 1912) by Members of Parliament and Ministers.

In fact, however, 'the idea that the reform of 1866 created a state audit wholly as the servant of Parliament was from the outset a serious over simplification'.[22] There were many more references to the Treasury in the 1866 Act than to Parliament: 'the Treasury reserved to itself detailed powers; it was responsible for deciding which departments were to submit accounts to the CAG and the manner in which such accounts were to be kept'.[23] Under the 1866 Act the CAG was directed to bring excess expenditures to the notice of the Treasury and to indicate to the Treasury any item requiring its special authority. In 1876 their Lordships of the Treasury reported that the 1866 Act had enabled them to exercise the control 'entrusted to them by constitutional usage' far more completely than previously. In addition, the CAG himself, though appointed by the Crown by Letters Patent under the Great Seal and subject to removal only by the Sovereign on an address from the two Houses of Parliament, is nominated by the Treasury, often from its own ranks. The Treasury also reserved to itself, under the 1866 and 1921 acts, the regulation of recruitment and salaries of the staff of the CAG in the EAD. 'This is a contrast with other countries, in which the state audit office, as a constitutional control over the executive departments of state, is accorded strict independence from those departments, particularly in matters of internal finance and personnel'.[24]

This fundamental weakness, and others referred to below, was illustrated in a masterly comparative study of state auditing by Dr E. L. Normanton in 1966.[25] Dr Normanton showed that the CAG was under more direction from the Executive than any other state auditor: 'at least in legal form, powers of executive direction could scarcely be more complete and they are incomparably more so than in any other Western country'.[26] He pointed out that the Comptroller General, heading the General Accounting Office in the United States, is an agent of the Congress and obtains the budget for his department directly from Congress after determining its requirements himself. The Comptroller General has statutory powers to direct principles, standards, forms and systems of accounting and no public authority is exempted from his investigations. In West Germany, the President of the State Audit and Federal Commissioner for Efficiency is a statutorily independent consultant to government, local and other public authorities. Ministers are bound to Consult the State Audit Office on major organizational and accounting changes and on the preparation of budgetary estimates. In France, the Cour des Comptes, whose members have the status of judges and are irremovable and entirely free from outside direction, reports to the President and to Parliament and carries out investigations on behalf of Parliament. In comparison with these state audit bodies, the CAG and the EAD are very closely controlled by the Executive to the detriment of Parliamentary authority.

Normanton has also pointed out that the audit carried out by the CAG was far narrower in scope and coverage than that of other state auditors. 'Everywhere, except in the UK, there appears to have been a strongly held view that *the uses of all government funds ought to be investigated, irrespective of where and by whom they were spent*; this principle might be expressed as, "no grant or subsidy without accountability!" '.[27] While state auditors in other countries can investigate all spenders of state funds, the CAG covers only about half of British public expenditure. The nationalized industries are not subject to a public audit (Herbert Morrison thought that the prospect would be unnerving for the managements of public enterprises and the CAG of the day was not in favour of undertaking the work)[28] and neither are a large number of other public agencies, including the British National Oil Corporation. Normanton remarked that 'more types of expenditure escape from constitutional audit in the United Kingdom than in any of the other powers of the West'.[29]

Furthermore, unlike other state auditors, the CAG does not examine the organizational effectiveness and administrative efficiency of departments, public bodies and private spenders of state funds. Originally set up to verify the 'regularity' of expenditure, ensuring that it was properly authorized, backed by statutory authority and used for the purpose for which it was voted, the CAG has been encouraged by the PAC since 1887 to examine expenditure for evidence of waste and extravagance and more recently to scrutinize departmental financial control and procurement procedures but not to examine whether the spending achieved its aims or was efficiently managed.

The greatest contrast with this narrow view of audit can be seen from a comparison with the General Accounting Office in the United States. Since the appointment of Elmer B. Staats as Comptroller in 1966 the GAO has greatly broadened the scope of its audit and in 1972 published 'Standards of Audit of Governmental Organizations, Programmes, Activities and Functions' which set out its tasks. The introduction to this document said that auditing was no longer a function concerned primarily with financial operations: it was now also concerned with whether governmental organizations were achieving the purpose for which programmes were authorized and funds made available. There were now three elements of audit:

1 Financial and compliance – the 'regularily' audit (now only some ten per cent of its work)

2 Economy and efficiency – whether the agency is managing or utilizing its resources in an economical and efficient manner and the causes of any inefficiencies or uneconomical practices, including inadequacies in management information systems, administrative procedures or organizational structure.

3 Programme results – whether the desired benefits or results are being achieved, whether the objectives established by the legislature of other authorizing body are being met and whether the agency has considered alternatives at a lower cost.

175

The congressional reports of the GAO in 1975 (including 199 to the Congress; 178 to congressional committees; 255 to members of Congress) show the value of 'programme results' enquiries, or 'effectiveness audits'. The GAO reported on, for example, the effectiveness of vehicle safety programmes, the management of Post Office activities, housing for the elderly, literacy programmes, equal opportunity programmes, crude oil pricing policy, energy conservation in selected public agencies and aid to Thailand. As well as providing objective assessments of the results of spending for Congress, the GAO produced over 400 reports for federal agency officials to aid them in reviewing programme results. The CAG in Britain has moved from element 1 above into element 2 but has not considered programme results, nor has the PAC attempted to move our state audit in this direction.

Finally, Normanton pointed to the low level of technical expertise possessed by our audit staff. Since the work of the EAD was enforcing the simple rules of regularity audit, it was not seen as requiring a high level of professional skill or training. The department was staffed by Executive grades (apart from the CAG himself) recruited as A-level school leavers with an average age at entry of 18. State auditors in France have to be qualified at post-graduate level in public finance (average age of entry, 27). The investigating staff of the State Audit Office in West Germany are graduates, and often post-graduates, with an average age at entry of 30. In 1975, the GAO in the United States employed 2,500 professional accountants, 530 graduate management specialists, 126 attorneys, 103 mathematicians, 36 engineers, 37 computer scientists and 177 economists and other social scientists. In 1969, of the 650 staff in the EAD, 10 had degrees and a further 10 had professional qualifications. Partly as a result of criticisms of its recruitment policy and partly due to the change in the Executive Officer entry (see Chapter 3) the EAD recruited graduates after 1975.* In addition, since 1975 all new entrants have been released from duty to study for a new professional qualification from the Chartered Institute of Public Finance and Accountancy. However, Normanton's observation that our audit system fixes 'the status and careers of the state audit staff at a level in the public service which is unquestionably and demonstrably the lowest of any major country in the Western world'[30] and his conclusion that ours is the only state audit in which the auditors are of a standing inferior to those whose decisions are being audited are still generally true. In every significant aspect: independence, scope and coverage, type of enquiry and staffing our state audit system has been subordinate to the Executive, with momentous consequences for Parliamentary

---

* By late 1979 185 EAD staff had degree-level qualifications.

control and scrutiny. Of course, Parliament has only itself to blame for this state of affairs, as Professor Stamp of the University of Lancaster has asserted: 'the main problem has been the supine and servile incompetence of the Public Accounts Committee in its efforts to curb the influence of the Treasury over the CAG' (Financial Times 11.2.80).

Normanton's work attracted academic attention for a time but its importance was lost on Parliament. The subject lay dormant until it was revived by the author and Robert Sheldon, MP, in a Fabian tract in 1973.[31] The tract proposed reforms in planning and management accounting in government, called for the implementation of the Fulton proposals and condemned the secretiveness of British government, advocating an act laying down the principle of 'the public's right to know' (which later became the main element in the freedom of information campaign, see below). On state audit, the authors called for the widening of the functions of the EAD to include studies of efficiency, organization and operating systems in all spenders of state money, public or private and the employment of professionally qualified staff in the EAD. The department, they said, should be totally independent of the Treasury and the Civil Service Department and should undertake studies at the request of the Public Accounts Committee and other Parliamentary committees.

After 1974 the author took part in debates in the House of Commons on the reports of the PAC and drew attention to the obsolescence of our audit arrangements and the Rt. Hon. Edward du Cann, MP. then Chairman of the PAC, expressed growing concern about the weaknesses in Parliamentary procedure for controlling public expenditure 'the whole business of government has changed vastly, unbelievable and unrecognizably since the (1866) statute was passed . . . we should find a way of inquiring into the whole subject of public accountability'.[32]

The first Parliamentary review of our state audit arrangements for over 100 years was carried out by the General Sub-Committee of the Expenditure Committee in the course of its study of the Civil Service in 1976–7. In a memorandum to the Committee submitted by the CAG[33], he said that for many years his audit had gone beyond questions of regularity and into 'value for money' or economy and efficiency in administration. His staff looked into the efficiency of departmental systems for monitoring and controlling expenditure: it did not, however, examine the operating efficiency of departmental management – in Britain this was a matter for the Executive itself with the central role being played by the Civil Service Department and the Treasury. Similarly, effectiveness (or results) audits of the kind carried out by the GAO in the United States were the responsibility of the department concerned 'which is, or should be, best equipped in expertise and resources to make

177

them and whose Minister is best placed to inject the necessary policy guidance'.[34] An effectiveness audit, he said, would require a statement of Governmental objectives and the means of measuring the degree of success in attaining them. It was likely to involve questions of policy, 'an area which the CAG and his department have over the years studiously avoided'.[35] In the course of being examined by the Committee the then CAG, Sir Douglas Henley, said 'I am, of course, totally independent even of Parliament'[36] and later commented that the efficacy of his audit had not been constrained by the control over his staffing by the Civil Service Department and that he did not think it 'very terrible' that the Treasury had the final word in determining the form of the accounts.

The committee was not impressed by the revelation of the way the CAG saw this work and expressed the opinion in its report that 'by comparison with other countries our system of public audit is out of date'.[37] It recommended that the Exchequer and Audit Act should be amended to state as a principle that the EAD might audit any accounts into which public money went, even if public money was not the bulk of receipts into such accounts. It also recommended that the CAG should take over the staff of local authority auditors from the Department of the Environment; that the EAD should be empowered to conduct audits of management efficiency and effectiveness of all that it audited financially and should recruit staff capable of carrying out these extended audits; that in future the CAG should be appointed after consultations with the PAC and that sources of recruitment outside the Civil Service should be considered. Most important, the committee considered that the CAG and the staff of the EAD should become part of the Parliamentary staff.

The Government's observations on these recommendations disagreed with the proposal that the coverage of the CAG's audit should be extended: the cost of reinforcing the EAD was not justifiable and bringing local authorities into its field of activity had very important constitutional implications for the autonomy of these authorities. The Government was also not willing to allow the audit to extend into policy considerations for which, it said, only Ministers could answer to Parliament, though it welcomed the intention of the CAG to develop further his operations into the fields of efficiency and value for money.* The recruitment policy and staffing of the EAD would be kept under review. In future, the chairman of the PAC would be consulted 'about the ap-

---

* If the EAD does develop in this way, it will not be long before it will be necessary for Ministers to answer its observations, because the value and efficiency of expenditure (unlike regularity) depends as much on policy decisions as on administration. This will call for a re-assessment of the purpose of the Accounting Officer.

pointment of a CAG before the Prime Minister advised the Queen on it'. Most important, to the recommendation that the CAG and the staff of the EAD should become Parliamentary staff, the Government replied that it considered it of cardinal importance that the CAG should not be subject to directions 'from any quarter' in the exercise of duties laid on him by statute.

The Expenditure Committee produced a report in reply to the Government's observations. In doing so, it examined Sir Douglas Henley again and for his appearance the Treasury produced a note on his status and functions. It included a statement of great constitutional importance. The 1866 Act had said: 'Every Appropriation Account shall be examined by the Comptroller and Auditor General on behalf of the House of Commons. ...' a phrase repeated, for example, in the definition of functions of the CAG produced by him for the PAC in 1916.

The Treasury in 1978 said:

'The CAG's relationship with Parliament derives from the fact that most of his reports are presented to Parliament and he has by long practice established a close relationship with the Public Accounts Committee at which his formal status is that of a witness'.[38]

There could be no clearer example of the bureaucracy taking power from Parliament.

In oral evidence, Sir Douglas Henley said 'I think it would not be right, as I have said, for Parliament or anyone else to as it were have the power to distract me from the way in which I and my Department ought to carry out that responsibility' (for statutory audit).[39] He later quoted 'a note about my department' which said 'the department is independent of all other public departments, including the Treasury, but at the same time it is an important instrument of the Treasury, since it is responsible for ascertaining that their directions relating to expenditure are duly obeyed; thus, the harmonious action and mutual support of two departments are essential to efficient financial administration' 'I think', said Sir Douglas, 'that sums it up'.[40] He said he did not think that the note was contradictory, when this was put to him by a member of the committee.

During the hearings of the same committee, Lord Peart, the Lord Privy Seal, and top officials of the Treasury and the Civil Service Department were challenged on whether or not the CAG was a servant of the House and simply replied that in their view he was independent.[41]

In its report on the Government observations, the Expenditure Committee said that it found the situation of the CAG disturbing as contrary to 'a proper constitutional principle that the auditor of the Executive should be independent of it'.[42] It is interesting that in April 1979, in an unprecedented move, a Treasury Under Secretary was transferred to the EAD as deputy to the CAG, linking the two departments even more closely.

In 1978 the National Executive of the Labour Party produced a statement on the reform of the House of Commons which proposed reforms in the system of state audit on the lines proposed by the Expenditure Committee and these were included in the Party's 1979 election manifesto.

In 1979 the PAC itself considered its work and the status and functions of the CAG, in the light of the recommendations made by the Expenditure and Procedure Committees. Its timid and confused report (April 1979, HC 330) dwelt mainly on the staffing problems which would be caused for the EAD if the scope and coverage of the audit were to be extended. It saw a risk that the 'independence of the audit could be jeopardized if the C and AG were to be appointed by the House and if his department were subject to requests for assistance from the House . . .' (para 15). It concluded that no changes should be made which would jeopardize the independent audit work by EAD 'which we believe to be essential for a proper surveillance of government spending by Parliament'. It never explained why it thought that an audit which was independent of the House could exercise more surveillance than one which was under direct Parliamentary control. The report included the report of a management review of EAD, which called for a more positive approach to audit management, standardized documentation throughout the EAD, better working papers, more training, greater central guidance on standards and procedures and the introduction of quality control reviews. It also said that a concern for economy in staffing in the EAD had been taken too far.

In January 1980 the Consultative Committee of Accounting Bodies produced a paper on the EAD which they submitted to the Treasury (why the Treasury and not the PAC?). The Committee took it upon themselves to assert that the CAG should be independent of both the government and Parliament. It also considered that the EAD should occasionally operate in conjunction with professional firms 'who have some of the capabilities required'. A *Financial Times* report (20.1.80) said that senior civil servants were predicting that the next CAG would be appointed from the accountancy profession. It was clear that the review of the Exchequer and Audit Act, due to be published as a green paper in early 1980, had prompted the professional accountants to try to move in on the EAD. This is a disturbing development. Though more accountants are needed in the EAD, an effectiveness audit, e.g. of anti-poverty, education, housing and industrial innovation programmes requires skills in the social sciences, technology and management far wider than professional accountants can bring to bear. Accountancy

180

training in Britain is notoriously narrow and unsuited to the examination of public policy issues.

The Procedure Committee, 1978

The Procedure Committee of 1977–8 produced a report proposing wide-ranging reforms in Parliamentary procedures aimed at giving Parliament greater powers of scrutiny of the Executive.

It reopened the question of the powers, functions and responsibilities of the CAG. Dr Normanton submitted evidence[43] calling for legislation to bring all public expenditure into the field of state audit, to give complete independence to the auditors and to enable Parliament to directly vote the administrative cost of the audit body. The author submitted evidence[44] proposing the combination of the Expenditure Committee and the PAC in a system of powerful investigatory committees, organized to match government departments and controlling the staff of the EAD. Mr Edward du Cann, MP, Chairman of the PAC, also proposed[45] the amalgamation of the Expenditure Committee and the PAC with terms of reference which included efficiency and effectiveness audit.

The Procedure Committee did not accept the proposal to combine the Expenditure Committee and the PAC but it did repeat the Expenditure Committee's recommendation to amalgamate the EAD with local authority audit, to establish the principle that all public expenditure should be audited and to define the EAD staff as servants of the House. In response to this report and to a Parliamentary row over the inability of the CAG to examine the accounts of the National Enterprise Board, the Government finally admitted the need for a review, by the Treasury, of the Exchequer and Audit Act and the new Conservative administration of 1979 accepted this proposal.

The Procedure Committee considered the performance of the House of Commons of two of its most important tasks: legislation and the scrutiny of the activities of the Executive, and proposed a further study of the control of finance, including the supply procedure and the role of state audit. Most of the report was concerned with the use made by the House of committees concerned with legislation, scrutiny and financial control. It said that the overwhelming weight of evidence favoured the development and rationalization of the committee system of the House but that some members, notably the then Leader of the House, Mr Michael Foot, had misgivings about the effects of committee work on the character of the House. 'In making our recommendations we have therefore taken great care to weigh the advantages of a rational and effective committee system against the need to retain the Chamber as the focus of the political and legislative work of Parliament and to pro-

181

tect, and if possible, enhance the opportunities of the individual member to influence the decisions of the House'.[46]

The first set of proposals from the Procedure Committee concerned the scrutiny of legislation. There was widespread dissatisfaction with the adversarial and superficial nature of the examination of bills in standing committee and strong support for changes which would enable the more thorough investigation of the merits of particular bills. From these concerns came the idea that bills should be examined by committees established in select committee form: i.e. able to summon witnesses and call for evidence. A compromise proposal was finally accepted 'the Public Bill Committee Procedure', in which the first three sessions of a standing committee on a bill could be held in select committee form with public hearings of oral evidence and written submissions.

At the time of writing, the Government had not given its views on these proposals. If they are accepted, they do offer the promise of a more thorough and detailed clarification of the objectives, purposes and likely effects of a piece of legislation but it would be unwise to hold out too many hopes for the new arrangement. What is most likely to happen is that during the initial investigatory stage of any controversial bill the opposition will muster expert witnesses to show that the legislation will be unworkable or deleterious in its effects and the government side will produce ministers and experts to show how beneficial the legislation will be. There will be a series of newsworthy confrontations and the Government will then force the bill through in the usual way without any significant changes.

A more radical proposal on legislation was that all, or most, bills should be timetabled, that is allocated a specific period of time to complete all their stages. It was pointed out that the lack of a fixed programme for a bill led to difficulties for the Government as oppositions used every means for delay and to tedium and inconvenience for Members. However, the committee considered that timetabling would remove a useful weapon from the opposition and that Government already had the means to 'guillotine' a bill if it felt it were necessary and that no change should be made to the existing procedures.

The most important proposals of the Procedure Committee were for a reformed structure of select committees. Despite the growth in select committees since 1964 and the changes in their powers, facilities and methods of work, 'the development of the system has been piecemeal and has resulted in a decidedly patchy coverage of the activities of governmental departments and agencies and of the major areas of public policy and administration'.[47] While some departments, such as the Overseas Development Ministry and the Ministry of Defence, were subject to continuous and detailed scrutiny other departments received scant attention. Some parts of some departments were regularly examined, while others were not. Committee responsibilities overlapped, e.g. the Committee on Nationalized Industries, the Science and Technology Committee and the Race Relations Committee all conducted enquiries in the same fields as the sub-committees of the Expenditure Committee. As a result of historical accident or sporadic pressures there was an incomplete and unsystematic scrutiny of the activities of the Executive. It was desirable that the different branches of the public service be 'subject to an even and regular incidence of select committee investigation into their activities'.[48]

The Committee accepted the argument for a structure of investigatory select committees based on the structure of government departments: a 'departmentally-related' committee system covering all the responsibilities of departments including nationalized industries and quasi autonomous non-governmental organizations. There were to be twelve of these committees, (with an average of ten members each), covering Agriculture; Defence; Education, Science and Arts; Energy; Environment; Foreign Affairs; Home Affairs; Industry and Employment; Social Services; Trade and Consumer Affairs; Transport and Treasury (including the CSD and the Ombudsman). The Expenditure Committee and the 'subject' select committees (e.g. Science and Technology) would be wound up. Government observations on committee reports should be produced within two months of the publication of a report and eight days in each session should be set aside for debates on the reports which could be on specific motions proposed by the reporting committee.

A number of witnesses had opposed the employment of a permanent staff by the new committees mostly on the grounds that experts would come to dominate the committee members. The Procedure Committee disagreed with this view. 'If the new select committees we propose are to call Ministers and civil servants to account, to examine the purposes and results of public expenditure programmes and to analyse the objectives and strategies behind the policies of departments, they will require full-time expert staffs.'[49] In addition, Members should be able to call on personal research assistance, paid centrally by the House. 'This would be particularly valuable for those Members who serve on select committees since it could give them a source of advice independent of the committee staffs.'

The Procedure Committee tackled the controversial question of the powers of select committees to send for persons, papers and records. Such committees were hampered by their inability to order the attendance of Ministers or to order the production of papers by most government departments and by the absence of any effective means of bringing a case of refusal to the attention of the House and of seeking the support of the House to enforce their wishes. 'We believe that the powers of committees and the procedure for enforcing those powers, need strengthening to bring them in line with the central requirement of select committees to secure access to the information held by the Government and its agencies'.[50] The Committee recommended that the select committees should have the power to order the attendance of Ministers to give evidence and to order the production of papers and records by all Ministers. In the event of a refusal to provide papers, the Committee recommended a procedure whereby a motion requiring them to be produced could be put before the House with precedence over other public business.

Finally, the Committee reported that the financial and statistical information presented to Parliament was inadequate for effective scrutiny. It proposed a review of this information by the Public Accounts Committee and the new Treasury Committee.

In February 1979, seven months after it reported, the Government allowed a debate on the Procedure Committee's recommendations. There was overwhelming support for them with the notable exception of the Leader of the House, Mr Foot, who strongly opposed the proposed new committee system as likely to weaken the power of the chamber of the House: 'the more powerful the committees have become in the United States, the more debased or ineffective have become the House of Representatives and, to some extent, the Senate'.[51] He foresaw a further draining away of attention from the Chamber and the strength of Parliament being increasingly transferred to such committees. The committees would become a shield for departments and would so be favoured by top civil servants. It would be a 'great error' for the House to proceed along these lines. It was a radical procedure – and radical meant tearing something up by its roots. The House should move carefully before coming to a decision in the next session of Parliament.

Soon after the May 1979 general election, the new Leader of the House, Mr St. John Stevas, put forward a motion to set up the new committee structure, which was passed. He resisted the proposal of the committee for a new procedure to enforce the production of papers for the committees but promised that departments would fully co-operate with them. At the time of writing, the oher recommendations of the Procedure Committee have not been debated and the Government's views on them are not known.

The Procedure Committee's proposals could be an important step forward in redressing the balance of power between Parliament and the Executive. However, much more remains to be done. In themselves, these proposals do no more than establish a new framework for scrutiny. If the committees do not establish their right to an adequate specialist support staff of, say, five full-time staff members per committee, and do not demand an improvement in the information from departments, including the provision of such papers as Programme Analysis Reviews, they will be no more effective than the Expenditure Committee was. If they go chasing after popular topics of the day rather than the systematic analysis of policies and spending programmes, the reform will come to nothing.

The Committees could examine both individual current issues and carry out an overall examination of the policy-making and management of departments, if necessary through sub-committees. The committee concerned with health and social services took this approach in its initial programme of work and decided to examine perinatal and neonatal mortality and all the government's expenditure plans in its field. All the other committees, however, have initially made the unfortunate decision to pursue individual issues: ammunition storage; the CAP on dairy products; the sale of council houses; overseas student fees; the 'sus' law; information services in the British Library. To be fully effective, the development of committee work should be accompanied by a massive change in the way MPs see their role. If the increasing constituency work of an MP and his work on legislative committees and back bench and party policy committees is to be added to by assiduous membership of well briefed and rigorously investigative select committees covering the whole range of public administration in Britain today, then we have to have full-time MPs with support staff of their own. The job will be too big for part-timers. During the drafting of the Procedure Committee's report an amendment was moved by the author putting this proposition, among others. 'We consider that the work of an assiduous Member of Parliament has increased so greatly that it should now be seen as a full-time job and that the arrangement of Parliamentary sittings to enable Members to pursue outside employment on the excuse that they need to "keep in touch" with the everyday world of the Courts and the City is contradictory to our idea of a modern and effective Parliamentary system.' The amendment proposed that the House should meet in the mornings, afternoons and evenings up to 7.30 pm and not at night. 'We are convinced that the present pattern of sittings is quite unnecessary, that it is left over from a more leisurely age when Parliament was dominated by the tradition of the gentleman amateur – a tradition, which we are glad to see, is fast disappearing from other aspects of our national life – and that it is high time that it was ended. A professional, full-time membership of the House has the right to fair remuneration and adequate accommodation and services'.[52]

The amendment was supported by all the Labour members of the Committee and was lost on the casting vote of the chairman.

The fact is that a Parliament which takes scrutiny of the Executive seriously requires a full time professionalism of its members and the only way to get it is to organize the sittings of the House to prevent Members from having outside jobs. Once this is done, the pressure for research assistants and other support staff (e.g. to help with constituency case work) and for proper accommodation and facilities could not be resisted by governments. Full timers would be able to devote the attention to committee work that it will now deserve and could at last be an effective countervailing power to the government bureaucracy.

Freedom of Information

Much of this book has been about information: the information required by departments to formulate policies, plans and spending programmes; the control information required to assess the efficiency and effectiveness of government; information for Parliamentary scrutiny. Much of this information exists but some of it will have to be provided by changes in the way departments conduct their affairs. Underlying the problem of information there is the issue of official secrecy. We have an exceptionally secretive system of government, most of it conducted under the cloak of the Official Secrets Act. For the past ten years, there has been growing dissatisfaction with this act inside and outside Parliament and increasing pressure for reform.

The first Official Secrets Act was passed in 1889: in Section 1 it dealt with spying and in Section 2 with breaches of official trust. In 1911, increasing concern about German espionage led to legislation of that year, which is still in force. The 1911 Act tightened up Section 1 and widened the effect of Section 2 of the 1889 Act. Clause 2 was not discussed at all in the debate in Parliament. This 'catch-all' clause establishes a criminal sanction on all those who communicate or receive any kind of official information without authority. Crude, and excessively severe, it permeates every part of central administration in Britain, making it a criminal offence to reveal not only policy studies carried out by departments but the detailed rules and regulations they operate, the organization of public offices, the responsibilities of Cabinet committees and the job descriptions of civil servants. These provisions are saved from absurdity only by the Attorney General's reluctance to prosecute under them.

The Fulton Committee proposed a reform of official secrecy in 1968 but nothing was done until the failure of prosecutions against the *Sunday Telegraph* for disclosing a report on the Nigerian war in

February 1971. In his summing up of the case Mr Justice Caulfield suggested that Section 2 of the Act should be 'pensioned off'. In April 1971 the Franks Committee was set up to review the Official Secrets Act, ostensibly to carry out the Conservative manifesto commitment of 1970 'to eliminate unnecessary secrecy concerning the workings of government'. The Franks Committee reporting in September 1972, was highly critical of Section 2: 'the main offence which Section 2 creates is the unauthorized communication of information (including documents) by a Crown servant. ... It catches all official documents and information. It makes no distinctions of kind and no distinctions of degree. All information which a Crown servant learns in the cause of his duty is "official" for the purposes of Section 2 whatever its nature, whatever its importance, whatever its original source. A blanket is thrown over everything; nothing escapes'.[53] Not only all Crown servants but all receivers of official information were also covered by Section 2.

The Franks Committee concluded that Section 1 of the Official Secrets Act should be replaced by an Espionage Act and Section 2 by an Official Information Act which would define general categories of official information unauthorized disclosure of which might injure 'the security of the nation or the safety of the people' and define particular items within these broad categories unauthorized disclosure of which might cause 'serious injury'. Franks proposed seven categories: defence and internal security; foreign relations; information relating to the value of sterling and reserves; cabinet papers; information likely to assist criminal activities; information about private citizens and the affairs of private concerns.

The Labour government of 1974 undertook to legislate on official secrecy. Its manifesto promised to replace Section 2 with a measure which 'put the burden on public authorities to justify withholding information'. However, the Home Secretary, Mr Rees, announced in 1976 proposals for an Official Information Act on the broad lines recommended by the Franks Committee, though rather more liberal in that sanctions would not be applied in the economic sphere nor would it necessarily be applied to all cabinet documents.

These proposals were widely criticized as still being too restrictive and the government did not pursue them. By this time there was widespread and active interest in the replacement of Part 2 by an Official Information Act embodying the 'right to know' on the lines of Swedish and American legislation. Such legislation was considered and rejected by the Franks Committee because they said it raised important constitutional questions going beyond its terms of reference and because such laws were felt not to have a direct effect on openness in government. The Swedish and American information laws establish a legally enforceable right of access to official information, subject to specific exceptions, e.g. for defence, foreign relations, internal security, law enforcement, cabinet documents, information entrusted to government by private individuals and information entrusted to government by companies where disclosure would harm their competitive position. They also establish the principle that decisions as to whether information falls within the exemptions from disclosure can be made by the courts or the Ombudsman. A bill on these lines was drawn up by a policy sub-committee of the National Executive of the Labour Party in 1978 and in the same year Mr Clement Freud, MP, introduced a similar private member's bill which was not supported by the Labour government and did not complete its committee stage.

The Conservative government of 1979 also proposed to legislate on official secrets but within three months the Home Secretary, Mr Whitelaw, had informed the National Council for Civil Liberties that a public right to see most government records (now endorsed by the Law Society) 'would not be appropriate'[54] and even a voluntary code of conduct on open government to be followed by departments 'would be open to the same objections'. It was clear that the government had in mind a bill on the lines proposed by the Franks Committee, limiting criminal penalties under Section 2. In October 1979 the government introduced a Protection of Official Information Bill which was widely criticized as repressive. It was suddenly withdrawn in November 1979, apparently because ministers had not realized how repressive it was, at the time of the Blunt case. Meanwhile, the Council of Europe had passed a resolution urging its nineteen member nations to enact open government laws modelled on the 200-year old provision in the Swedish constitution: a resolution already followed by Holland, France, Norway and Denmark and now under active consideration by other governments. The demand for the increased public accountability of government has made some progress in recent years: most notably in the creation of departmentally related select committees. Our state audit system is at last being examined, but by the Treasury, which is not a good augury for its result. The next battle is for more information: a massive improvement in the regular statistical and financial reports made by departments and the introduction of open government through freedom of information legislation. No recent government shows any inclination to improve the information it gives and the battle will be long and hard.

References

1. GARRETT, J., MP, *Memorandum to the First Report from the Committee on Procedure*. Session 1977–8, HC 588, Appendix 44, p. 141, para. 1.

188

2. *Report from the Committee on National Expenditure*, (7 July 1903).
3. *House of Commons debates*, (26 July 1905), col. 411.
4. *House of Commons debates*, (17 April 1912), col. 360.
5. *Select Committee on Procedure, Report*, (November 1932), HC 129.
6. *Committee on Procedure, Third Report*, (October 1946), HC 189.
7. *Select Committee on Procedure*, Session 1964–5, (1965), HC 303.
8. *House of Commons debates*, (27 October 1965), col. 184.
9. *House of Commons debates*, (14 November 1967), col. 260.
10. *Select Committee on Procedure*, Session 1968–9, (1969), HC 410.
11. *Select Committee of the House of Commons*, (1970), Cmnd. 4507.
12. *Select Committee on Procedure*, Session 1970–71, HC 538.
13. *Expenditure Committee, Sixth Special Report*, (1971–2), HC 476.
14. *Government Observations on the Expenditure Committee's Sixth Special Report*, (1973), Cmnd. 5187.
15. *House of Commons debates*, (15 January 1974), col. 488.
16. *House of Commons (Administration)*, (1975), HC 624.
17. *Expenditure Committee, Eleventh Report*, Session 1976–7, (July 1977), HC 535.
18. *Expenditure Committee, Third Report*, Session 1978–9, (Debruary 1979), HC 163.
19. ROBINSON, A., *Parliament and Public Spending*, (Heinemann, London, 1978), p. 139.
20. *Select Committee on Procedure, Third Report*, (1946), HC 189, para. 40.
21. *House of Commons debates*, (5 August 1921), col. 1886.
22. NORMANTON, Dr E. L., 'Public Accountability', *Memorandum to the Committee on Procedure* (1977–78), Vol. III. Appendix 43, p. 133.
23. ibid., p. 133.
24. ibid., p. 134.
25. NORMANTON, E. L., *The Accountability and Audit of Governments*, (Manchester University Press, 1966).
26. ibid., p. 273.
27. ibid., p. 137.
28. ibid., p. 325.
29. ibid., p. 373.
30. ibid., p. 272.
31. GARRETT, J. and SHELDON, R., 'Administrative Reform, the next step', *Fabian tract* 426, (1973).
32. *House of Commons debates*, (9 December 1976), col. 663.
33. *Expenditure Committee, Eleventh Report*, (July 1977), Vol. II, p. 582.
34. ibid., p. 584.
35. ibid., p. 585.
36. ibid., p. 595.
37. ibid., Vol. II, para. 153.
38. *Expenditure Committee, Twelfth Report*, July 1978), HC 576, Appendix 1, para. 4.
39. ibid., p. 29.
40. ibid., p. 30.
41. ibid., p. 18.
42. ibid., p. xiii.
43. *Select Committee on Procedure*, 1977–8, Vol. III, p. 139.
44. ibid., p. 144.
45. ibid., Vol. II, p. 134.
46. ibid., Vol. I, para. 1.8.
47. ibid., Vol. I, para. 5.14.

48. ibid., Vol. I, para. 5.15.
49. ibid., Vol. I, para. 6.39.
50. ibid., Vol. I, para. 7.10.
51. *House of Commons debates*, (20 February 1979), col. 292.
52. *Select Committee on Procedure*, (1977–78) Vol. I, p. 58.
53. *Departmental Committee on Section 2 of the Official Secrets Act*, Home Office (1972), Cmnd. 5104, para. 17.
54. 'Closed Mind on Open Governing', *Observer*, (19 August 1979).

X

A Programme of Reform

This book may be said to span the rise and fall of the management movement in the British Civil Service. Most of the new ideas of the late 1960s, which reformers thought would greatly improve the effectiveness of the Civil Service – unified grading, a powerful Civil Service College, programme budgeting, programme analysis review, policy planning units, accountable management, management review, efficiency audits, management by objectives – have now faded away. The innovative and optimistic atmosphere of the late 1960s has given way to a sour hostility between the Civil Service unions and the government and between politicians and the Service. Governments concerned to reform the Service by the introduction of new techniques and ways of thinking have given way to governments concerned simply to hack it down in size. The age of good husbandry has, as it were, given way to the age of slash and burn.

The ideas of the reformers have had some effect: many areas of the Service are better managed than they were and the worst features of the administrative style of management which dominated the Service for many decades are disappearing. But change has been piecemeal and has depended upon developments in individual departments usually encouraged and sponsored by the CSD but without clear support from top management. The principles of change typified by the Fulton Report of 1968 and the reorganization of central government in 1970 were hindered by the opposition of the higher Civil Service to new ideas but, most important, they were thwarted by the lack of political interest in fundamental change. Ministers would not devote the time and effort to what most of them see as peripheral and boringly technical questions. Ministers also lost the goodwill of Civil Service unions in their pursuit of ill thought-out schemes for across-the-board cuts in Civil Service employment and in their determination to hold down public sector pay even if they could not hold down the pay of anybody else.

In spite of efforts to do so, nobody has shown the diagnosis and the prescriptions of the Fulton Committee to be wrong and, as we have seen, later studies have endorsed them. Many of the ideas of the 'new style of government' of 1970, though mixed up with a lot of irrelevance about the virtues of large-scale business management, would have produced more rational and systematic means of planning and control in government. The fact that these initiatives have withered does not mean that the arguments are lost. A future government will again have to tackle the question of Civil Service reform, to be implemented over a decade or more, with each advance building on the one before and carrying management and the staff unions along with it. The British Civil Service, for all its strengths, is not organized or managed in a way which has enabled it to cope with the problems of modern Britain and our machinery for Parliamentary and public scrutiny is clearly inadequate to meet the requirements of an alert and informed democracy.

A programme of reform should include:

1 The resumption of progress towards a unified grading structure, so as to simplify the grading structure, facilitate forms of organization which bring together the skills and experience required for the tasks to be undertaken and to give technically qualified specialists the opportunity to fit themselves for top jobs.

2 The establishment of a national college of public administration, concerned with teaching the management of administrative processes, for entry to which the best young Civil Service managers of all backgrounds could compete, provided they had relevant qualifications and experience.

3 A wholesale reform of our government accounting and statistical information so that Parliament and the public can scrutinize the purpose and results of public expenditure programmes and the performance of the accountable units which manage them.

4 A Freedom of Information Act, placing the responsibility on government for withholding information.

5 A new Exchequer and Audit Act which establishes our state audit as accountable to Parliament, independent of the Executive and capable of examining the management of all spenders of state funds.

6 Arrangements for providing House of Commons departmental select committees with sufficient staff and management information to enable them properly to scrutinize the Executive.

7 The establishment of policy planning units and Ministerial *cabinets* of specialist advisers in departments, to allow the more rational examination of policy options and plans under the direction of Ministers.

8 The establishment of high-level efficiency reviews of departments under the direction of the Civil Service Department.

9 The honouring of pay research in the Civil Service and the development of personnel management so that the support of junior civil servants can be enlisted in improving and modernizing the Service.

Such a programme needs political commitment at the highest level and the recognition of the importance of an effective Civil Service in dealing with the risks and opportunities we face as a nation.

Index

195